WEB-BASED COMMUNICATIONS, THE INTERNET, AND DISTANCE EDUCATION

WEB-BASED COMMUNICATIONS, THE INTERNET, AND DISTANCE EDUCATION

Edited by Michael G. Moore and Geoffrey T. Cozine

Readings in Distance Education Number 7
The American Center for the Study of Distance Education
College of Education
The Pennsylvania State University

The Readings in Distance Education Series is published by The American Center for the Study of Distance Education at The Pennsylvania State University. This series is designed to provide instructional and resource material for students, educators, training specialists, and other professionals working in the field of distance education. Comprised of a selection of articles from *The American Journal of Distance Education,* each Readings focuses on a particular aspect of distance education practice and research.

Editorial and Publishing Staff

The American Center for the Study of Distance Education
College of Education
The Pennsylvania State University
110 Rackley Building
University Park, PA 16802-3202

Phone: 814-863-3764
Fax: 814-865-5878
E-mail: ACSDE@psu.edu
Web site: http://www.ed.psu.edu/ACSDE/

TABLE OF CONTENTS

TABLE OF CONTENTS (continued)

Preface

Distance Learning and the Internet

Online, Web-based communication—seen by many as the key technological innovation of the last decade of the twentieth century—has attracted the attention of college educators to the idea of distance education in a way that no earlier technology managed to do. By some estimates, by 2002, 85 percent of American colleges will offer online courses to over 2 million students. Even these numbers may be dwarfed by enrollments in the private, for-profit sector, where some 3 million people already study in programs accredited by the Distance Education and Training Council (www.detc.org). Furthermore, growth is likely to accelerate as technology develops, with the cost of bandwidth falling, the increasing reach of the principal "pipes" (such as digital satellite transponders and fiber-optic cable) for broad bandwidth, and "last-mile" solutions (such as digital subscriber lines and coaxial cable) becoming more prevalent.

With such growth of the technology, knowledge of how to best apply it—in delivering instructional programs and in facilitating the purposeful learner-instructor and learner-learner interactions that differentiate communication in education from other uses of the same technology—lags very far behind. There are a number of plausible explanations why this is so. One is that the educators, both in the classroom and in the administration, are unable or unwilling to make the necessary organizational and structural changes in their institutions to take best advantage of the technology. Simply giving high-powered machines like computers and modems to classroom teachers may extend their influence and improve the quality of their teaching, but it can only do so marginally. Significant improvements require machines and humans to be reorganized into delivery systems that are more sophisticated than those existing before. In other words, it is organizational technology that lags behind communications technology. Lagging also is what we might call "pedagogical technology," i.e., the understanding of the perspectives on learning and the methods of teaching that best take advantage of the technology. Many teachers still tend to regard themselves not as organizers of learning environments, but as owners and controllers of information, a rather absurd self-image given the infinite amount of information now at everyone's fingertips via the World Wide Web.

A second reason why educational applications lag behind technological developments is the disconnect between current practice and previous research and theory. Driven not only by technological excitement—but also by a new consumerist approach to selling educational services in which marketing favors only the new—fewer educators have the time or inclination to check out the viability of their new initiatives against what is already known from research, theory, and experience. The fact is that there are very few teaching-learning issues that arise in using new technology that were not recognized, and fairly well explored, when distance education depended on technologically simpler forms of communication. These basic issues concern how people learn when they are separated for all or most of the time from their instructors; how both content and process can best be structured, organized, and presented to those learners so that each can best interact with that content in his or her own way; what degree of interaction (with an instructor or with other learners) is needed for any given content area and any particular type and level of learner; and, finally, how people and machines are to be organized so that the delivery of information, guidance, support, and facilitation of interaction is optimal and cost-effective. These issues, explored quite extensively in the past, remain the issues to be further explored as we learn to adapt the new technology to the old purposes.

The American Journal of Distance Education has published a growing number of articles related to Web-based delivery of distance learning, and a selection of these have been brought together in this book of readings. These articles have all been subject to peer review, and each author has been required to set the article in a theoretical context, at least showing how the findings of the article relate to previous research. The articles here are far from perfect, but they are the best, and, as such, they are indicative of the current state of the art. They are offered here in a single volume in the hope that they will prove valuable in informing and guiding readers—whether instructors, administrators, researchers, or students—as they enter and begin to explore this exciting world of online distance education. We hope that, as readers understand better what is known about distance education via the Web, it will become more clear how much is not known, and that, by linking the questions about the application of this new technology to the theories and knowledge acquired through research in earlier technologies, the general quality of research and practice in this field will be advanced.

I extend my thanks to the authors who provided the articles reproduced here, the referees who helped those authors, and, in particular, Geoffrey T. Cozine and other members of The American Center for Study of Distance Education staff, whose hard work makes this and other publications possible.

Michael G. Moore

Performance and Perceptions of Distance Learners in Cyberspace

Peter Navarro and Judy Shoemaker

Vol. 14 No. 2 2000

Abstract

This study compared the performance and perception of cyberlearners to that of traditional learners. A study of several hundred undergraduate students taking an introductory economics course at the University of California suggests that cyberlearners learn as well as, or better than, traditional learners regardless of characteristics such as gender, ethnicity, academic background, computer skills, and academic aptitude and that they do so with a high degree of satisfaction. CD-ROM-based lectures, electronic testing, threaded electronic bulletin boards, and online discussion rooms all appear to be effective instructional technologies. The CD-ROM-based lectures that simulated the traditional classroom experience were regarded as being both the most essential and most enjoyable instructional medium.

Introduction

Can cyberlearners perform as well as, or better than, traditional learners? Can age, gender, aptitude, and other such factors be used to predict performance? What impact does a student's perception of various interactions within a "virtual community" have on performance? Why do some students prefer a cyberlearning environment to the traditional classroom? Can there be an acceptably high degree of "customer," or student, satisfaction with a cybercourse, and how might this affect student performance? What kinds of attitudes are students likely to have with regard to different instructional technologies, such as CD-ROM-based lectures and online discussion rooms? How easy to use are the new cyberlearning technologies? What kinds of new instructional technologies are most essential—and enjoyable—to students? How might student attitudes toward the various technologies relate to performance and satisfaction? What kinds of technical problems are students likely to encounter in a cybercourse, and how might these problems affect performance and satisfaction?

These questions of student performance, performance prediction, perceived interactions, satisfaction, attitudes toward technology, and technical constraints are at the core of any comprehensive, empirical analysis of the efficacy of distance learning. Moreover, these questions are particularly important as major colleges and universities race to develop online course capability in a rapidly emerging cybereducation market. Critical issues that remain unresolved range from the effectiveness of cyberlearning (Burdman 1998; Saba 1996) to the quality of students' learning experiences when the students are geographically dispersed (Dillman et al. 1995; El-Khawas 1995).

The strongest critics of the online revolution warn of the emergence of "digital diploma mills" that lack crucial personal interactions, not only between students and professors, but also among students as well. In this online revolution, the critics see a depersonalization of the learning process and an empty pedagogy that stresses memorization rather than synthesis and analysis (Burdman 1998; Saba 1998; Young 1998, 1997; Gross 1997; Monaghan 1995).

Cyberlearning advocates, on the contrary, argue that online education provides students with better and faster access to information, allows for more individualized instruction, accommodates different learning styles, and increases students' satisfaction with their courses (Baker, Hale, and Gifford 1997; Sun Associates 1997). These advocates also argue that the new computer-assisted technologies can promote not only greater student involvement in learning, but also more individual responsibility for learning. In doing so, cyberlearning is said to promote a "constructivist theory" of learning in which students actively construct an internal representation of knowledge by interacting with the learning materials (Kosakowski 1998; Zhang 1998; Sun Associates 1997; Kerka 1996; Sherry, L. 1996; Steiner 1995).

This paper compares the performance and perception of cyberlearners to that of traditional learners. It begins with a review of the literature, discusses the data sample and research design, and presents results.

A Review of the Literature

Comparative Studies. The issue of student performance traces its roots to the early 1920s, when correspondence courses emerged as the first challenge to the traditional classroom (Burdman 1998; Pascarella and Terenzini 1991; Rumble and Harry 1982). Numerous studies have compared the performance of distance learners to that of traditional learners (Russell 1998; Baker, Hale, and Gifford 1997; Souder 1993; Moore and Thompson 1990; Delbeq and Scates 1989; DeLoughry 1988; Eiserman and Williams 1987; Stone 1987, 1988). The broad consensus among these performance studies is that there appears to be "no significant difference" in learner achievement between the two modes. In most studies, distance learners appear to perform as well as traditional learners (Russell 1998; Moore and Thompson 1990; US Congress 1989; Eiserman and Williams 1987). However, the vast majority of these studies have focused on the efficacy of older learning technologies, such as telecourses (Moore 1989). There are relatively few studies that rigorously compare distance learning in the newer, multimedia cyberlearning format with traditional learning. Moreover, much of the new cyberlearning literature is based on case study material rather than on carefully controlled statistical studies (Escalada and Zollman 1997; Lewis, Treves, and Shaindlin 1997; Collins 1996). Two notable exceptions to this lack of statistical studies are McCollum (1997) and Brewer and Erickson (1997). Furthermore, while Grimes, Nielsen, and Niss (1988) have examined the efficacy of teaching economics in a telecourse delivery system, there have been few, if any, studies examining the specific effectiveness of teaching economics in cyberspace.

In this study, we hypothesized that cyberlearners perform as well as, or better than, traditional learners, as measured by test grades.

Predictive Factors

The amount of research on predicting the success of distance learners is inadequate. It has concentrated largely on demographic correlates of student success (Cookson 1989). Some of these studies have demonstrated that academic success in a distance learning environment is related to such things as age (Souder 1993; Rekkedal 1983), gender (Oxford et al. 1993; Carr and Ledwith 1980), marital status (Dille and Mezack 1991), and occupation (Carr and Ledwith 1980). A number of studies have also examined the role of personality traits in predicting performance. For example, Dille and Mezack (1991) found that more successful learners (in terms of academic achievement) had a "greater internal locus of control"—a trait characterized by the belief that personal achievement is due to ability and effort, as opposed to luck or situational factors. In addition, the distance learners who achieved higher grades tended to be more self-sufficient, rather than group oriented, and less compulsive.

In this study, we hypothesized that factors such as gender, ethnicity, and age as well as aptitude, distance from campus, and academic major may help predict performance. However, we did not consider occupation or marital status because we were working with an undergraduate sample rather than the more typical adult population of distance learners. Finally, while we recognized the importance of personality traits in predicting performance, we decided to leave that as a topic for future research.

The Role of Learner Interactions

Numerous studies have stressed the critical importance of addressing various types of learner interactions in the educational process (Hillman, Willis, and Gunawardena 1994; Moore 1992; Garrison and Baynton 1987; Shuy 1987; Smeltzer and Davy 1987; Ellis and Mathis 1985; Holmberg 1983; Bruffee 1982; Salomon 1981; Daniel and Marquis 1979; McCroskey and Andersen 1976; Flanders 1970). The need for learner-centered environments in distance education is, likewise, well established (Wagner and McCombs 1995; Wolcott 1995; Willis 1994), particularly in terms of interpersonal interactions within virtual communities (Dede 1996; Miller, McKenna, and Ramsey 1993; Silvernail and Johnson 1992; Walker and Hackman 1992; Garrison 1990).

Moore (1989) and Moore and Kearsley (1995) provide a framework for studying interaction in distance education. They identify three closely related types: learner-instructor, learner-learner, and learner-content. In this framework, learner-learner interaction serves as a motivational tool. However, such interactions are also thought to be necessary for certain kinds of social skill learning, such as communication or group-process skills. In contrast to this, because learner-content interaction allows learners to engage in knowledge construction, some believe that it requires only a mental response and does not require system interactivity (Smith and Dillon 1999). The various kinds of interactions have been viewed as a tool that corrects learning and enhances meaning (Wagner 1994); that promotes higher-order learning, such as analysis, problem solving, and synthesis (Weston and Cranton 1986); and that assists learners in processing new learning and remaining motivated (Knowles 1980). From this perspective, education has been viewed, at least partly, as a social process in which interactions play an integral part (Bruffee 1982; Salomon 1981). For example, students experiencing higher levels of interaction have been shown to have more positive attitudes (Garrison 1990; Hackman and Walker 1990; Ritchie and Newby 1989) and higher levels of achievement (Learmont 1990; Hunt 1987; Walberg 1984; Simonson 1979; McCroskey and Andersen 1976). Up to this point, however, the reported effects of interactions on distance learning have been mixed (Ritchie and Newby 1989; Kataoka 1987; Wergin 1986; Weingand 1984; Perin 1983; Cohen, Ebeling, and Kulik 1982; Anderson 1978; Chu and Schramm 1967).

In this study, we used Moore's (1989) framework to focus on student perceptions of both learner-learner and learner-instructor interactions and also on how these perceptions may affect a student's performance. Specifically, we hypothesized that performance is positively correlated with a student's perception of various interactions. We also examined how students relate, in a learner-content context, to the various instructional technologies used in an online experiment.

Student Satisfaction and Self-Selection

An issue closely related to both student performance and student interactions is student satisfaction. Few studies have assessed the extent to which students are satisfied with distance learning (Harrison et al. 1991; Barker 1987; Barron 1987; Lienau 1987; Abel and Creswell 1983). Biner, Dean, and Mellinger (1994) observed that, when satisfaction measures are incorporated into research efforts, they are often given little attention in the final publication (Souder 1993; Wagner 1987). This is a surprising gap in the literature because, as Biner (1993) has noted, high distance learner satisfaction should result in lower dropout rates. Satisfied distance learners are less likely to withdraw from classes for nonacademic reasons, while dissatisfied distance learners are more likely to have low motivation. Pascarella et al. (1996) found a positive relationship between students' satisfaction with instruction and their subsequent success in a course. Ritchie and Newby (1989) found that a more positive attitude may help students finish a course of study. Similarly, Sherry, Fulford, and Zhang (1998) found that, when learners perceive the level of interaction to be high, they are more satisfied with instruction than when they perceive the level to be low. In examining this issue, Biner, Dean, and Mellinger (1994) used factor analysis to identify some of the important determinants of student satisfaction. Included in their list are attitudes toward the instructor and instruction, the technology used, and the degree of communication between the students and the instructor.

From the above observations, we hypothesized that (1) student satisfaction is positively correlated with performance; (2) student satisfaction is positively correlated with satisfaction with the instructor, the course, and the technology; (3) student satisfaction is positively correlated with perceptions of various types of interactions; and (4) student satisfaction is inversely correlated with the incidence of technical problems. We did not examine the relationship of student satisfaction to the dropout rate. This is a potentially important relationship; however, it was not testable with our undergraduate sample because there was virtually no dropout rate and, hence, no variance to examine.

On the issue of self-selection, little appears to be known yet as to why some students might prefer a distance learning environment. However, Biner et al. (1995) have shown that distance (telecourse) students tend to be more intelligent, emotionally stable, trusting, compulsive, passive, and conforming than traditional college students.

Technical Issues and Attitudes toward Technology

Effective instructional design and techniques have been identified as crucial elements in student achievement (Whittington 1987). Hudson and Boyd (1984) identified the performance of hardware and software as equally important factors in testing the outcomes of student distance learning projects. In this study, we measured the extent of technical problems experienced by students and attempted to determine whether the incidence of such problems was correlated with student performance or with student satisfaction. We also examined the issue of effective instructional design by gauging student attitudes toward the different instructional technologies used, e.g., CD-ROM lectures and online testing. Bruning et al. (1993) illustrated how analyzing the attributes associated with a particular medium or delivery system can help us learn how to design effective distance education courses.

The Data Sample

This study was conducted in the fall quarter of the 1998–1999 academic year. At the beginning of the quarter, the 200 students enrolled in an introductory macroeconomics course were given the option of taking the class in cyberspace or in the traditional classroom. While 151 students chose the traditional format, 49 students chose the cyberspace option.

A chi-square test of independence at the 95% level failed to yield evidence to show that the two groups were different in terms of gender, ethnicity, class level, major, school, and average SAT scores for both math and verbal skills. However, the traditional learners were more likely to have previously taken introductory microeconomics. Thus, everything else being equal, we might expect a slightly better performance from these students relative to the cybergroup. Nonetheless, the cyberlearners were found to have slightly higher grade point averages than the traditional learners. This might signal a slightly better performance potential for the cyberlearners relative to the traditional learners.

Cyber vs. Traditional Teaching Formats

The teaching format used with the traditional learners involved three hours of lecture and one hour of discussion per week. These students attended class and used a standard introductory textbook. In contrast, the only face-to-face interaction that the cyberlearners had with the instructor came at the beginning of the course, since these students were not required to attend class. Instead, class lectures were provided on CD-ROM, an electronic testing center was used to administer weekly online quizzes, a threaded electronic bulletin board was used for asynchronous class discussions, an online discussion room was available for synchronous discussions, and students had twenty-four hour e-mail access to the instructor for additional asynchronous communications. Each of these instructional technologies was designed to address a particular pedagogical issue.

The CD-ROM employed in the cybercourse was The Power of Macroeconomics (Irwin/McGraw-Hill 1998). It was specifically designed to simulate the classroom lecture experience and included eleven separate lectures on topics such as fiscal and monetary policy. Although it served as a lecture substitute, the primary pedagogical purpose of the CD-ROM was to provide visual and audio stimulation, which have been determined to be an important part of enhancing the learning process (Moore 1989).

Each week, students were expected to successfully complete a twenty-question, multiple-choice quiz based on the assigned textbook reading. From a pedagogical perspective, the primary goal of this testing was to ensure that each student kept up with the weekly reading and to provide students with immediate feedback, as the quizzes were graded online. Souder (1993) has noted the importance of prompt feedback.

The purpose of the threaded electronic bulletin board, from an administrative perspective, was to post the class syllabus, reading list, computer lab and exam schedules, and other administrative notices. From a pedagogical perspective, a primary function of the board was to promote asynchronous learner-instructor, as well as learner-learner, policy discussions.

The primary pedagogical purpose of the online discussion room was to stimulate synchronous interactions of the same type. In effect, the chat room served as a cybersurrogate for the traditional professor and teaching assistant's office hours. It also provided a meeting room for students.

Cyberlearners also had e-mail access to the professor, teaching assistant, and technical support staff. They were guaranteed a reply within twenty-four hours, and a reply typically came on the same day. From a pedagogical perspective, e-mail allows for customized and individualized instruction.

Research Design and Performance Results

Two evaluation instruments were used in the study. First, at the end of the course, final exams with fifteen identical questions were administered to both the cyberlearners and the traditional learners. The exams consisted entirely of short essay questions that required some application of macroeconomic principles. Using blind scoring, one individual graded both the cyberlearner and the traditional learner responses.

Second, students were administered an attitudinal survey. Part A of the survey presented questions related to issues such as commuting distance to campus, access to computers, level of computer skills, the primary reason for taking the course, opinions regarding workload, and the overall quality of the course. Part B of the survey was administered only to the cyberlearners. It focused on issues such as the evaluation of various instructional technologies, e.g., the CD-ROM and electronic testing center.

Cyberlearners performed significantly better on the final exam than the traditional learners. The mean score for the cyberlearners was 11.3 ($SD = 2.6$, $n = 48$), while the mean score for the traditional learners was 9.8 ($SD = 2.5$, $n = 145$). With a t-test statistic of 3.70, this result was statistically significant at the 0.01 level. (Throughout this study, where the total n is less than the sample size previously mentioned [$n = 200$], there were nonresponses by some students to the particular instrument.)

Cyberlearners also performed better on the final exam when the results were analyzed by gender, ethnicity, or class level using a two-way analysis-of-variance test. There was, likewise, no statistical difference between economics majors and non–economics majors or between students in the school of social sciences and those in other schools, such as engineering, biological sciences, and humanities.

To test the hypothesis that the cyberlearner group would achieve a higher level of performance because of a slightly higher average GPA, we also conducted an analysis of covariance test. No statistical difference was found to suggest that a higher average GPA could explain the difference in performance.

Results from the Attitudinal Survey

We hypothesized that students with greater access to a personal computer and the Internet and those with higher-level computer skills would be more likely to select the cyberlearning option. We also hypothesized that students who lived farther from campus would be more likely to select cyberlearning, as would students for whom English was not their first language. None of these hypotheses were borne out. Table 1 indicates that there was no statistical difference between the traditional learners and the cyberlearners for any of these variables. (Chi-square tests were used to examine the data. An alpha level of 0.05 [$p < 0.05$] was used as the significance level for all statistical tests.) We were particularly surprised by the finding of no significant difference on the distance to campus variable.

To further probe the question of self-selection, cyberlearners were asked about their primary reason for taking the Web-based version of the course, while traditional learners were asked why they chose not to take this version. In a multiple-choice response format, 44% of the cyberlearners cited "convenience" as their primary reason for enrolling in the Web-based version of the course. In addition, 28% indicated a desire to learn at their own pace, 20% opted for the cybercourse because they were not required to attend class, 2% took the class to improve their computer skills, and 7% cited other reasons.

A similar survey revealed that 49% of the traditional learners did not enroll in the Web-based version of the course because they felt "more comfortable in a traditional classroom environment." Of the remaining students, 20% "didn't think they would learn as much," 15% were unaware that the choice was being offered, 8% said the cybercourse was originally scheduled at a bad time (these students were unaware that the course would be taught in cyberspace and that attendance would not be necessary after the first day), and 7% cited other reasons.

Table 1. Self-Selection Hypotheses and Survey Data

Item	Item	Traditional Learner (N=89)	Cyberlearner (N=46)	Statistical Test
Distance to campus	On campus	23%	20%	Chi square = 0.98
	Very close	40%	37%	$df = 4, p = 0.91$
	2–5 miles	19%	26%	
	6–10 miles	3%	4%	
	10+ miles	15%	13%	
Access to a computer at home	Yes	91%	91%	Chi square = 0.006
	No	9%	9%	$df = 1, p = 0.939$
Access to the Internet at home	Yes	88%	80%	Chi square = 1.454
	No	12%	20%	$df = 1, p = 0.228$
Location of computer used most	Home	78%	65%	Chi square = 3.763
	On-campus lab	22%	33%	$df = 2, p = 0.152$
	Other	0%	2%	
Computer skills	No experience	2%	0%	Chi square = 6.609
	Novice	24%	28%	$df = 4, p = 0.158$
	Intermediate	54%	41%	
	Advanced	20%	26%	
	Expert	0%	4%	
First language	English	26%	41%	Chi square = 5.57
	English and other	26%	11%	$df = 2, p = 0.06$
	Other	47%	48%	

Attitudes toward Instructional Technologies

Table 2 presents the results from part B of the attitudinal survey, which dealt with the instructional technologies that were considered "most essential" by the cyberlearners. The CD-ROM lectures were regarded as the most essential by 83% of the cyberlearners, while only 15% cited the textbook. However, 44% of the cyberlearners did cite the textbook as the second most essential course component. The electronic testing center, featuring the weekly online quizzes, was cited as the third most essential component of the course by 50% of the cyberlearners.

A majority of the cyberlearners (68%) regarded the CD-ROM as the "most enjoyable" learning component. It was followed by the electronic bulletin board at 14%, the online discussions at 11%, the electronic testing center at 9%, and the textbook at 2%.

One interpretation of these results is that both a threaded bulletin board and an online discussion room can be valuable components of any online course, at least in terms of maintaining student interest. It would also appear that well-executed CD-ROM lectures are certainly an acceptable surrogate for traditional classroom lectures, as made evident by these lectures being cited as both the most essential and most enjoyable course component.

Table 2. Essential Instructional Technologies

Item	Option	Count (N=46)	Percentage
Most essential component for learning course material	CD-ROM	38	83%
	Electronic testing center	0	0%
	Electronic bulletin board	0	0%
	Online chats	1	2%
	Textbook	7	15%
Second most essential component for learning course material	CD-ROM	7	15%
	Electronic testing center	16	35%
	Electronic bulletin board	2	4%
	Online chats	1	2%
	Textbook	20	44%
Third most essential component for learning course material	CD-ROM	3	7%
	Electronic testing center	23	50%
	Electronic bulletin board	6	13%
	Online chats	2	4%
	Textbook	12	26%

Learner-Instructor and Learner-Learner Interactions

Table 3 provides the survey results from part B regarding learner-instructor and learner-learner interactions and whether or not the cyberlearners felt they had adequate opportunities to develop and defend their opinions and positions and to express themselves in writing.

After taking the course, 72% of the cyberlearners felt that there were adequate opportunities for learner-instructor interactions. However, only 45% indicated that there were adequate opportunities to interact with other learners. These results suggest that one potential problem with online courses may not necessarily be the lack of learner-instructor interaction, but the more subtle problem of insufficient learner-learner interactions.

Of the 46 cyberlearners taking the course, 85% indicated that they had adequate opportunities to develop and defend their opinions and positions. In addition, 64% indicated that they had adequate opportunities to express themselves in writing and to practice their writing skills. These results suggest that a threaded electronic bulletin board, coupled with an online discussion room, is an effective tool for stimulating thought and debate.

Table 3. Cyberlearner Attitudes toward Interactions

Item	Option	Count (N=46)	Percentage
Adequate opportunities to interact with the professor	Yes	33	72%
	No	13	28%
Adequate opportunities to interact with other students	Yes	20	45%
	No	24	55%
Adequate opportunities to develop and defend opinions and positions	Yes	39	85%
	No	7	15%
Adequate opportunities for self-expression in writing or practicing writing skills	Yes	29	64%
	No	16	35%

Technical Problems

Table 4 presents the results of part B of the survey that were concerned with the frequency of technical problems. At least 20% of the cyberlearners encountered frequent technical problems, while 46% indicated that technical problems were rare.

Table 4. Frequency of Technical Problems

Item	Option	Count (N=46)	Percentage
Frequency of technical problems	Never	0	0%
	Rarely, 1–2 times	21	46%
	A few times, 3–5 times	16	35%
	Frequently, more than 5 times	9	20%

Based on student responses, the most frequent and serious technical problem was a slowdown of the computer server during the weekly electronic quizzes.

Student Satisfaction

In terms of the perceived course quality and student satisfaction with the course, traditional learners had a mean response of 3.80 on a scale of 1 (poor) to 5 (excellent), as compared to a mean score of 4.09 for the cyberlearners. While the difference was not statistically significant, these results do suggest a relatively high degree of satisfaction among cyberlearners with a strong majority of students from both groups appearing to be very satisfied with their learning experience. Almost 90% of the cyberlearners responded positively to the question of whether or not the university should offer more Web-based courses.

Linking Performance with Interactions, Student Satisfaction, and Technical Problems

Table 5 presents the correlations between student performance and selected items on the attitudinal survey.

Table 5. Performance and Attitudinal Survey Items

Attitudinal Survey Item	Correlation Coefficient with Performance
Frequency of technical problems	-0.35*
Learner-instructor interactions	0.10
Learner-learner interactions	0.24
Course quality (student satisfaction)	-0.10

* $p < 0.05$ indicates statistical significance

The values of the correlation coefficients provide some weak evidence in support of our hypotheses. Performance was negatively correlated with the frequency of technical problems and positively correlated with both learner-instructor and learner-learner interactions. However, none of these three correlation coefficients was statistically significant. Only course quality appeared to be correlated at a statistically significant level with student performance; that is, the students' performance appeared to improve as their perception of course quality did. Based on these results, we urge that further studies examine these important relationships.

Conclusions

The results of this study strongly suggest that cyberlearners can learn as well as, or better than, traditional learners regardless of characteristics such as gender, ethnicity, academic background, computer skills, or academic aptitude. This study also suggests that cyberlearners who succeed do so with a high degree of "learner satisfaction." Our experience indicates that a cyberapproach should have the following features: (1) multimedia lectures that simulate the classroom experience; (2) a very active threaded electronic bulletin board; (3) online discussion groups; and (4) electronic testing of important course content with instant feedback.

Two important reasons for students to self-select a cyberlearning option are scheduling convenience and the ability to learn at their own pace. CD-ROM-based lectures that simulate the traditional classroom experience, electronic testing, a threaded electronic bulletin board, and an online discussion room all appear to be both effective and preferred instructional technologies, with the CD-ROM-based lectures being regarded as the most essential and most enjoyable.

Finally, while the experimental cybercourse in this study appeared to offer sufficient opportunities for learner-instructor interactions, over half of the cyberlearners sought more learner-learner interactions. This suggests that interaction, specifically among learners, is an important area of cybercourse design that needs more attention.

References

Abel, J. D., and K. W. Creswell. 1983. A study of student attitudes concerning instructional TV. *Educational and Industrial Television,* October, 72–9.

Anderson, R. M. 1978. Evaluation of graduate engineering education by television at Purdue University. *Proceedings of the Institute of Electrical and Electronics Engineers* 66: 918–26.

Baker, W., T. Hale, and B. R. Gifford. 1997. From theory to implementation: The mediated approach to computer-mediated instruction, learning and assessment. *Educom Review* 32 (5). Retrieved June 8, 1998 from the World Wide Web: http://www.educause.edu/web/pubs/review/reviewArticles/32542.html

Barker, B. O. 1987. Interactive instructional television via satellite: A first year evaluation. *Journal of Rural and Small Schools* 2 (1): 18–23.

Barron, D. D. 1987. Faculty and student perceptions of educating using television. *Journal of Education for Library and Information Science* 27 (4): 257–71.

Biner, P. M. 1993. The development of an instrument to measure student attitudes toward televised courses. *The American Journal of Distance Education* 7 (1): 62–73.

Biner, P. M., M. L. Bink, M. L. Huffmann, and R. S. Dean. 1995. Personality characteristics differentiating and predicting the achievement of television-course students. *The American Journal of Distance Education* 9 (2): 46–60.

Biner, P. M., R. S. Dean, and A. E. Mellinger. 1994. Factors underlying distance learner satisfaction with televised college-level courses. *The American Journal of Distance Education* 8 (1): 60–71.

Brewer, S. M., and D. R. Erickson. 1997. A tale of two classrooms. *Journal of Computing in Teacher Education* 13 (3): 20–2.

Bruffee, K. A. 1982. CLTV: Collaborative learning television. *Educational Communications and Technology Journal* 30: 26–40.

Bruning, R., M. Landis, E. Hoffman, and K. Grosskopf. 1993. Perspectives on an interactive satellite-based Japanese language course. *The American Journal of Distance Education* 7 (3): 22–38.

Burdman, P. 1998. Cyber U. *Anaheim (California) Orange County Register*, 13 September, sec. 1, p. 9.

Carr, R., and F. Ledwith. 1980. Helping disadvantaged students. *Teaching at a Distance* 18: 77–85.

Chu, G. C., and W. Schramm. 1967. *Learning from television: What the research says.* Washington, DC: National Association of Educational Broadcasters.

Cohen, P. A., B. J. Ebeling, and J. A. Kulik. 1982. A meta-analysis of outcome studies of visual-based instruction. *Educational Communications and Technology Journal* 29: 26–36.

Collins, M. A. J. 1996. A successful experiment with an electronic bulletin board in a large class. *Journal of College Science Teaching* 26 (3): 189–91.

Cookson, P. S. 1989. Research on learners and learning in distance education: A review. *The American Journal of Distance Education* 3 (2): 22–34.

Daniel, J. S., and C. Marquis. 1979. Interaction and independence: Getting the mixture right. *Teaching at a Distance* 14: 29–43.

Dede, C. 1996. The evolution of distance education: Emerging technologies and distributed learning. *The American Journal of Distance Education* 10 (2): 4–36.

Delbeq, A., and D. C. Scates. 1989. *Distance learning through telecommunications: A review of lessons learned.* Report to the American Assembly of Collegiate Schools of Business. St. Louis, MO.

DeLoughry, T. J. 1988. Remote instruction using computers found as effective as classroom sessions. *The Chronicle of Higher Education* 34 (2): 15–21.

Dille, B., and M. Mezack. 1991. Identifying predictors of high-risk among community college telecourse students. *The American Journal of Distance Education* 5 (1): 24–35.

Dillman, D. A., J. A. Christenson, P. Salant, and P. D. Warner. 1995. What the public wants from higher education: Work force implications from a 1995 national survey. ERIC, ED 388193.

Eiserman, W. D., and D. D. Williams. 1987. Distance education in elementary and secondary schools: A review of the literature. In *Statewide evaluation report on productivity studies related to improved use of technology to extend educational programs.* Logan, UT: Wasatch Institute for Research and Evaluation. ERIC, ED 291350.

El-Khawas, E. 1995. *Campus trends 1995: New directions for academic programs.* Higher Education Panel Report, no. 85. ERIC, ED 386089.

Ellis, L., and D. Mathis. 1985. College student learning from televised versus conventional classroom lectures: A controlled experiment. *Higher Education* 14: 165–73.

Escalada, L. T., and D. A. Zollman. 1997. An investigation on the effects of using interactive digital video in a physics classroom on student learning and attitudes. *Journal of Research in Science Teaching* 34 (5): 467–89.

Flanders, N. A. 1970. *Analyzing teaching behavior.* Reading, MA: Addison-Wesley.

Garrison, D. R. 1990. An analysis and evaluation of audioteleconferencing to facilitate education at a distance. *The American Journal of Distance Education* 4 (3): 13–24.

Garrison, D. R., and M. Baynton. 1987. Beyond independence in distance education: The concept of control. *The American Journal of Distance Education* 1 (3): 3–15.

Grimes, P. W., J. E. Nielsen, and J. F. Niss. 1988. The performance of nonresident students in the "Economics U$A" telecourse. *The American Journal of Distance Education* 2 (2): 36–43.

Gross, P. 1997. Engaging the disengaged: How is it different when using distance education? In *Walking the tightrope: The balance between innovation and leadership.* Proceedings of the 6th Annual International Conference of the Chair Academy, Reno, NV, February 12–15. ERIC, JC 970 185.

Hackman, M. Z., and K. B. Walker. 1990. Instructional communication in the televised classroom: The effects of system design and teacher immediacy on student learning and satisfaction. *Communication Education* 39: 196–206.

Harrison, P. F., F. Saba, B. J. Seeman, G. Molise, R. Behm, and D. W. Williams. 1991. Dimensions of effectiveness: Assessing the organizational, instructional and technological aspects of distance education programs. Paper presented at the Annual Conference of Educational Communications Technology, February 13–16, Orlando, FL.

Hillman, D. C. A., D. J. Willis, and C. N. Gunawardena. 1994. Learner-interface interaction in distance education: An extension of contemporary models and strategies for practitioners. *The American Journal of Distance Education* 8 (2): 30–42.

Holmberg, B. 1983. Guided didactic conversation in distance education. In *Distance education: International perspectives*, ed. D. Sewart, D. Keegan, and B. Holmberg, 114–22. New York: St. Martin's Press.

Hudson, H. E., and C. H. Boyd. 1984. Distance learning: A review for educators. ERIC, ED 246 872.

Hunt, W. C. 1987. Teaching and learning in the affective domain: A review for educators. ERIC, ED 288 871.

Irwin/McGraw-Hill. 1998. *The power of macroeconomics* [CD-ROM]. Boston: Irwin/McGraw-Hill.

Kataoka, H. 1987. Long-distance language learning: The second year of televised Japanese. *The Journal of Educational Techniques and Technologies* 20: 43–50.

Kerka, S. 1996. *Distance learning, the Internet, and the World Wide Web.* Columbus, OH: ERIC Clearinghouse on Adult, Career, and Vocational Education. ERIC, ED 395214.

Knowles, M. 1980. *The modern practice of adult education.* New York: Cambridge.

Kosakowski, J. 1998. *The benefits of information technology.* Syracuse, NY: ERIC Clearinghouse on Information and Technology. ERIC, ED 420302.

Learmont, D. 1990. Affective differences between host-site and remote-site distance learners participating in two-way interactive television classrooms for high school course credit. Ph.D. diss., University of South Dakota, Vermillion.

Lewis, D. C., J. A. Treves, and A. B. Shaindlin. 1997. Making sense of academic cyberspace: Case study of an electronic classroom. *College Teaching* 45 (3): 96–100.

Lienau, L. 1987. Evaluation of teaching/learning at a distance. Paper presented at the Third Annual Conference on Teaching and Learning at a Distance, August 3–6, Madison, WI.

McCollum, K. 1997. A professor divides his class in two to test value of on-line instruction. *The Chronicle of Higher Education*, 21 February, 43 (24), sec. A23.

McCroskey, J. C., and J. F. Andersen. 1976. The relationship between communication apprehension and academic achievement among college students. *Human Communication Research* 3: 73–81.

Miller, J. W., M. C. McKenna, and P. Ramsey. 1993. An evaluation of student content learning and affective perceptions of a two-day interactive video learning experience. *Educational Technology* 33 (6): 51–5.

Monaghan, P. 1995. Technology and the unions: Faculty labor leaders air hopes and concerns as colleges enter the electronic era. *The Chronicle of Higher Education,* 10 February, 41 (22), sec. A17.

Moore, M. G. 1989. Effects of distance learning: A summary of the literature. Paper for US Congress, Office of Technology Assessment.

———. 1992. Editorial. The 1995 distance education research symposium: A research agenda. *The American Journal of Distance Education* 9 (2): 1–6.

Moore, M. G., and G. Kearsley. 1995. *Distance education: A systems view.* Belmont, CA: Wadsworth Publishing.

Moore, M. G., and M. M. Thompson. 1990. *The effects of distance learning: A summary of literature.* Revised edition. ACSDE Research Monograph Number 15. University Park, PA: The American Center for the Study of Distance Education, The Pennsylvania State University.

Oxford, R., Y. Park-Oh, S. Ito, and M. Sumrall. 1993. Factors affecting achievement in a satellite-delivered Japanese language program. *The American Journal of Distance Education* 7 (1): 11–25.

Pascarella, E. T., and P. T. Terenzini. 1991. *How college affects students: Findings and insights from twenty years of research.* San Francisco: Jossey-Bass Publishers.

Pascarella, E. T., E. J. Whitt, A. Nora, M. Edison, L. S. Hagedorn, and P. T. Terenzini. 1996. What have we learned from the first year of The National Study of Student Learning? *Journal of College Student Development* 37 (2): 182–92.

Perin, P. 1983. Communication interactive de groupe et mediatisation. *Psychologie-Francaise* 28: 289–96.

Rekkedal, T. 1983. Enhancing student progress in Norway. *Teaching at a Distance* 23: 19–24.

Ritchie, H., and T. J. Newby. 1989. Classroom lecture/discussion vs. live televised instruction: A comparison of effects on student performance, attitude, and interaction. *The American Journal of Distance Education* 3 (3): 36–43.

Rumble, G., and K. Harry, eds. 1982. *The distance teaching universities.* London: Croom Helm.

Russell, T. L. 1998. *The "no significant difference" phenomenon.* 4th ed. Raleigh, NC: North Carolina State University.

Saba, F. 1996. Introduction to distance education. *Distance Education Report.* Retrieved 15 August 1998 from the World Wide Web: http://www.distance-educator.com/intro.htm

———. 1998. Discontent with the use of technology in higher education. *Distance Educator* 2 (8). Retrieved 15 August 1998 from the World Wide Web: http://www.distance-educator.com/

Salomon, G. 1981. *Communication and education.* Beverly Hills: Sage Publications.

Sherry, A. C., C. P. Fulford, and S. Zhang. 1998. Assessing distance learners' satisfaction with instruction: A quantitative and qualitative measure. *The American Journal of Distance Education* 12 (3): 4–28.

Sherry, L. 1996. Issues in distance learning. *International Journal of Educational Telecommunications* 1 (4): 337–65.

Shuy, R. W. 1987. Research currents: Dialogue as the heart of learning. *Language Arts* 64: 890–7.

Silvernail, D. L., and J. L. Johnson. 1992. The impact of interactive televised instruction on student evaluations of their instructors. *Educational Technology* 32 (6): 47–50.

Simonson, M. R. 1979. Media and attitudes. *Educational Communication and Technology Journal* 27: 217–36.

Smeltzer, L. R., and J. A. Davy. 1987. Teleconferencing: Reach out to train someone. *Personnel Administrator* 32 (6): 211–9.

Smith, P. L., and C. L. Dillon. 1999. Comparing distance learning and classroom learning: Conceptual considerations. *The American Journal of Distance Education* 13 (2): 6–23.

Souder, W. E. 1993. The effectiveness of traditional vs. satellite delivery in three management of technology master's degree programs. *The American Journal of Distance Education* 7 (1): 37–53.

Steiner, V. 1995. What is distance education? Retrieved 26 August 1998 from the World Wide Web: http://www.wested.org/tie/dlrn/ distance.html

Stone, H. R. 1987. Comparative characteristics analysis of on-campus resident and off-campus video-based engineering graduate students and their implications. *Institute of Electrical and Electronic Engineers, Transactions on Education* 30 (2): 12–8.

———. 1988. Variations in the characteristics and performance between on-campus and video-based off-campus engineering graduate students. *Journal of Continuing Higher Education* 36 (1): 18–23.

Sun Associates. 1997. Educational technology integration: Basic technology tools for educators. Retrieved 3 June 1998 from the World Wide Web: http://www.sun-associates.com/resources/ bastools.html

US Congress, Office of Technology Assessment. 1989. *Linking for learning: A new course for education* OTA-SET-430. Washington, DC: Government Printing Office.

Wagner, E. D. 1994. In support of a functional definition of interaction. *The American Journal of Distance Education* 8 (2): 6–29.

Wagner, E. D., and B. L. McCombs. 1995. Learner centered psychological principles in practice: Designs for distance education. *Educational Technology* 35 (2): 32–5.

Wagner, N. 1987. Operation and evaluation of the instructional television system at Arizona State University. Paper presented at the Third Annual Conference on Teaching and Learning at a Distance, August 3–6, Madison, WI.

Walberg, H. 1984. Improving the productivity of America's schools. *Educational Leadership* 41 (8): 19–27.

Walker, K., and M. Hackman. 1992. Multiple predictors of perceived learning and satisfaction: The importance of information transfer and non-verbal immediacy in the televised course. *Distance Education* 13 (1): 81–92.

Weingand, D. E. 1984. Telecommunications delivery of instruction: A comparison with the traditional classroom. *Journal of Education for Library and Information Science* 25: 3–13.

Wergin, W. F. 1986. Televising graduate engineering courses: Results of an instructional experiment. *Engineering Education* 77: 109–16.

Weston, C., and P. A. Cranton. 1986. Selecting instructional strategies. *The Journal of Higher Education* 57 (3): 259–88.

Whittington, N. 1987. Is instructional television educationally effective? A research review. *The American Journal of Distance Education* 1 (1): 47–57.

Willis, B., ed. 1994. *Distance education: Strategies and tools.* Englewood Cliffs, NJ: Educational Technology.

Wolcott, L. L. 1995. The distance teacher as reflective practitioner. *Educational Technology* 35 (1): 39–43.

Young, J. R. 1997. Rethinking the role of the professor in an age of high-tech tools. *The Chronicle of Higher Education*, 3 October, 44 (6), sec. A26–A28.

———. 1998. A year of Web pages for every course: UCLA debates their value. *The Chronicle of Higher Education*, 15 May, 44 (36), sec. A29.

Zhang, P. 1998. A case study on technology use in distance learning. *Journal of Research on Computing in Education* 30 (4): 398–419.

Distance Education for Dentists: Improving the Quality of Online Instruction

Heiko Spallek, Peter Berthold, Diarmuid B. Shanley, and Rolf Attstrom

Vol. 14 No. 2 2000

Abstract

This study describes the development and the evaluation of quality assurance criteria for online dental education. These criteria were developed by the authors and evaluated by oral health professionals through an Internet survey. The survey indicated that oral health professionals ranked the creation of scientifically based, frequently updated courses that clearly define their educational goals and objectives as highly important.

Introduction

The peer review process ensures that contributions to scientific journals meet acceptable standards. This process and its inherent standards do not exist in the field of online education (Eysenbach and Diepgen 1998). Since online education has the potential to reach a very broad audience, the authors of this article developed quality assurance criteria to ensure that online educational materials meet similarly rigorous standards for publication.

Schleyer and Pham's (1999) review of 157 online continuing dental education courses found that their instructional quality was poor. Only 28% of these courses scored questions online. Many of the courses neglected to include basic information, such as the name(s) of the author(s) (29%), the intended audience (81%), and the goals and objectives (77%). To date, the best approach used for identifying quality indicators is that of the Subcommittee on Educational Software established by the Accredited Standards Committee Medical Devices 156 (Task Group on Dental Informatics). Based on this subcommittee's recommendations, Schleyer and Johnson (1999) developed preliminary guidelines for the design of educational software. These guidelines cover several areas of instructional software design, such as pedagogical issues, subject matter, language, grammar, format, surface features, questions, feedback, invisible functions, and offline materials.

Sophisticated technological design, however, does not substitute for the quality of a program's educational content or for its scientific validity. If online educational material is to gain credibility with professional and educational accreditation authorities throughout the world, it must be educationally and scientifically based.

In November 1997, a workshop on interactive periodontology was held in Copenhagen, Denmark, on behalf of the European Project in Dental Education (Attstrom 1997). As a result of this workshop, a pilot model for dental education called "Virtual Interactive Periodontology" (VIP) was developed. VIP is an online learning resource. Dental educators from around the world contribute material to VIP that can be accessed by students from all of the contributing institutions. The creation of VIP made it necessary to develop and evaluate quality assurance criteria for this submitted material.

The authors of this project developed a set of quality assurance criteria for online instruction and then evaluated them by conducting an Internet survey of oral health professionals. The criteria were designed in a manner that would encourage authors to contribute to interactive learning within a variety of curricula. This included a peer review process that would allow academics to apply their online contributions toward their tenure and promotion requirements. We anticipate that the set of quality criteria we identified will evolve into standards that will facilitate the sharing of peer-reviewed, educational online material within and between dental educators in countries worldwide. This approach offers enormous potential for idea and information sharing, as well as for reducing research and program duplication. For example, if authors who are about to write an interactive program can see that a similar program has already been developed and peer reviewed, then they may redirect their efforts toward another area of study, a similar program of distinctly higher standards, or one with a more relevant educational content. Currently, the use of online educational material by institutions other than the one where the material was developed is very restricted because there is no peer review process based on predetermined criteria. As dental schools in both developed and developing countries continue to experience difficulty in faculty recruitment, the production of peer-reviewed, interactive learning programs offers one approach to addressing this problem by providing a source of high quality, online educational materials from which dental faculty can draw. Perhaps a more significant consequence is that, if an Internet program has not been peer reviewed, it would be subject to a more critical analysis and would thereby improve the overall quality and public opinion of Internet programs in general. International peer review could contribute to the globalization of dental education and might lead to a cross-acceptance of dental degrees between different countries without the need for repeating entire parts of a dental curriculum or qualifying examinations.

Methods

During the 1997 workshop on interactive periodontology in Denmark, a group of five respondents, including one dental informatician[1], designed and compiled a set of basic quality criteria for hypermedia documents in periodontal education. In order to validate the survey design, fifty dentists from an electronic periodontal discussion group were randomly selected to receive a questionnaire; thirty-one completed it. The results of this pilot survey were then used to finalize and develop a cross-sectional survey. This survey was designed using the methods developed by Dillmann (1978) and was made available through Temple University's Web server at http://www.temple.edu/dentistry/di/survey/sr0898/ In order to ascertain the respondents' attributes, behaviors, beliefs, and attitudes, the survey included closed-ended questions with ordered answers as well as open-ended questions. Three of these questions were about demographics, four questions were about computer knowledge, seven questions were about experiences with online learning material, and four questions were about quality assurance criteria (one of these four questions was further subdivided into fourteen sections). Responses to the surveys were entered directly into a Web-server application based on Oracle 8 (see Figure 1).

The online survey was widely publicized among the dental community. An estimated 8,000 dentists were contacted via e-mail and through publicly available electronic discussion groups, such as the ones compiled by the College of Dentistry at The University of Iowa (Quinn 1999). In addition, the science, medicine, and dentistry Usenet newsgroup (news:sci.med.dentistry) was used to contact oral health professionals. Two follow-up reminders were sent to all groups after four and eight weeks respectively.

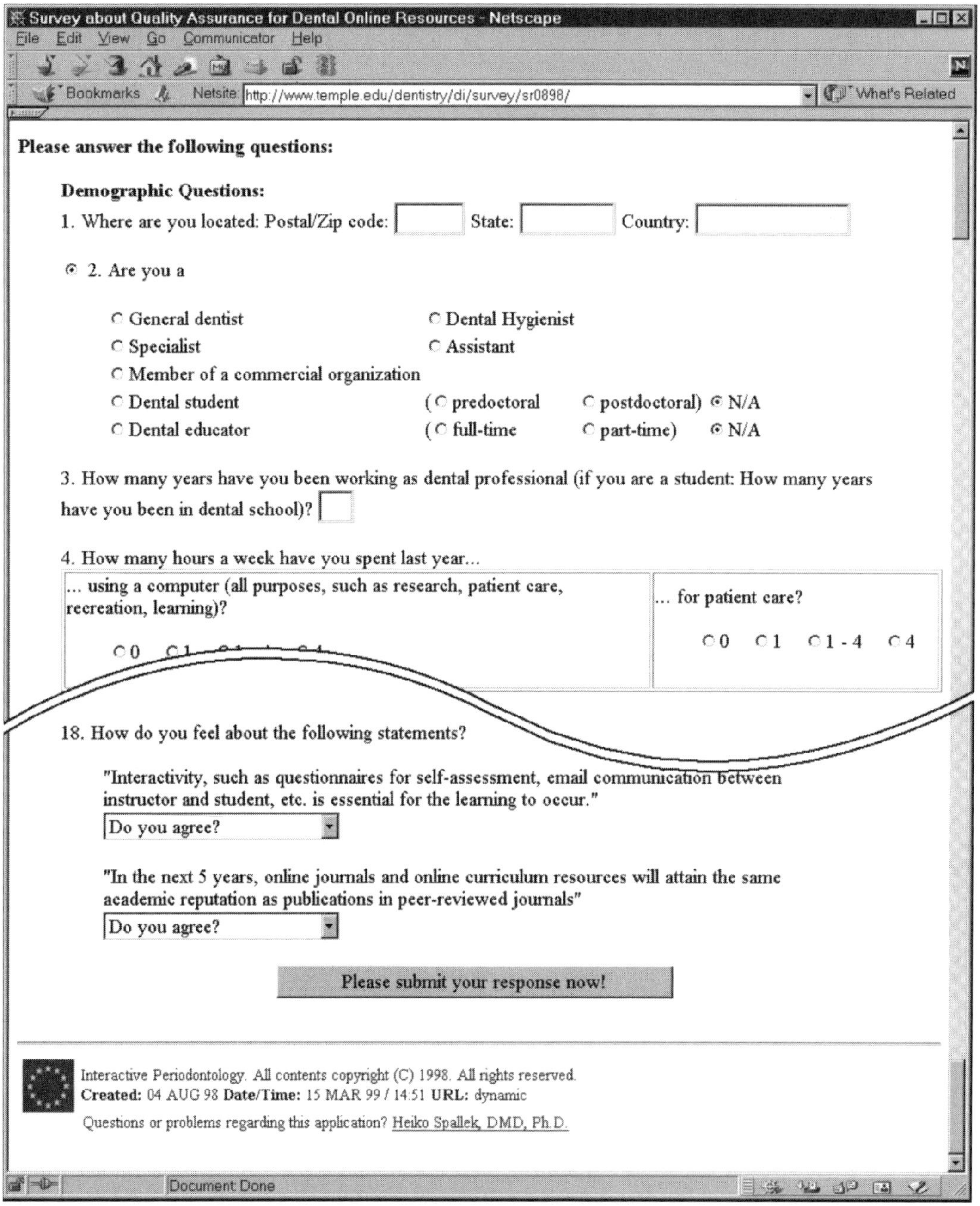

Figure 1. Web-Based Survey of Quality Assurance Criteria

Results and Discussion

Demographic and Computer Experience. Between August and October 1998, 218 responses were received from 38 different countries. The largest number of respondents came from three countries—the US (115), Canada (15), and Germany (11). Of those respondents, sixty-two were dental educators, seventy-eight were general dentists, forty-four were specialists, eighteen were dental students, and four were dental hygienists. Twelve respondents did not provide information about their occupation.

Regarding their use of computers, 193 respondents (88%) stated that they spent four hours per week using a computer in the last year. Their computer activities included research, patient care, recreation, and learning. This means that, during a forty-hour work week, respondents spent approximately 10% of their time on the computer. Ninety-four respondents rated their computer knowledge as "moderate," eighty-four said it was "extensive," and thirty-three considered themselves "experts."

Since respondents were solicited from online mailing lists and newsgroups (solely accessible via the Internet), it can be assumed that the respondents had an interest in and knowledge of computing and Internet applications.

Former Experience with Online Learning. Of the 218 respondents, 58 had participated in online courses in areas other than dentistry, and 57 had participated in online courses in dentistry (25 of these respondents selected both options). The remaining respondents did not participate in online courses. The majority of respondents who had taken online courses were satisfied with the overall quality of their most recent course (9 [10%] were "extremely satisfied"; 68 [75%] were "satisfied"; 13 [14%] were "unsatisfied"; and 4 [4%] were "extremely unsatisfied"). In 6 cases (7%), respondents were dissatisfied because of a lack of in-depth course material or because of the instructor's lack of knowledge. In 4 cases (4%), instructional design deficiencies, such as "It was basically scrolling text with a few images," were cited as problems. "No interaction" was also cited as a cause for dissatisfaction by 5 (6%) of the respondents. In addition, 80 respondents (89%) experienced technical difficulties with online courses. However, the most frequently mentioned problems were the speed of transmission (62% of all technical difficulties) and system crashes (19% of all technical difficulties).

Need for Quality Assurance in Online Learning. Of the 218 respondents, 148 (68%) agreed that there is a need for an international quality assurance committee for online educational material in dentistry (82 [38%] "strongly"; 66 [30%] "somewhat"); 36 (17%) respondents stated that they "do not agree"; 20 (9%) neither agreed nor disagreed; and 14 (6%) did not answer the question. The respondents ranked the criteria for quality online continuing education in order of importance (see Table 1). If the criteria are grouped by content ("scientifically based," "regularly updated," etc.) and instructional design ("consistent look and feel; aesthetics," "prompt feedback to any answered question," etc.), then, overall, the respondents ranked the content criteria higher than the instructional design criteria.

Table 1. Quality Assurance Criteria as Ranked by Respondents (Closed-Ended Questions)

Quality Assurance Criteria Courses should...	**Very Important**	**Important**	**Not Important**	**Not Important at All**	**Total Number of Responses**
be scientifically based.	138	51	11	1	201
be regularly updated (current).	127	71	2	0	200
be easy to navigate through.	122	55	8	1	186
have defined educational objectives.	104	89	7	1	201
stimulate learning.	101	90	7	1	199
be created by appropriately qualified academics.	82	84	30	8	204
be at an appropriate level for the intended participants.	71	111	14	3	199
be peer reviewed.	68	101	25	7	201
be structured so that the participant can determine the pace.	64	112	21	1	198
give prompt feedback to any answered question.	60	127	10	1	198
contain context-sensitive help.*	55	109	32	2	198
have a consistent look and feel; aesthetics.	45	85	63	6	199
include self-assessments.	44	111	37	6	198
adapt to the performance of the participant.	31	107	49	10	197

*a help system that takes into account the action a user is currently performing

In the survey, 162 respondents (74%) agreed with the following statement (76 [35%] "strongly"; 86 [39%] "somewhat"): "Interactivity, such as questionnaires for self-assessment, e-mail communication between instructor and student, etc., is essential for learning to occur." Of the total number of respondents, 27 (12%) disagreed, 22 (10%) neither agreed nor disagreed, and 7 (3%) did not respond to the statement.

The respondents were also asked to indicate their agreement with the following statement: "In the next 5 years, online journals and online curriculum resources will attain the same academic reputation as publications in peer-reviewed journals." Out of the total number of respondents, 119 (55%) agreed with this statement (52 [24%] "strongly"; 67 [31%] "somewhat"); 55 (25%) disagreed; 31 (14%) neither agreed nor disagreed; and 13 (6%) did not respond to the statement.

Fifty-three respondents used the opportunity to submit suggestions for additional quality criteria for online learning materials. The categorization of these additional criteria can be seen in Table 2.

Table 2. Frequency of New Suggestions for Additional Quality Assurance Criteria (Open-Ended Questions)

Additional Quality Assurance Criteria	Frequency
Need for up-to-date references (online and traditional)	12
Proof of authors' expertise, such as "Credentials of course creator/instructor"	8
Need for evaluations against comparable traditional educational approaches, such as "are we really accomplishing something with this modality"	5
Downloadable course information, such as "(high quality) pictures and graphics downloadable for future reference"	5
Clinical relevance	4
Requests of translations into languages other than English	3
Other (mentioned only once or twice)	16
Total	53

Computer Knowledge vs. Survey Participation. While this study is only a first attempt at developing and evaluating quality assurance criteria for online learning material, it has demonstrated that there is a worldwide interest among those in the dental community who use online resources on a regular basis. The respondents' professional backgrounds, their use of the Internet, and their educational experiences make their views valuable in determining quality criteria.

However, this survey had limitations because the respondents were self-selected instead of being chosen at random. Respondents were biased in their use of computers in general and in their use of the Internet in particular. Because they had their own e-mail accounts and had used a dental discussion group at least once prior to our survey, we can assume that they have a positive attitude toward the Internet. In addition, all respondents had to be familiar with the concept of Internet addresses and how to access a given Web site to submit their responses. Another factor that cannot be measured is the possibility that instructors in higher education, and in medicine or dentistry in particular, may lack competence in or knowledge of educational techniques.

For these and other reasons, it is difficult to draw conclusions in terms of the overall evaluation of online courses by dentists. It would have been beneficial to extend this evaluation to dentists who do not use the Internet and who were, consequently, excluded from this survey. Even though that option was outside the scope of this project, it should be pursued in future research.

Current Status vs. Need for Quality Assurance. The results of this survey indicate that a majority of the respondents are relatively satisfied with the quality of the online courses they have taken. However, some of the respondents criticized instructional design and the lack of in-depth material, which mirrors the results of other studies (Schleyer and Johnson 1999). Almost all of the respondents who had taken online courses in the past had experienced some kind of technical problem.

Respondents widely recognized the need for quality assurance criteria. They rated the creation of scientifically based, frequently updated courses that clearly define their educational objectives as "highly important." Despite the fact that the majority of respondents experienced technical difficulties in previous online courses, they did not fully agree with the more technically oriented quality criteria, such as the call for context-sensitive help. Other educational aspects, such as the inclusion of self-assessment tests, the adaptation of courses to the performance of the participant, and the need for a consistent look and feel, were rated as much less important by the respondents than they were by the group that set up these criteria in the first place.

Information technology increasingly influences educational developments in many fields of academia. One example of this is the VIP project, where dental schools from different countries contribute educational resources, such as clinical pictures, video clips, glossaries, and entire online courses to a shared educational repository. In addition, an example of applied standards in education is the growing number of standardized tests that can be taken in a computerized format. The Graduate Record Examination (GRE), the Graduate Management Admission Test (GMAT), and the Test of English as a Foreign Language (TOEFL) are examples of general-purpose tests (Educational Testing Service Network 1999). The North East Regional Boards of Dental Examiners (NERB) in the US is an example of a dental license test that can be taken online as well. Despite the fact that educators and students might resist this development, computerized test taking is likely to be transformed from optional to mandatory in an increasing number of cases.

As the trend toward electronic media in oral health education increases, the need to establish criteria for quality assurance in this new medium becomes increasingly important. These online programs must gain the same credibility as traditional ones. Already, there are examples of electronic publications in dentistry on the Internet that recommend the use of certain procedures or materials. However, the scientific content and background of several of these publications is less than adequate, and their credibility is further undermined when the authors are not identified.

Scientifically sound quality criteria will enhance the credibility of electronically published learning material among professionals and professional organizations. The application of quality assurance criteria is essential if electronic programs are to receive widespread application and recognition by the larger academic community. Whatever our aspirations may be for the so-called "electronic curriculum" or the "virtual" dental school of the future, progress can be made only if the programs produced are built on a modular basis and are of the highest quality in content, science, and technology. They must facilitate student access to information in a user-friendly, interactive manner. Without peer review and quality assessment, it is likely that considerable resources will continue to be wasted on programs of unsound educational and scientific content regardless of the most sophisticated technological advances.

Conclusion

This project identified quality assurance criteria for the development of online dental education material that focus on scientifically based, frequently updated courses that provide clearly defined educational goals. The authors had these criteria evaluated by oral health professionals who currently use the Internet and, therefore, are the most likely consumers of online learning material in this area.

Authors of online continuing education courses can use the results of this survey to develop new courses and to modify existing ones. It is anticipated that this project will also encourage authors to contribute to interactive curricula as the science of interactive learning grows at an increasing pace. Ultimately, oral health deals with the well-being of our patients, and it is our obligation as practitioners and researchers to maintain the highest standards for our educational material.

The quality assurance criteria developed from this and other projects can be implemented through gradual adoption by different professional groups and associations. This adoption should be characterized by the collection of feedback from different user groups. All involved should seek agreement on a commonly usable set of policies as well as on a continuously evolving repertoire of criteria that identify quality. Once the policies have been discussed, reviewed, and verified by the scientific community, it is very likely that they will be adopted and applied by universities, specialist organizations, regulating agencies, and international accrediting authorities.

The authors of this article will continue to promote the adoption of quality assurance criteria by various universities, specialist organizations, and regulating agencies. The establishment of an internationally recognized "seal of approval" for online educational material based on these criteria would be an excellent means of encouraging the development of such material.

Note

1. Dental informatics is the application of computer science principles to dentistry for the purpose of treatment, research, and education.

Acknowledgements

This project is supported by the Council for the Renewal of Undergraduate Education, Sweden. The authors want to thank Dr. Titus Schleyer for his thoughtful recommendations regarding the development of standards in dental education and Ms. Maryellen Fitzpatrick for her kind review of the manuscript.

References

Attstrom, R. 1997. Proceedings of the 1st Workshop in Interactive Periodontology. A European Project in Dental Education. [online]. Copenhagen, Denmark. Available at http://interactive.odparod.lu.se/ workshop/proceedings/sumproc.html

Dillmann, D. A. 1978. *Mail and telephone surveys*. New York: John Wiley & Sons, Inc.

Educational Testing Service Network 1999. [online]. Educational Testing Service. Available at http://www.ets.org/

Eysenbach, G., and T. L. Diepgen. 1998. Towards quality management of medical information on the Internet: Evaluation, labelling, and filtering of information. *British Medical Journal* 317: 1496–502.

International Committee of Medical Journal Editors. 1988. Uniform requirements for manuscripts submitted to biomedical journals. *British Medical Journal* 296: 401–5.

Quinn, J. 1999. Electronic discussion groups in dentistry. [online]. Iowa City: Dows Institute for Dental Research, The University of Iowa. Available at http://indy.radiology.uiowa.edu/Beyond/Dentistry/leslie.html

Schleyer, T., and L. Johnson. 1999. Guidelines for the design of educational software. Accredited Standards Committee Medical Devices 156 (Task Group on Dental Informatics). [online]. Philadelphia, PA: Temple University School of Dentistry. Available at http://www.temple.edu/dentistry/di/edswstd/

Schleyer, T., and T. Pham. 1999. Online continuing dental education. *Journal of the American Dental Association* 130: 848–54, 877–8.

Deterrents to Participation in Web-Based Continuing Professional Education

Kathy J. Perdue and Thomas Valentine

Vol. 14 No. 1 2000

Abstract

This study examined the perceptions of certified public accountants concerning deterrents to participation in Web-based continuing professional education. A survey instrument was mailed to a random sample of the Georgia Society of Certified Public Accountants' membership, and 444 usable surveys were returned. Four broad dimensions of deterrence to participation in Web-based education were identified through factor analysis. The two most influential deterrents were Concerns about Electronically Mediated Communication and Concerns about the Quality of Course Offerings. The other two were Concerns about Access to Technology-Associated Resources and Concerns about the Availability of Necessary Personal Resources. The vast majority of respondents reported that they had access to the technology and that they perceived themselves as having the personal characteristics necessary for participation in Web-based education activities. However, the proportion of respondents using Web-based education for continuing professional learning in 1998 was minimal.

Introduction

Despite the proliferation of opportunities for continuing professional education (CPE) using Web-based courses or programs, the current utilization of these opportunities by certified public accountants (CPAs) appears to be limited (Nacinovich 1998). A study conducted for the Georgia Society of Certified Public Accountants by Perdue and Valentine (1998) found that respondents believe distance education, including the use of the Internet, is an effective way to learn. In addition, the study found that the vast majority of respondents reported having adequate access to the technology necessary for participation in a variety of distance education activities. However, with the exception of print-based distance education, the percentage of respondents actually using distance education for CPE was minimal.

Research concerning continuing education via distance education is in its early stages and consists primarily of a few descriptive studies of multiple groups of professionals (Grundnoski 1992; Scalter 1990) conducted before the Web became available as an education medium. As a result, there is little empirical research concerning the use of Web-based education by professional groups and virtually none concerning deterrents to that use. Because a variety of organizations—including state and national professional associations, public education institutions, and private educational organizations—are beginning to investigate the development of Web-based courses for accountants (Carlozzi 1998; Khan 1997; Nacinovich 1998), the need to fill this gap in the literature is a timely one. If Web-based education is to live up to its true potential, program planners need to know why CPAs are not participating in this form of distance learning.

Purpose of the Study

The purpose of this study was to identify deterrents to participation in Web-based CPE by CPAs. The central questions explored in this study were

1. What is the relative importance of specific deterrents to participation in Web-based continuing professional education by certified public accountants in Georgia?
2. Can individual deterrents be reduced to a more parsimonious, conceptual framework through factor analysis?

Methodology

Instrumentation. The instrument used in this study was a mailed, self-completion survey designed to gather information about deterrents to participation in Web-based CPE. There were seven major steps in the development process of the study survey instrument.

The first step, concept clarification, resulted in an operational definition of "deterrent" based on the writings of Darkenwald and Valentine (1985). For this study, a deterrent is identified as *a force working in combination with other forces to reduce the chance that an individual will elect to participate in a particular Web-based educational opportunity.*

The second step, development and refinement of the pilot survey item pool, involved developing a list of potential deterrents to participation and evaluating those items for inclusion in the survey. That list was gathered from the following four sources:

- a computer-based literature search of adult continuing education and distance education articles using a variety of databases,
- interviews conducted with continuing education professionals of the Georgia Society of CPAs,
- interviews with education providers who develop and deliver CPE courses and programs for CPAs,
- interviews with practicing CPAs.

The initial list of 242 deterrent items was then refined by three separate groups of reviewers: the researchers, a small panel of adult educators, and a trio of licensed CPAs practicing in Georgia who represented the varying practice arenas of accounting. A rigorous process of analyzing each potential item for semantic equivalents served to eliminate item redundancy and ultimately reduced the potential pool to sixty-five unique items that formed the core content for the pilot survey instrument.

The third step in the overall instrument development process was to design an optimal format to capture respondent data. Several formats were developed and evaluated by CPE administrators, providers, participants, and the researchers. The response scale at which we arrived is depicted in Table 1.

Table 1. Sample Survey Item

	Strongly Disagree	←		→		Strongly Agree
1. I don't have the *computer hardware* necessary to participate in Web-based CPE courses..	1	2	3	4	5	6

The fourth step in developing the survey instrument was to add ten items intended to collect personal and professional information on study participants. These items included (1) age; (2) years certified as a CPA; (3) gender; (4) arena of accounting practice; (5) formal education; (6) prior use of the Internet to purchase goods or services; (7) total hours of CPE completed during the last reporting cycle (a two-year period); (8) hours of self-study CPE during the last reporting cycle; (9) hours of Web-based CPE during the last reporting cycle; and (10) hours of Web-based CPE to be completed in the next reporting cycle.

Step five, the prepilot review of the proposed survey instrument, consisted of critiques by three separate groups including adult educators, the researchers, and practicing CPAs. In the next step, an empirical pilot test was conducted in which 266 attendees at the 1998 Georgia Society of CPAs' Southeastern Accounting Show completed the survey. Frequency analysis of the responses was undertaken to make certain that items exhibited a sufficient amount of variance. The intercorrelations among items were calculated to make sure that items were not redundant. Step seven resulted in a final survey containing sixty-seven items. Fifty-seven items measuring specific deterrents used a Likert-type scale indicating the extent to which participants agreed or disagreed with each one. Ten personal and professional variables provided the respondents with open-ended or selection responses.

Sampling and Data Collection. The sample was randomly selected from the 1997–1998 Membership Directory of the Georgia Society of CPAs. A total of 800 CPAs were randomly chosen from the directory, which represented approximately 8,000 CPAs from twenty-two membership chapters. In October 1998, respondents were mailed a copy of the survey. After three follow-ups, 444 respondents had returned usable surveys, yielding a final raw response rate of 56%.

Description of Respondents. The 444 respondents ranged in age from twenty-five to seventy-two with a mean age of 42.5 years. The respondents' number of years as a licensed CPA ranged from 0.5 to 46 years with a mean of 13.6 years. The number of CPE hours completed during the last reporting period ranged from 0 to 300 hours with a mean of 79.2 hours. The number of these hours completed using some form of self-study (any CPE conducted without instructor assistance) ranged from 0 to 120 with a mean of 15.5 hours. The number of total hours completed using Web-based courses ranged from 0 to 40 with a mean of 0.2 hours. Out of 444 respondents, 98.4% indicated no use of Web-based courses during the last reporting period.

A majority (63.1%) of the respondents were male. With respect to employment, 50.7% of the respondents were employed in the arena of public practice, 36.7% in industry, 4.1% in government, 1.6% in education, and 6.9% in other areas. With respect to formal education, 66.5% of respondents held a bachelor's degree, 30.8% held a master's degree, 1.6% held a doctorate degree, and 1.1% marked "other." The majority (55.5%) had used the Internet to purchase goods or services.

Data Analysis. Responses were analyzed using SPSS for Windows. Item means were tabulated and ranked to address research question 1: What is the relative importance of specific deterrents to participation in Web-based CPE by CPAs in Georgia? Because there was not sufficient theoretical basis for predicting the factor structure of deterrents to Web-based CPE for CPAs, exploratory factor analytic procedures were utilized to address research question 2: Can individual deterrents be reduced to a more parsimonious, conceptual framework through factor analysis? A principal components analysis was employed to extract the initial factors. In order to obtain uncorrelated factors with the simplest possible structure, we utilized orthogonal rotation using the Varimax procedure to reach a final solution. The selection of a factor solution was based upon at least three criteria: (1) ability to interpret meaning, (2) minimization of crossloaders to enhance parsimony, and (3) avoidance of factors containing too few items. After the factor solution was selected, factor scores were computed for each individual factor using additive indices. These indices were used to restrict inclusion in the factor scores to those items with a criterion loading that exceeded 0.55, a level without crossloaders. The intercorrelations between scores were computed and analyzed to determine the extent to which the factors were related.

Findings

Findings in Relation to Research Question 1. The survey contained fifty-seven items that attempted to assess respondents' degree of deterrence. Item means ranged from 1.55 to 4.20 on a 1 (strongly disagree) to 6 (strongly agree) point scale. Only thirteen of the items demonstrated a mean at or above 3.5. The top ten items describe the greatest deterrents to respondents' participation in Web-based CPE and are depicted in Table 2. Of these top ten items, seven involve educational technology preferences. The remaining three items describe concerns with evaluation, time constraint, and security.

Table 2. Top Ten Deterrents

Rank	Item #	Item	M	SD
1	17	I prefer hearing CPE lectures in person rather than reading them on a *computer screen.*	4.20	1.55
2	57	It has never occurred to me to participate in Web-based CPE courses to complete my CPE requirements.	4.03	1.80
3	16	I prefer face-to-face interaction with the *instructor* rather than electronic communication used in Web-based CPE courses.	4.01	1.59
4	13	I prefer traditional classroom instruction over Web-based CPE courses.	4.00	1.53
5	18	I prefer hearing CPE lectures in person rather than hearing them through a *computer speaker.*	3.93	1.58
6	15	I prefer face-to-face interaction with my *peers* rather than electronic communication used in Web-based CPE courses.	3.89	1.59
7	14	I prefer using printed materials over the kind of electronic materials (e.g., computer screens, e-mails) used for Web-based CPE courses.	3.86	1.51
8	41	I am concerned that I don't know how to evaluate the quality of a Web-based CPE course before enrolling in it.	3.79	1.65
9	37	I am concerned that I might have too many interruptions in my office or home to participate in Web-based CPE courses.	3.79	1.73
10	53	I am concerned about submitting *personal* information over the Internet in order to participate in a Web-based CPE course.	3.77	1.79

Table 3 depicts the ten bottom-ranked deterrents, that is, those that provide the least deterrence to participation in a Web-based CPE course. The means for these bottom ten items range from 1.55 to 2.22. Conceptually, all of these items fall into the "access to resources" category—seven related to technology-associated resources, two related to personal resources, and one related to political resources.

Table 3. Bottom Ten Deterrents

Rank	Item #	Item	M	SD
48	11	I don't have the *patience* to learn how to use the Web for a Web-based CPE course.	2.22	1.36
49	7	I don't have the authority in my work environment that allows me to download the necessary computer software from the Internet (e.g., browsers, sounds, video, graphics applications).	2.08	1.70
50	26	I am concerned that the cost of *purchasing the computer hardware* needed to participate in Web-based CPE courses is too high.	2.03	1.35
51	3	I don't have the *technical knowledge* necessary to participate in Web-based CPE courses.	1.89	1.31
52	8	I don't have reliable enough access to the *Internet* to participate in Web-based CPE courses.	1.89	1.46
53	2	I don't have the *computer software* necessary to participate in Web-based CPE courses.	1.86	1.52
54	4	I don't have the *confidence* necessary to participate in Web-based CPE courses.	1.83	1.23
55	27	I am concerned that the cost of *connecting to the Internet* is too high to justify participating in Web-based CPE courses.	1.80	1.18
56	9	I don't have reliable enough access to *electronic mail (e-mail)* to participate in Web-based CPE courses.	1.79	1.42
57	1	I don't have the *computer hardware* necessary to participate in Web-based CPE coruses.	1.55	1.29

Findings in Relation to Research Question 2. Although ten of the factors initially extracted by principal components analysis met the Kaiser criterion for retention (a minimum eigenvalue of 1.0), a more parsimonious solution was pursued. Seven terminal factor solutions representing two, three, four, five, six, seven, and eight components were computed using the Varimax procedure. An examination of the scree plot of factor variances also supported the selection of a four-factor solution. After inspection of the rotated factor matrices, the four-factor solution was selected as the most conceptually meaningful representation of the data, accounting for 54% of the variance. Tables 4 through 7 present the items comprising each of the four factors. Only items with loadings of 0.55 or greater were used to define a given factor. The variance explained by the four factors were 18.6%, 13.0%, 11.8%, and 10.2% respectively.

Table 4. Factor I: Concerns about the Quality of Course Offerings

Item No.	Deterrent Item	Loading Value	Item Mean	Scale Rank
49	I am concerned about the *relevancy* of course content in a Web-based CPE course.	.72	2.44	39
48	I am concerned about the *accuracy* of course content in a Web-based CPE course.	.71	2.42	40
50	I am concerned that other people might not place as high a value on Web-based CPE courses as on other forms of CPE.	.69	2.67	33
46	I am concerned that CPE credits may not be properly documented by the provider of a Web-based CPE course.	.68	2.74	32
47	I am concerned that the State Board of Accountancy will not recognize CPE credits earned in a Web-based CPE course.	.68	2.91	29
52	I am concerned about submitting *financial* information over the Internet in order to participate in a Web-based CPE course.	.65	3.68	11
42	I am concerned that I can't get a course recommendation from other CPAs who have taken a Web-based CPE course.	.63	3.22	19
51	I am concerned about submitting *written comments* over the Internet in order to participate in a Web-based CPE course.	.62	2.58	34
43	I am concerned that a Web-based CPE course would take too long to complete.	.62	3.36	16
53	I am concerned about submitting *personal* information over the Internet in order to participate in a Web-based CPE course.	.61	3.77	10
31	I am concerned that electronic discussion in Web-based CPE courses would lack focus.	.61	3.02	25
41	I am concerned that I don't know how to evaluate the quality of a Web-based CPE course before enrolling in it.	.60	3.79	8
40	I am concerned that a Web-based CPE course might not provide printed reference materials for me to use in my work.	.59	3.38	15
30	I am concerned that electronic communication could be misinterpreted during participation in Web-based CPE courses.	.58	2.49	38
32	I am concerned that Web-based CPE courses might not provide immediate feedback.	.57	3.11	22

The items comprising Factor I: Concerns about the Quality of Course Offerings look at quality from two perspectives—self-evaluation of the course quality and perceived evaluation of the course quality by others. The twelve deterrent items dealing with self-assessment of quality reflect professional, security, and personal concerns. Five variables (Items 49, 48, 42, 43, and 40) reflect professional concerns; three variables (Items 52, 51, and 53) reflect security concerns; and four variables (Items 31, 41, 30, and 32) reflect personal concerns. The three items that examine the ways others might assess the course offerings reflect concerns about others in general (Item 50) and concerns about CPE-associated organizations in particular (Items 46 and 47). The item means for this factor ranged from 2.42 to 3.79 with an average of 3.03. Only Factor II: Concerns about Electronically Mediated Communication had a higher items mean.

Table 5. Factor II: Concerns about Electronically Mediated Communication

Item No.	Deterrent Item	Loading Value	Item Mean	Scale Rank
16	I prefer face-to-face interaction with the *instructor* rather than electronic communication used in Web-based CPE courses.	.87	4.01	3
15	I prefer face-to-face interaction with my *peers* rather than electronic communication used in Web-based CPE courses.	.87	3.89	6
17	I prefer hearing CPE lectures in person rather than reading them on a *computer screen.*	.85	4.20	1
18	I prefer hearing CPE lectures in person rather than hearing them through a *computer speaker.*	.84	3.93	5
13	I prefer traditional classroom instruction over Web-based CPE courses.	.83	4.00	4
14	I prefer using printed materials over the kind of electronic materials (e.g., computer screens, e-mails) used for Web-based CPE courses.	.73	3.86	7
20	I don't believe that Web-based CPE courses have sufficient advantages to justify using them for CPE.	.57	2.75	31

The conceptual content of Factor II included rejection of electronically mediated interpersonal interactions and of electronically mediated CPE. The two deterrent items indicating rejection of electronically mediated interpersonal interactions included preferences for interaction both with CPE instructors (Item 16) and with respondents' peers (Item 15). The five variables reflecting rejection of electronically mediated CPE included both preferences regarding specific aspects of Web-based CPE and opinions of Web-based CPE in general. Four of these variables (Items 17, 18, 13, and 14) cluster into preferences regarding specific aspects of Web-based CPE, while one variable (Item 20) is concerned with Web-based CPE in general. The item means for this factor ranged from 2.75 to 4.20. With an average of 3.80, Factor II: Concerns about Electronically Mediated Communication had the highest items mean of the four factors.

Table 6. Factor III: Concerns about Access to Technology-Associated Resources

Item No.	Deterrent Item	Loading Value	Item Mean	Scale Rank
8	I don't have reliable enough access to the *Internet* to participate in Web-based CPE courses.	.79	1.89	52
1	I don't have the *computer hardware* necessary to participate in Web-based CPE courses.	.78	1.55	57
2	I don't have the *computer software* necessary to participate in Web-based CPE courses.	.78	1.86	53
9	I don't have reliable enough access to *electronic mail (e-mail)* to participate in Web-based CPE courses.	.76	1.79	56
27	I am concerned that the cost of *connecting to the Internet* is too high to justify participating in Web-based CPE courses.	.75	1.80	55
26	I am concerned that the cost of *purchasing the computer hardware* needed to participate in Web-based CPE courses is too high.	.71	2.03	50
3	I don't have the technical knowledge necessary to participate in Web-based CPE courses.	.65	1.89	51

The items comprising Factor III address three types of resources—Web-based, financial, and specialized knowledge. Four variables (Items 8, 1, 2, and 9) reflect concerns about Web-based technology resources; two variables (Items 27 and 26) reflect concerns about financial resources; and one variable (Item 3) addresses concerns about specialized knowledge resources. The item means for all of these variables are relatively low, ranging from 1.55 to 2.03. With an average of 1.82, Factor III: Concerns about Access to Technology-Associated Resources had the lowest items mean of the four factors.

Table 7. Factor IV: Concerns about the Availability of Necessary Personal Resources

Item No.	Deterrent Item	Loading Value	Item Mean	Scale Rank
11	I don't have the *patience* to learn how to use the Web for a Web-based CPE course.	.71	2.22	48
10	I don't have the *time* to learn how to use the Web for a Web-based CPE course.	.67	2.31	41
4	I don't have the *confidence* necessary to participate in Web-based CPE courses.	.63	1.86	54
6	I don't have the *skill* to download the necessary computer software from the Internet (e.g., browsers, sound, video, graphics applications) in order to participate in Web-based CPE courses.	.62	2.24	47

The conceptual content of Factor IV: Concerns about the Availability of Necessary Personal Resources included two deterrent items that address personality characteristics (Items 11 and 4) and two items that address external constraints of personal time and specialized skill (Items 10 and 6). The item means for this factor ranged from 1.83 to 2.31 with an average of 2.15. Only Factor III: Concerns about Access to Technology-Associated Resources had a lower items mean.

Discussion

Research question 1 called for us to determine the relative importance of deterrents to participation in Web-based CPE by CPAs in Georgia. It is interesting to note that the highest-ranking items relate to concerns about the specifics of electronic education and interaction. Most of these concerns were attitudinal in nature and revealed a desire for preserving the manner in which CPAs have traditionally completed their CPE requirements. Whether or not this conservative outlook is typical of CPAs, or other professionals, can only be established through replication studies.

Specifically, seven of the top ten highest-ranking deterrents deal directly with CPAs' concerns about the specifics of electronic education. Their preference for traditional classroom education, lectures, and printed materials supports the literature indicating a resistance to change (Rogers 1995). Moreover, their concern about electronic interaction with instructors and peers supports the literature stating that the lack of face-to-face interaction is a primary stumbling block for electronic education (Eastmond 1995; McCormack and Jones 1998; Moore and Kearsley 1996; Nguyen, Tan, and Kezunovic 1996; Webb and Street 1997; Wiesenberg and Hutton 1995).

Other factors that served as individual deterrents ultimately had much lower ratings for this group of CPAs. Clearly, the reason they are not participating in Web-based CPE is not principally related to difficulty in accessing necessary resources, particularly those associated with technology; six of the ten lowest-ranking individual deterrents involve problems with hardware, software, and network connectivity. Rapid changes in technology and its continued widespread use are apparent in the accounting profession. Consequently, technology-associated resources have become necessary tools for conducting business, thereby making these resources more available to CPAs than to the general population.

Items dealing with the CPAs' knowledge, patience, and confidence in interacting with Web-based CPE, as well as having the authority to download software from the Internet, also appear in the ten lowest-ranking items. This ranking suggests that CPAs are not deterred nearly as much by these factors. Again, the difference is partially accounted for by the contextual arena of the study. As professionals, CPAs regularly use technology in their business activities. The utilization of technology, combined with their education and training, may serve to enhance CPAs' knowledge and skills and to build their confidence in interacting with Web-based CPE.

Research question 2 called for us to determine if individual deterrents could be reduced to a more parsimonious, conceptual framework through factor analysis. Our analysis allowed us to reduce the individual items to four factors. Whereas research question 1 dealt with specific deterrents, the use of factor analysis in research question 2 allowed us to think in terms of theoretical and practical implications. In essence, we found it valuable to consider four factors.

Factor I: Concerns about the Quality of Course Offerings. With a mean rating of 3.03, this is the second most influential factor in terms of its power to deter CPAs from participating in Web-based CPE. CPAs are simply not convinced about the quality of Web-based course offerings. Professionally, CPAs are concerned about the relevancy and accuracy of Web-based course content, their inability to obtain printed materials or course recommendations from other CPAs, and the issue of how long a Web-based course would take to complete. This supports Gantz (1997) and Hawkins (1997), who state that the biggest obstacles to Web-based education are the accuracy of course content and the richness of the offerings. The CPAs also expressed concerns about the quality of security when submitting financial or personal information and written comments over the Internet. This supports Wiesenberg and Hutton's (1995) claim that learners participating in Web-based education were anxious about putting their written word out on the Internet, due to the uncertainty of its future use. It also supports Nguyen, Tan, and Kezunovic (1996) and McCormack and Jones (1998), who state that learners' concerns about the security of the Web is a significant challenge to overcome.

CPAs were also concerned that electronic discussions would lack focus and could be misinterpreted, that they did not know how to evaluate the quality of a Web-based course, and that Web-based courses might not provide immediate feedback. Concerns about how others perceive the quality of courses include the value placed on Web-based courses relative to other forms of CPE as well as concerns about the documentation of Web-based CPE courses and acceptance of those credits by their State Board of Accountancy or other administrative agency.

Factor II: Concerns about Electronically Mediated Communication. With a mean rating of 3.80, this derived factor is the most influential in terms of deterring participation in Web-based CPE by CPAs. This factor's mean is twice as high as Factor III: Concerns about Access to Technology-Associated Resources. Collectively, the variables suggest a resistance to change among respondents. Specifically, they suggest a resistance to changing the way that CPE has been traditionally conducted. This resistance is reflected as a rejection of electronically mediated interpersonal communication. CPAs clearly prefer face-to-face interaction with instructors and their peers over the electronically mediated communication used in Web-based courses. This supports previous studies by Moore and Kearsley (1996) asserting that interaction is critical for education facilitated at a distance. It also supports the assertions of Simoff and Maher (1997) and Webb and Street (1997) that state that the loss of face-to-face interactivity is a considerable challenge in the design of Web-based courses.

Also evident are concerns about the use of electronic communication being extended to all facets of education. The CPAs polled in this study prefer hearing lectures in a traditional classroom setting over listening to lectures spoken through a computer speaker or reading them on a computer screen. They also prefer print materials to e-mail. This is in agreement with McCormack and Jones (1998), who argue that students taught through traditional education methods may have difficulty in adapting to a new method of education. In general, most respondents do not believe that Web-based CPE courses have enough advantages over traditional CPE courses to justify using them. This supports the previous study by Perdue and Valentine (1998), which indicates that, while these CPAs had access to technology-associated resources, they preferred to maintain the status quo.

Factor III: Concerns about Access to Technology-Associated Resources. This derived factor has the least influence in deterring CPAs from participating in Web-based CPE. With the lowest average items mean of 1.82, Factor III indicates that lack of participation in Web-based CPE courses is not principally related to difficulty in accessing the necessary technology-associated resources. This is congruent with findings of earlier research (Perdue and Valentine 1998) stating that most CPAs have access to the technology-associated resources necessary to participate in Web-based CPE.

The content of Factor III is best reflected in three types of resources: Web-based technology, financial, and specialized knowledge. While the literature reflects that a lack of access to technology is a significant barrier to participation in Web-based education (Filipczak 1995; Gantz 1997; Khan 1997; Lockheed Idaho Technologies Co. 1995; Mak and Mak 1995; McCormack and Jones 1998; Owston 1997; Webb and Street 1997; Wulf 1996), by and large, CPAs indicate that they have access to the required technology. This is in contrast to what is generally reported in the literature and indicates that the importance of this barrier is specific to a given population.

It is also important to note that CPAs, an extremely cost-conscious group of professionals, do not perceive the cost of acquiring the needed technology as significant. Again, this is in conflict with the literature that indicates cost as a major barrier to Web-based education (Dillon 1997; Lockheed Idaho Technologies Co. 1995; McCormack and Jones 1998; Owston 1997). As discussed in research question 1, this difference may be explained by the CPAs' adoption of technology to perform their professional duties.

Factor IV: Concerns about the Availability of Necessary Personal Resources. With an average items mean of 2.15, this is the second least influential factor in deterring participation in Web-based CPE by CPAs. Only Factor III: Concerns about Access to Technology-Associated Resources is lower. Collectively, the variables suggest that CPAs perceive themselves as having the personal resources necessary for participation in Web-based CPE.

Specifically, Factor IV deals with personal characteristics and external constraints. Concerns about personal characteristics included respondents' fears that they lacked both the patience to learn how to use the Web and the confidence necessary to participate in Web-based CPE courses. Overall, however, the CPAs indicated that they perceived themselves as having both the patience and the confidence to participate in Web-based CPE. This fails to support the literature indicating that lack of the necessary personal characteristics is a barrier to participation in Web-based education (Eastmond 1995; Filipczak 1995; McCormack and Jones 1998; Romiszowski 1997). This is partially accounted for by the CPAs' level of education and work experience, as well as by the detailed nature of the work they have selected to perform.

Concerns about external constraints included lack of time to learn how to use the Web and lack of skill in downloading the necessary computer software. As with the personal characteristics, the CPAs indicated that these external constraints did not deter them from participating in Web-based CPE. This again fails to support the literature claiming that lack of time and necessary technical skills deter participation in Web-based education (Filipczak 1995; McCormack and Jones 1998; Webb and Street 1997; Wulf 1996). CPAs believe they have the skill set necessary for participating in Web-based CPE.

Implications

This study provides both practical and theoretical contributions to the fields of distance education and CPE. Examining the dimensions of and the perceived deterrents to professional participation in CPE via Web-based courses will better prepare continuing professional educators to address these factors and to facilitate increased program participation. The identification of deterrents to participation in Web-based CPE for CPAs may, therefore, result in the development of more responsive programming.

This study provides a better understanding of deterrents to Web-based training for one particular group of adult learners—CPAs. The results of this study provide program planners with valuable insights into the dimensions of influence on professional accountants. These individual deterrent items can be used as a list of crucial elements that must be addressed in planning future programs and in communicating about such programs.

The study identified four deterrent factors, which can be used as a broader framework for identifying the issues that should be addressed when selecting course offerings and designing promotional messages. The issues of quality and electronically mediated communication will need to be considered in the development of course offerings using a Web-based format. These same issues will need to be addressed in marketing Web-based courses to CPAs, ensuring that a thorough presentation of the Web-based educational process is communicated and that appropriate training is available.

In addition to practical implications, this research provides theoretical contributions to the fields of distance education and CPE. Taken together, the four factors comprise a partial theory of the forces that deter CPAs from participating in Web-based education. As such, they hold promise both for advancing the theory base and guiding research in the future. They also have heuristic value for administrators and policymakers seeking to develop and market course offerings. It is possible that these four broad theoretical constructs relate to other groups, such as medical or legal professionals, but caution should be used in generalizing beyond the study population.

Further studies are needed to extend the current research and to investigate Web-based CPE from a broader perspective. First, there is an important limitation in this study: the results cannot be statistically generalized to CPAs outside the state of Georgia or to other professionals. Additional research is needed to replicate this study with similar populations of CPAs on a regional and national level. Doing so would aid in the understanding of the forces that deter CPAs as a population from participating in Web-based CPE. Also needed is a replication of the study with other professional groups, such as medical and legal professionals. Although many of the deterrent items seem universally valid, some of the items are not. Given the rate at which Web-based education is proliferating, additional research is needed to identify deterrents in different professional contexts.

There is also a need for further research to identify and describe distinctive types of learners as defined by their perceived deterrents to participating in Web-based CPE. The research objectives would be to divide the research population into distinct subgroups using cluster analysis and, then, to describe the identified subgroups in terms of personal and professional variables. This would allow program planners to know how deterrent forces manifest themselves among a population of potential learners.

Finally, there is a need to investigate deterrents to Web-based CPE through qualitative research. The use of interviews and focus groups would reveal a more comprehensive, in-depth understanding of the deterrent factors. Certainly, Factor II: Concerns about Electronically Mediated Communication represents the most influential factor that exists. Perhaps a qualitative study in which a group of CPAs is interviewed could determine the actual extent of CPAs' discomfort with the lack of face-to-face interaction versus their discomfort with the medium utilized in Web-based CPE courses.

References

Carlozzi, C. L. 1998. Learning for the future. *Journal of Accountancy* 186 (1): 42–4.

Darkenwald, G. G., and T. Valentine. 1985. Factor structure of deterrents to public participation in adult education. *Adult Education Quarterly* 35 (4): 177–93.

Dillon, N. 1997. Internet-based training passes audit. *Computerworld,* 3 November, 47–8.

Eastmond, D. V. 1995. *Alone but together: Adult distance study through computer conferencing.* Cresskill, NJ: Hampton Press.

Filipczak, B. 1995. Putting the learning into distance learning. *Training,* October, 111–8.

Gantz, J. 1997. Web-based training can help IT organizations. *Computerworld,* 9 July, 37.

Grundnoski, A. T. 1992. A descriptive study of attitudes and behavior toward professional continuing education by distance means within five professional groups in Marquette County, Michigan. Ph.D. diss., Michigan State University, East Lansing.

Hawkins, D. T. 1997. Web-based training for online retrieval: An idea whose time is coming. *Online,* May–June, 68–9.

Khan, B. H. 1997. *Web-based instruction.* Englewood Cliffs, NJ: Educational Technology Publications.

Lockheed Idaho Technologies Co. 1995. A study of advanced training technology: Emerging answers to tough questions. Washington, DC: US Department of Energy.

Mak, L., and S. Mak. 1995. Web in action: Applications and hesitations. Paper read at First Australian World Wide Web Conference, 30 April–2 May, at New South Wales, Australia.

McCormack, C., and D. Jones. 1998. *Building a Web-based education system.* New York: Wiley Computer Pub.

Moore, M. G., and G. Kearsley. 1996. *Distance education: A systems view.* Belmont, CA: Wadsworth Publishing.

Nacinovich, M. 1998. CPE: Lights, camera, action? *Accounting Technology*, April, 38–43.

Nguyen, A. T. A., W. Tan, and L. Kezunovic. 1996. Interactive multimedia on the World Wide Web: Implementation and implications for the tertiary education sector. Paper read at Second Annual World Wide Web Conference, July, at Goldcoast, Australia.

Owston, R. D. 1997. The World Wide Web: A technology to enhance teaching and learning? *Educational Researcher,* March, 27–33.

Perdue, K. J., and T. Valentine. 1998. Beliefs of certified public accountants toward distance education: A statewide Georgia survey. *The American Journal of Distance Education* 12 (3): 29–41.

Rogers, E. M. 1995. *Diffusion of innovations*. 4th ed. New York: Free Press.

Romiszowski, A. J. 1997. Web-based distance learning and teaching: Revolutionary invention or reaction to necessity? In *Web-based instruction*, ed. B. H. Khan. Englewood Cliffs, NJ: Educational Technology Publications.

Scalter, K. 1990. An investigation of national and international approaches to teleconferencing in continuing and distance education. Ph.D. diss., Boston University.

Simoff, S. J., and M. L. Maher. 1997. Web-mediated courses: The revolution in on-line design education. Paper read at Third Australian World Wide Web Conference, July, at Lismore, New South Wales, Australia.

Webb, G., and M. A. Street. 1997. A theoretical framework for Internet-based training at Sydney Institute of Technology. Paper read at Third Australian World Wide Web Conference, July, at Lismore, New South Wales, Australia.

Wiesenberg, F., and S. Hutton. 1995. Teaching a graduate program using computer mediated conferencing software. Paper read at Annual Meeting of the American Association for Adult and Continuing Education, November, at Kansas City, MO.

Wulf, K. 1996. Training via the Internet: Where are we? *Training and Development* 50 (5): 50–5.

A Distributed Collaborative Science Learning Laboratory on the Internet

Laura R. Winer, Martine Chomienne, and Jesús Vázquez-Abad

Vol. 14 No. 1 2000

Abstract

A Distributed Collaborative Science Learning Laboratory (DCSLL) was designed, prototyped, and pilot-tested as the "Electrical Circuit Simulator." This laboratory was part of a module on electricity within an introductory distance course for postsecondary students on the scientific method. The concept of a DCSLL emerged from work in distance education and new technologies, cooperative/collaborative learning, and science education. Instructional design principles derived from these areas are presented, and their implementation in the DCSLL is described, followed by results from the pilot test. Analysis of the results led to the articulation of six instructional design guidelines, identified as being key to the development of such learning environments.

Introduction

One area that has proved particularly resistant to implementation in a distance education context is the laboratory component of science courses. In order to offer distance students a full range of courses, however, new ways must be found to provide this aspect of science courses. A growing interest in collaborative work within the distance education community focuses on reducing high attrition rates, finding ways to provide cognitive and metacognitive support, as well as addressing individual differences, both cognitive and affective. In exploring the potential of Internet-based collaborative learning, we were able to articulate preliminary principles based on existing work and use them as guides for the design of a prototype Distributed Collaborative Science Learning Laboratory (DCSLL). The prototype was pilot-tested, and the results obtained were used to elaborate and clarify the design principles.

Origins of a DCSLL

The concept of a DCSLL emerged from work in distance education, cooperative/collaborative learning, and science education.

Distance Education and New Technologies. The defining characteristic of distance education is the distribution of students across time and space, from the instructor or tutor and, often, from each other. The learners are usually adults who normally work part- or full-time while taking courses. Bourdeau and Bates (1997) provide guidelines for instructional design specific to a distance education context. The challenges facing the instructional designer include (1) responding to the high attrition rate caused by student isolation, lack of a sense of belonging, and problems in sustaining motivation and commitment; (2) adapting to individual cognitive and affective profiles; and (3) providing adequate cognitive and metacognitive support to the learners. New technologies and collaborative approaches offer the promise of alternative means and methods that may help meet these challenges.

Dede (1996) discusses the implications of new media for distance education. He identifies three new forms of distributed learning: collective knowledge webs (complementing traditional information sources), virtual communities (complementing face-to-face interaction), and immersive experiences in shared synthetic environments (extending learning-by-doing in real-world settings). These three forms of distributed learning are presented as providing extensions of learning-by-doing in a collaborative mode. However, we feel that collective knowledge webs and virtual communities can be more accurately described as "collaboration in discourse" and that immersive experiences in shared synthetic environments enter the realm of "collaboration in action." By collaboration in discourse, we refer to learning situations in which sharing is based on conversation, whereas collaboration in action refers to learners acting together to complete tasks.

The introduction of new technologies also has implications for the nature of interactions. Hillman, Willis, and Gunawardena (1994) add the relationship between the learner and the technological interface to the standard learner-content, learner-instructor, and learner-learner interactions. This learner-interface interaction is especially significant when working within mediated communication. While many think this is merely a novice's problem that will expire on its own as the population becomes more technologically sophisticated, Hillman et al. point out that even experienced drivers may have problems operating the windshield wipers on rented cars. The analogy is worthwhile because each technological environment has its own idiosyncrasies that must be learned, no matter how "standardized" they are.

Many authors, notably Anderson and Garrison (1995); Dede (1996); and Hillman, Willis, and Gunawardena (1994), have identified the need for appropriate instructional design research that exploits the potential of new technologies as the key to successful future developments in distance education.

With computer technologies creating opportunities for increased collaboration, distance education is moving from an individual, solo endeavor to one that links the learner to others and involves him or her in social exchange and communication with both the tutor and other learners. For example, Thach and Murphy (1994) present a continuum of interactions that moves from collaboration by the designers, to student-to-student, class-to-class, and, finally, institution-to-institution. Along the same lines, Anderson and Garrison (1995) present the concept of a community of learners in which the emphasis is on developing, extracting, and refining existing knowledge from the group, rather than following a teacher transmission of knowledge model. This group interdependence does entail a loss of some of the flexibility and independence that distance education learners have typically enjoyed. However, Anderson and Garrison found that most of the students enrolled in courses requiring group interactions found the trade-off between reduced independence and increased interactivity one that was worthwhile. Similarly, Garrison (1993) highlights the potential for new technologies to sustain two-way communication and, therefore, facilitate the development of learning environments that move away from the traditional (distance education) behaviorist orientation to learning.

Cooperative/Collaborative Learning. According to the Oxford English Dictionary, the terms "cooperative" and "collaborative" share the same meaning and have equivalent etymologies. Nevertheless, one finds the words used both interchangeably and in opposition to each other, and the distinctions made in some fields contradict those made in others. We have chosen the term "collaborative" for our work based on Salomon's (1992) view; however, in the following discussion, we respect and use the particular author's choice of vocabulary.

The essential elements of traditional collaborative learning are face-to-face interaction, positive interdependence, individual accountability, cooperative social skills, and group processing (Johnson and Johnson 1976). (Obviously, the requirement for face-to-face interaction would have to be replaced if we are to create collaborative learning activities in a distance education environment.) Slavin (1983) concluded that the effects of cooperative learning are primarily motivational, since working together toward a group goal creates peer support for individual learning, and that, in turn, increases individual motivation both to achieve and to help others. Abrami et al. (1995) also found that "there is little doubt that cooperative learning produces superior results when the objective is the promotion of positive attitudes and feelings toward learning, classmates, and self" (196). As anyone familiar with distance education knows, motivation is key. Therefore, the potential for cooperative learning to increase a student's motivation by adding to their sense of belonging and commitment makes it worth investigating. Although distance learners are already motivated enough to initiate their own learning activities, their high attrition rates could be decreased by improving the quality and quantity of interactions.

Distribution and Collaborative Learning. The concept of distribution refers to different kinds of distribution: across time, across space, and across individuals. In distance learning, learners are distributed geographically and temporally. To complicate this situation further, the resources needed for a given learning activity may also be at a distance from the student and/or the teacher. In addition to overcoming the traditional pedagogical challenges, distribution introduces additional challenges to supporting authentic collaborative work; it increases the complexity of coordination and communication and also introduces logistical hurdles such as working together on tasks, exchanging documents, and arranging meetings.

Collaborative learning may also be seen as different individual cognitive systems working together toward a common goal. For example, in a collaborative approach, each student working on a laboratory activity brings his or her own cognition to the activity. They not only bring their existing knowledge, belief systems, and cognitive abilities, but they also bring their own way of building new knowledge. Team cognition is thus distributed among its members, and team learning is, to some extent, dependent on the characteristics of this distribution. When different tasks are assigned to each member of a team, the interaction between each individual's cognition and the specific task assigned will influence the group outcome. The concept of distributed cognition has implications, therefore, not only for the way in which a group will work, but also for what the results of that work will be. Thus, depending on the composition of the team, the team may choose to work by dividing roles and/or tasks according to the competencies that particular individuals bring to the team. They should implement a strategy that either exploits an individual's strengths or strengthens their weaknesses.

The Science Learning Laboratory. The science laboratory is seen as central to science teaching by those who believe that it promotes positive attitudes toward science, scientific inquiry, conceptual development, and technical skills (Collette and Chiappetta 1994). Constructivist views of science learning consider the laboratory to be the primary instructional environment for involving students in scientific inquiry. However, given the widespread use and importance of laboratory instruction in science education, it is surprising how little we know about the effects of lab work on learning (Gallagher 1987; Lazarowitz and Tamir 1994).

The laboratory is an environment that not only characterizes (in popular culture) science as a profession, but also sets it apart from most other disciplines, such as the humanities and social sciences (White 1988). As a learning environment and an instructional strategy, the science laboratory includes practical work within planned learning experiences that take place in a purposely assigned environment (Lazarowitz and Tamir 1994). While a physical space or an assigned, structured sequence of tasks often defines science laboratories, the science learning lab does not necessarily require either of these elements. The important aspect of a science learning lab is the controlled nature of both the actions and the environment that ultimately permits students to generalize beyond the specific instance under study. As such, a "laboratory" may be conducted in a traditional, controlled environment or out in the field with a teacher-provided protocol or a student-generated one.

For those who see the laboratory as practical work that leads to concept formation and the formulation of theories, each experiment should begin with an existing theory and knowledge base and the identification of a problem that then leads to a hypothesis, a plan, and, finally, the execution of an experiment (Arons 1993; Lazarowitz and Tamir 1994). Accordingly, science laboratories should provide concrete experiences, ways to help students confront their misconceptions, opportunities for developing process and technical skills, and opportunities to construct knowledge. Even though these objectives are aimed at the individual, concerns related to the role of social interaction in knowledge construction and motivation make it worthwhile to look at what cooperative learning can contribute to instructional models of laboratories.

Cooperative Learning in Science. A large-scale survey of student results in introductory physics courses found that the use of interactive engagement methods in the classroom can significantly improve course effectiveness (Hake 1998). In chemistry, Nurrenbern (1995) states that tasks in a cooperative learning activity must require students to make independent contributions toward task completion, as well as requiring some group decision making on the process itself. These are presumably the main characteristics to consider when designing an activity.

While noting the scarcity of research on cooperative science laboratory learning, Lazarowitz and Tamir (1994) report on studies that show cooperative work to be superior to competitive and individual work in terms of cognitive achievement but inferior in terms of process skills. However, when learner abilities were taken into account, no conclusive statements could be generated from the results of the different studies. Not surprisingly, cooperative learning is superior to competitive approaches when there are cooperative tasks to be carried out, while competitive groups are superior for tasks emphasizing individual achievement.

In science education, the concept of cooperative learning is often viewed as being essentially synonymous with group learning. The advantages of cooperative learning are seen in its elimination (or at least reduction) of competitiveness between students and/or of student isolation by including team-building and team-learning activities (Collette and Chiappetta 1994; Jones 1989). This makes it an approach that is appropriate and effective for teaching and learning science (Hassard 1992).

The Challenge: Setting up a DCSLL through the Internet

Goal. Our project focused on exploring new applications of information and communication technologies in distance science learning. Our overall goal was to create principles for designing technological and teaching environments that would support distance learners in the collaborative learning of scientific concepts. Our educational partner was the CCFD (Centre collégial de formation à distance/Center for College Distance Education), based in Montreal. The center's mandate is to provide college-level (postsecondary, preuniversity) distance teaching for the province of Quebec. In conjunction with the RECTO (Réseau de chercheurs pour la téléformation opérationnalisée/Network of Researchers for Operational Teleteaching) project and funded by the Fonds de l'autoroute de l'information (Information Highway Fund), the center has created a new course designed to take advantage of the information highway (Potvin, Chomienne, and Boutin 1996).

The CCFD chose a new introductory course on the scientific method for the project. The course objective was to familiarize non–science majors with the fundamentals of the scientific method so that they would be able to apply it in simple problem-solving contexts, specifically those involving concrete physical phenomena. A key element in the course's learning activities was the distribution (in both time and space) of the virtual laboratory experiences. Because this was a new course, it provided an opportunity to incorporate information and communication technologies as an integral part of the design. The course material was designed for a hypermedia Web site and required both synchronous and asynchronous inter- and intrateam communication using tools such as electronic mail, chat rooms, teleconferences, and computer audioconferences.

The course designers chose physics as the content area from which to teach the scientific method, and they developed a modular course with a common starting point—a chapter on the history of the scientific method. Students then completed three modules consisting of mechanics, optics and sound waves, and electricity. The course materials contained embedded exercises and hypertext links. The module on electricity was chosen to be the testbed for the design of a prototype DCSLL.

Description of the Prototype

In designing the electricity laboratory, we created three experiments for the learners to conduct. These experiments were not designed for deductive verification of laws and principles. To produce individual syntheses, some of the activities within the DCSLL component of the course covered concepts through concrete manipulation; these then served as a basis for negotiating a collective synthesis. Other activities reviewed a concept so that the learners could gain a better understanding of it on both a qualitative and quantitative level. Still others used the concepts discussed to gain new knowledge through teamwork. The specific instances where collaboration came into play are identified in Figure 1.

In the first experiment, experimentation was conducted with real artifacts, and measurements were taken using real instruments. In the other two, experimentation was carried out by simulation, and the measurements were computerized. Collaboration began only during the interpretation/conclusion phases of the first two experiments. The third experiment required the learners to plan their experimentation from the beginning, and then collaborate during both the analysis and interpretation/conclusion phases.

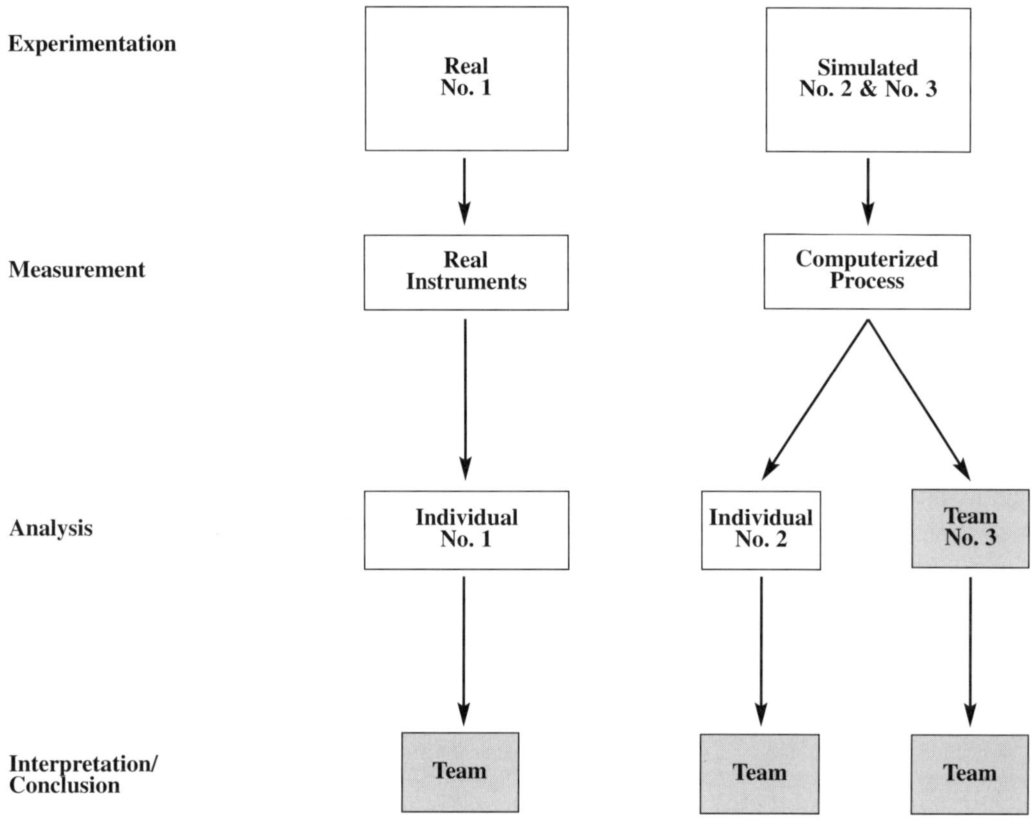

Figure 1. Collaboration in the Electricity Laboratory Experiments

Design Principles. The principles applied in the design of the DCSLL came from four contributing areas: instructional design for distance education, science learning laboratories, information and communications technology, and collaborative learning. The design principles are presented in a tabular format in the results section.

The Three Electrical Circuit Simulator Experiments. Experiment 1 consisted of a qualitative exploration of the behavior of simple circuits and involved concrete manipulation of common electrical equipment—light bulbs, batteries, electrical wiring, etc. The experiment was carried out with real (as opposed to simulated) objects, and measurements were taken using real instruments. The learners analyzed their data individually, while the interpretation of results and the development of conclusions were conducted as a team.

Experiment 2 examined the relationship between current, potential, and resistance in a simple electric circuit (Ohm's law). Experimentation involved a number of activities using a simulator.

The data measurement phase was done automatically by the computer. The learners analyzed their results individually, and again, both the interpretation and conclusions were the result of a team effort.

Experiment 3 studied the distribution of current and potential in a circuit (Kirchhoff's laws). Experimentation consisted of a number of activities using a simulator. The team planned the experiment before collecting the data. Although data measurement was automated, the data analysis, interpretation, and conclusion phases were all conducted as a team.

Pilot-Testing the Science Learning Laboratory

The prototype DCSLL on basic concepts of electricity was pilot-tested at the CCFD in July 1997 using a team of three participants who were representative of the target population. Results indicate that distance collaboration in the context of a distributed science learning laboratory is possible. During the pilot test, the participants showed their commitment and interdependency in the learning process.

Method. Data were gathered using the following means: group interviews with the three participants (both before and after the pilot project), students' assignments, and participant observation by the three research team members. Interview questions examined content and also probed the participants' ideas about science labs, collaborative work, and computer-based learning activities. Observations focused on the interactions as well as on the technical and conceptual areas that posed difficulties.

Logistics and Computer Platform. To simulate distance, the three participants worked in different rooms, each equipped with a workstation and telephone that enabled telephone conferencing.[1] The workstations themselves were PCs with Windows 95 and Internet access. Using a browser (either Explorer or Netscape), the participants accessed the laboratory site with a user name and password. By clicking on a desktop shortcut, they loaded NetMeeting, through which they could share a whiteboard, use the annotation tools (the hand, the highlighter, etc.), type in comments and information, and use the screen capture tool. When necessary, the research team provided on-the-spot technical support.

Results

The pilot test provided feedback on the success and appropriateness of the different design principles used to create the DCSLL. Each set of principles is presented in Tables 1–4 with the principle articulated in the left column and the results observed during the pilot test in the right column. Of course, since these results are based on a very limited number of participants, the significance of the results should be viewed with circumspection. The results of the pilot test were used to define new technical specifications for the revised version of the laboratory that has been implemented in the CCFD course.

Table 1. Distance Education

Prototype Design Principles	Results
1. Begin with an individual task, and then provide a personal workspace accessible at all times to respect different cognitive and affective profiles.	This proved important. Participants made frequent recourse to the personal workspace to work at their own speed and to try things out for themselves.
2. Develop readable, comprehensible learning materials that are easily followed.	The collaborative aspects made this both more important and more difficult because shared, not just individual, understanding was a factor.
3. Develop a variety of learning activities.	This proved entirely feasible.
4. Anticipate errors and prevent them when appropriate.	Conceptual errors were anticipated during the design phase. Nonproductive technical errors were prevented. Productive errors, which we did not seek to prevent, did not occur with this group.

Table 2. The Science Learning Laboratory

Prototype Design Principles	Results
1. Practical exercises within planned learning experiments carried out in an appropriate environment.	This proved feasible. Collaborative work raised the participants' awareness that scientists generally work as a team.
2. Inductive approach: discovery of laws based on a prediction followed by experimentation and comparison of the prediction with the experimental results in order to foster cognitive conflict.	The approach based on cognitive conflict did not suit all participants; this has implications for the tutor. Participants were not always comfortable making predictions and had to be convinced of the importance of their "lay" predictions.
3. Allow learners to design and conduct their own experiments.	The participants specifically asked to go further (i.e., designing their own circuits on the computer).
4. Progression from qualitative data to quantitative data to graphic representation to formal representation by mathematical equations.	The progression was effective, and the participants established their own mathematical equations. They grasped the relationship between the various representation systems.
5. Free the learners from nonauthentic or nonproductive work by using the computer in "emancipatory" mode. The learner should remain an active participant; do not automate too many of the tasks.	The procedures were not too difficult, so the participants had no trouble following the steps.

Table 3. Information and Communication Technologies

Prototype Design Principles	Results
1. Written, audio, and visual communication.	Both audio communication by telephone and shared visualization of individual results enhanced the learning experience.
2. Common work and visualization screen shared by all participants.	Having a shared work and visualization screen proved essential.
3. Preservation of autonomy and balance by carefully limiting application sharing.	Care must be taken in sharing applications, such as the simulator. This is related to the importance of a personal workspace; a shared simulator would have encroached on this.

Table 4. Collaborative Learning

Prototype Design Principles	Results
1. Positive interdependency without face-to-face interaction.	The learning environment enabled the development of positive interdependency; the audio communication successfully replaced face-to-face interaction.
2. Develop competencies (related to content and the collaborative method) and individual accountability.	Individuals became accountable for their own learning and that of the team as a whole.
3. Include sharing of the analysis and data interpretation.	The participants arrived at the planned learning outcomes.

Guidelines for the Design of a DCSLL

The results of the pilot test from the DCSLL on electricity enabled us to make a number of recommendations to instructional designers wishing to develop distance science learning laboratories. A DCSLL, such as the one we envisaged and realized, is a complex learning environment integrating contributions from different fields. The instructional design recommendations particular to this environment reflect the integration of the different contributing areas and address the complexity and challenges of their design. Some of these recommendations are equally applicable to learning environments that involve only some of the contributing areas, but in an environment as complex as a DCSLL, each of the following recommendations is essential.

1. Provide both a separate workspace for the individual and a common space for the team. Even in collaborative learning situations where the team is the functional unit, the individual learner should retain his or her autonomy. An individual workspace permits each learner to proceed at his or her own pace, to confront common misconceptions individually and not just be "pulled along with the crowd," and to confront idiosyncratic interpretations or conceptions about the concepts under study. The common space is necessary to allow the team to pool their findings and work together to accomplish the learning tasks.

2. Conduct formative evaluations of the learning materials with groups of learners to ensure that the instructions and vocabulary are not only internally consistent, but also subject to the same interpretation.
3. Offer a variety of learning activities. When feasible and appropriate, hands-on activities should be included to provide students with the opportunity to engage in concrete manipulation. Learners should be able to initiate experiments in addition to following predetermined protocols. Learning activities should progress from active to symbolic, and data generated should progress from qualitative to quantitative.
4. Error analysis must distinguish between productive and nonproductive errors, so as to permit the former and prevent the latter.
5. Technology should enhance the learning experience by providing experimental opportunities that would otherwise be unavailable, by facilitating data manipulation and analysis, and by supporting communication (written, video, and audio) among team members and with the tutor.
6. Each learner's contribution must be necessary, but not sufficient, for both the individual and the group to succeed in the learning activity. No one student should be able to complete the learning activities individually.

Conclusion

The test results of the prototype's pilot project, the "Electrical Circuit Simulator," demonstrated the feasibility of a Distributed Collaborative Science Learning Laboratory. However, due to the somewhat artificial setting of the pilot project, certain questions remain unanswered. For example, do the increased sources of feedback in a peer collaboration context improve the quality and nature of the interaction between students and tutors? Should opportunities for constructive technical errors be created? What are the implications for the tutor's role in an approach based on cognitive conflict? Under what conditions and in what form is asynchronous communication appropriate? What are the various roles played by the learners in a DCSLL? Many of these issues may be addressed in a real delivery of this Internet-based course to clients of the CCFD.

In conclusion, the Distributed Collaborative Science Learning Laboratory appears to be a practical way to provide authentic lab experiences and reduce student isolation while respecting the fundamental constraints of distance education. Careful attention must be paid to design and management issues raised by this new instructional approach, and the increased technical complexity of the learning environment must be taken into account when designing the instructional activities. Overall, it seems that the DCSLL approach is a way to support learning within a distance context that allows distance education students to engage in collaboration in action as well as collaboration in discourse.

Notes

1. Technological limitations prevent multipoint, Internet-based audio conferencing from offering satisfactory results. Therefore, in order to test the design principles without being limited by current technology, conventional telephone conferencing was substituted.

Author's Note: This article reports on work undertaken as part of a project in the TeleLearning Network of Centres of Excellence Research Program of the Canadian government (http://www.telelearn.ca). Additional funding was received from the Information Highway Fund (Fonds de l'autoroute de l'information) of Quebec and the Canadian Office of Learning Technologies. The authors would like to acknowledge Dr. Jacqueline Bourdeau of the Université du Québec à Chicoutimi for her support as project leader. The lead author was a research associate at the Faculty of Education of Université de Montréal while the work reported was carried out.

References

Abrami, P. C., B. Chambers, C. Poulsen, C. De Simone, S. d'Apollonia, and J. Howden. 1995. *Classroom connections: Understanding and using cooperative learning*. Toronto: Harcourt Brace.

Anderson, T. D., and D. R. Garrison. 1995. Transactional issues in distance education: The impact of design in audioteleconferencing. *The American Journal of Distance Education* 9 (2): 27–45.

Arons, A. B. 1993. Guiding insight and inquiry in the introductory physics laboratory. *Physics Teacher* 31: 278–82.

Bourdeau, J., and A. Bates. 1997. Instructional design for distance learning. In *Instructional design: International perspectives: Solving instructional design problems*, ed. S. Dijsktra, N. Seel, F. Schott, and R. Tennyson, 369–97. Mahwah, NJ: Lawrence Earlbaum Associates.

Collette, A. T., and E. L. Chiappetta. 1994. *Science instruction in the middle and secondary schools*. New York: Merrill/Macmillan Publishing Co.

Dede, C. 1996. The evolution of distance education: Emerging technologies and distributed learning. *The American Journal of Distance Education* 10 (2): 4–36.

Gallagher, J. J. 1987. A summary of research in science education, 1985: Research on laboratory work in science instruction. *Science Education* 71 (3): 351–5.

Garrison, D. R. 1993. A cognitive constructivist view of distance education: An analysis of teaching-learning assumptions. *Distance Education* 14 (2): 199–211.

Hake, R. 1998. Interactive-engagement versus traditional methods: A six-thousand student survey of mechanics test data for introductory physics courses. *The American Journal of Physics* 66 (1): 64–74.

Hassard, J. 1992. *Minds on science*. New York: Harper Collins.

Hillman, D. C. A., D. J. Willis, and C. J. Gunawardena. 1994. Learner-interface interaction in distance education: An extension of contemporary models and strategies for practitioners. *The American Journal of Distance Education* 8 (2): 30–42.

Johnson, D., and R. Johnson. 1976. *Learning together and alone*. Englewood Cliffs, NJ: Prentice-Hall.

Jones, R. M. 1989. Cooperative learning in the elementary science methods course. *Journal of Science Teacher Education* 1 (1): 1–3.

Lazarowitz, R., and P. Tamir. 1994. Research on using laboratory instruction in science. In *Handbook of research on science teaching and learning*, ed. D. L. Gabel, 94–128. New York: Macmillan Publishing Co.

Nurrenbern, S. C. 1995. *Experiences in cooperative learning: A collection for chemistry teachers*. Madison, WI: The Institute for Chemical Education, University of Wisconsin, Madison.

Potvin, C., M. Chomienne, and D. Boutin. 1996. *Devis pédagogique, culture scientifique et technologique, ensemble 2* (Instructional design, science and technology literacy, part 2). Document de travail (Working document). Montreal: CCFD.

Salomon, G. 1992. What does the design of effective CSCL (computer supported collaborative learning) require and how do we study its effects? *SIGCUE Outlook* 21 (3): 62–8.

Slavin, R. E. 1983. When does cooperative learning increase student achievement? *Psychological Bulletin* 94: 429–45.

Thach, L., and K. L. Murphy. 1994. Collaboration in distance education: From local to international perspectives. *The American Journal of Distance Education* 8 (3): 5–21.

White, R. 1988. *Learning science*. Oxford: Blackwell.

An Argument for the Application of Copyright Law to Distance Education

Tomas A. Lipinski

Vol. 13 No. 3 1999

Abstract

This article presents a legal analysis of the application of copyright law to distance education environments, particularly as it applies to Web-based instruction and the construction of electronic reserves, or so-called virtual libraries. The author argues that revision of copyright law to allow for the reproduction, display, and performance of works in these settings is consistent with national policy and existing and developing copyright law. The dangers of moving toward a schema of universal or compulsory licensing of information products and services are also explored. Finally, the author suggests several possible components that new legislation or "fair use" guidelines might include.

Intellectual Property Rights

According to Clinton administration rhetoric, the concepts of commerce and education are essential and compatible elements of the National Information Infrastructure's (NII) grand design. When completed, "the development of a national information infrastructure [will] enable all Americans to access information and communicate with each other using voice, data, images or video at anytime, anywhere" (IITF 1993, 5). As Grosso (1994) and Johnston, Handa, and Morgan (1997, 35–65) observe, providing safe and secure networks for e-commerce is the administration's most effective strategy for encouraging private investment in the NII. Linking education to e-commerce also plays a key role in the administration's design for the NII in two ways. According to Kalil (1995), the NII will provide new opportunities for education, which, in turn, will spur increased public interest in the NII. The United States Advisory Council on the NII (USACNII 1996) also supports its construction as an opportunity for the preservation and growth of both private and public sector interests.

The administration's first step in coordinating construction of the NII was to prepare the way for private sector investment. In terms of intellectual property rights, this meant identifying areas in need of legislative reform. The administration's blueprint for copyright revision is contained in the now-infamous White Paper report (IITFIPR 1995), which advocated expanding ownership rights. While the incentive and reward component of our copyright law must be promoted, IITFIPR asserted that it must not override its underlying rationale, that of societal benefit. Recent cases, such as *Fogerty v. Fantasy, Inc.* (1994, 527), have forwarded the preeminence of the public benefit component: "Because copyright law ultimately serves the purpose of enriching the general public through access to creative works, it is peculiarly important that the law's boundaries be demarcated as clearly as possible." The *Fogerty* court quoted from an earlier case, *Feist Publications, Inc. v. Rural Telephone Service Co.* (1991, 349–350), stating

> The primary objective of copyright is *not* to reward the labor of authors, but "to promote the Progress of Science and useful Arts." To this end, copyright assures authors the right

> to their original expression, but encourages others to build freely upon the ideas and information conveyed by a work. (emphasis added)

Recent legislation has conversely preserved both the incentive and reward components of our copyright law. For example, in passing The Sonny Bono Copyright Term Extension Act (US Congress 1998), the House Committee on the Judiciary commented that

> [e]xtending copyright protection will be an incentive for US authors to continue using their creativity to produce works, and provide copyright owners generally with the incentive to restore older works and further disseminate them to the public. (US Congress 1998a, 6)

In terms of user rights, section 404 of the Digital Millennium Copyright Act (US Congress 1998b, 2889) contains a provision that now allows qualifying libraries and archives to make "three copies or phonorecords" of published works "if the existing format in which the work is stored has become obsolete." This is a significant extension of the rights of nonprofit institutions under the copyright law.

> This provision is intended to permit libraries and archives to ensure that copies of works in their collections continue to be accessible and useful to their patrons....a format will be considered obsolete only if the machine or device necessary to render perceptible a work stored in that format is no longer manufactured or reasonably available in a commercial marketplace. (US Congress 1998c, Comments to section 403)

Congress has demonstrated a consistent, favorable attitude toward the preservation of "fair use" rights and has been receptive to the need to adopt existing laws and concepts to new technologies and situations. This bundle of rights, carved out from the copyright owner's exclusive rights, is an extension of a fair use of the owner's work. The term "fair use" is used in two distinct contexts in this article. First, it describes the statutory rights of users of copyrighted material defined in Title 17 of the US Code section 107 (US Code 1998). This statute requires that four factors be considered in determining whether the use is fair or not: (1) the purpose and character of the use, (2) the nature of the copyrighted work, (3) the amount and substantiality of the portion of the work used, and (4) the effect of the use upon the potential market for the work. The second context in which the term "fair use" is used represents a broader reference to the concept of copyright users' rights or, in the alternative, a limitation on the copyright owner's exclusive rights. This general concept is preserved throughout the copyright laws, i.e., Title 17 of the US Code, and is articulated in sections 108 and 109, for example. However, the drafters of the White Paper (IITFIPR 1995, 226) considered and rejected a blanket exception to the copyright laws for nonprofit institutions. While Congress has attempted to preserve the incentive and reward components of our copyright laws as new technologies have developed, it has also seen fit to preserve the "fair" rights of libraries and archives in new technology environments. Users in educational settings should have the same opportunity to benefit from new forms of technology and information dissemination. Unless educational institutions are secure in their fair use of copyrighted material, the development of distance education programs will wither instead of grow, and a critical component of this administration's vision for the NII would remain unfulfilled.

The Law and (Il)logic of Copyright in Distance Education Environments

At present, distance education is dominated by two distinct scenarios operating side by side. The first scenario is one in which instruction is presented live and, then, simultaneously distributed via network technology and/or stored for later transmission. This is the "classic" distance education protocol and the scenario that most closely resembles and impacts users' rights as elucidated in Title 17 US Code section 110. Another scenario that is rapidly gaining prominence is Web-based instruction in which students are provided access to copyrighted material via postings or links from a course Web site. The material loaded on or linked to the class Web site raises, at the least, copyright issues of reproduction and display.

It is not argued here that the copyright owners' rights of reproduction, display, and performance do not apply to Internet, online, or Web environments or that those owners' rights should be ignored. Indeed, copyright owners' rights do apply, and these rights should not be ignored. This conclusion is documented with case law support from Street (1998), Stuckey (1998), and Rosenor (1997) and by actual cases such as *Playboy Enterprises, Inc. v. Frena* (1993) and *Marobie-FL, Inc. v. National Association of Fire Equipment Distributors and Northwest Nexus* (1997). However, the question posed here is whether distant students should be penalized from receiving what would otherwise be an allowable display or performance if they were live and in front of the teacher.

The Inadequacy of Existing "Fair Use" Guidelines in Distance Education Settings

It appears that existing copyright law, including the expression of that law in various so-called "fair use" guidelines, excludes certain forms of instruction. As a result, students working in those formats are treated differently under copyright law merely because the law did not foresee the extent and range of technology now applied in educational settings. Gasaway (1996, 76–7) observes that copyright law and its applications limit some students in their access to otherwise available copyrighted material because of the medium or location of their instructional environment. This appears to be in direct opposition to the technologically intensive environment that the designers and visionaries of the NII had in mind.

The use of electronic reserve is an integral component of many distance education courses. Remote students may need to access a collection of course readings from a distance, and students in a Web-based course may find readings posted on the Web site or a link to the host institution's electronic library reserve. However, the existing Fair Use Guidelines for Electronic Reserve Systems (reprinted in Bielefield and Cheeseman 1997, 195–9) suggest that "[t]he total amount of material included in electronic reserve systems for a specific course as a matter of fair use should be a small proportion of the total assigned reading for a particular course." This might be fine for a campus of students with convenient access to on-site reserve rooms, but the reality of education in the NII environment is that some students may never make a single physical visit to the campus or library of the host institution. Likewise, the recent Fair Use Guidelines for Distance Learning (reprinted in Bielefield and Cheeseman 1997, 139–44) allow for either live broadcast or session recording for later transmission. However, it is not clear whether the initial loading (reproduction) of copyrighted material on a course Web site would be considered a fair use. In a live or traditional class setting, this is not needed since the instructor, consistent with existing law, merely brings the material to class for performance or display.

The distance guidelines also limit the educational institution. For example, section 1.2 of the guidelines indicate that "[t]hey [the instructors] may not...allow such transmissions to result in copies for students unless they have permission to do so, any more than face-to-face instructors may make copies of audiovisual works for their students without permission" (reprinted in Bielefield and Cheeseman 1997, 140–1). It is true that audiovisual works are not allowed to be reproduced for students under any classroom guideline or fair use concept, yet the law differentiates between an instructor who makes a copy of a videotape for each student and an educational environment in which a student may do so, after first obtaining the video from the library reserve or from the general collection. What is the difference between a student being able to get a tape from the library and making a copy, if the student so chooses, and the instructor placing the tape on a course Web site from which the student could, but is not required to, make his or her own copy? The distance guidelines use the phrase "result in copies" to suggest incorrectly that the school or library is responsible for the subsequent acts of its users. However, this is contrary to both the letter and spirit of the legal responsibility charged to libraries associated with educational institutions. Under Title 17 US Code section 108, nonprofit libraries are not responsible for contributory infringement arising from the provision of the access and means by which its patrons might make infringing copies. In fact, the White Paper authors point out that qualifying libraries are the only such entity that have been granted this statutory immunity (IITFIPR 1995, 111, footnote 357). In return for this immunity, the library must post a warning notice by its photocopier. Likewise, under Title 17 US Code section 109, a "nonprofit library or nonprofit education institution" may rent, lease, or lend software (providing the access for its patrons to software that, in turn, those patrons could illegally copy) without a threat of liability, as long as a similar warning notice is placed upon the software that is rented, leased, or lent. The warning notices are prescribed in regulations issued by the US Copyright Office (CFR 1998).

In addition, the distance guidelines state that "[r]eception must be in a classroom or other similar place devoted for instruction or any other site where the reception can be controlled by the eligible institution" (reprinted in Bielefield and Cheeseman 1997, 143). However, this does not allow for reception through Web-based instruction or by remote students accessing the virtual "classroom" from home or through a personal computer. Yet, tele-educating, like telecommuting, is something contemplated by the designers of the NII. Furthermore, if a *National Geographic* video may be "performed" from semester to semester under Title 17 US Code section 110, why, according to the distance guidelines, is a "[p]erformance of an entire copyrighted work or a large portion thereof [able to] be transmitted only once for a distance learning course?" (reprinted in Bielefield and Cheeseman 1997, 143).

Viewing and Reading Material in a Web-Based Instructional Environment

The White Paper (IITFIPR 1995, 72) implies that browsing the Web (viewing an image on a computer screen) is a "display" for purposes of the copyright owners' exclusive right to control use of their work under Title 17 US Code section 106. Therefore, copyright owners may proscribe, for example, a student's use of material viewed on the course Web site as the viewing is a "display" subject to the control of the copyright owner. Case law, however, suggests a contrary interpretation. Courts have struggled to apply traditional photocopying scenarios to Internet browsing with less-than-convincing articulation. Since humans cannot perceive a digital image in its elemental form of sequential zeros and ones, the representation of those zeros and ones in a visual or sensory image is required. Browsing computer screens or Web pages, therefore, is the functional equivalent of reading. This is the result reached in *Religious Technology Center v. Netcom On-Line Communications Services, Inc.* (1995). The court reasoned that

> Netcom's act of designing or implementing a system that automatically and uniformly creates temporary copies of all data sent through it is not unlike that of the owner of a copying machine who lets the public make copies with it. [footnote omitted] Although some of the people using the machine may directly infringe copyrights, courts analyze the machine owner's liability under the rubric of contributory infringement, not direct infringement. *(Religious Technology Center 1995,* 1369)

The court also observed that browsing was allowed in digital environments even though it makes a "copy" in the computer's RAM.

Hugenholtz (1996, 92) reaches a similar conclusion, observing that, "[i]n the 'paper' world, the act of reading a document or viewing a television program does not qualify as a restricted act. This may be different in the digitally networked environment." Nonetheless, Hugenholtz concludes that "[t]he mere reception or consumption of information by the end user has traditionally remained outside the scope of the copyright monopoly. The transition into the digital networked environment does not, as such, seem to justify such a radical extension of the exclusive right" (Hugenholtz 1996, 93). The *Religious Technology Center* decision is consistent with the Hugenholtz observation. If it could be reasoned that libraries do not pay twice for materials read or otherwise accessed in its "paper" collection (once for the initial acquisition, then a second time for its actual use), then it should be no different in digital environments.

An Argument for the Application of Copyright Law to Distance Education: Primary and Secondary Reproduction

The reproduction right of a copyright owner is implicated in the context of Web-based instruction. For example, the entire course content, including previously copyrighted material as well as material created by the instructor, is, in essence, copied or posted onto the course Web site, and in some distance systems, students can copy the posted material. In addition, the class Web site is often created in conjunction with an electronic reserve component maintained by the institution's library. Is this, or should this be, allowed under existing concepts of fair use? The answer is yes for the following reasons.

First, there should be no difference between print and digital formats in reserve construction. The electronic reserve guidelines should allow for the placement of an entire course's reading list onto an electronic reserve, either in a library setting or on a class Web site. Second, there should be no difference under the law between a traditional library reserve and an electronic reserve created and maintained by an institution's library or one created for convenience by faculty in Web-based instruction (assuming legitimate copies are used). The copyright law should accommodate the reality of digital technology use in education. While there is opportunity for students to duplicate entire course content and readings from an electronic reserve or class Web site, the library or host institution should not be regarded as a contributory infringer simply because it provides copyrighted materials to remote students through a "virtual library."

In *Marobie-FL, Inc. v. National Association of Fire Equipment Distributors (NAFED) and Northwest Nexus* (1997), the court concluded that Northwest Nexus, the online service provider, could not be held liable for direct infringement (i.e., primary reproduction) or vicarious liability *(Marobie-FL* 1997, 1179). The court reasoned that

> Although plaintiff correctly points out that Northwest provided a service somewhat broader than the service provided by the Internet access provider in *Religious Technology Center,* the court nevertheless finds that Northwest only provided the means to copy, distribute or display plaintiff's works, much like the owner of a public copying machine used by a third party to copy protected material. Like a copying machine owner, Northwest did not actually engage in any of these activities itself. Accordingly, Northwest may not be held liable for direct infringement. *(Marobie-FL* 1997, 1178)

The question remains whether the distance institution should be liable for contributory infringement by students, i.e., secondary reproduction. Applying the *Marobie-FL* court's photocopier analogy and the principle of Title 17 US Code section 108 (Limitations on exclusive rights: Reproduction by libraries and archives) to digital education environments, it seems logical to conclude that nonprofit educational entities should likewise be immune from claims of contributory infringement for unauthorized student copying in Web-based or other remote learning settings. Arguably, the educational institution is different from the passive conduit of an Internet access provider *(Marobie-FL* direct infringement immunity) or the library that maintains a photocopier for patron use but otherwise does not reproduce, display, or distribute copyrighted material. The question is whether an educational institution in a distance environment acts as an actual disseminator of copyrighted material or, like a library photocopier or electronic reserve, merely provides the means by which students might achieve similar results. The distinction might become critical should a court need to resolve the issue. However, it should be noted that NAFED, the entity that actually uploaded protected material in the *Marobie-FL* case, is a nonprofit, tax-exempt trade association. NAFED *was* liable when it uploaded three volumes of clip art onto its Web site for members' use.

In the discussion of distance education and possible amendment to the existing provisions of Title 17 US Code section 110, the danger of misuse by subsequent users is misleading. The focus of the existing education exemption is on the rights of copyright owners (to perform and to display) and the primary actor, the educational institution, not a student's ability (as a secondary user) to reproduce that display or redisplay the copyrighted work. Suddenly, the concept of secondary or residual impact is raised. It is not argued that this may or may not be problematic within the general copyright law, but the issues are separate. If Congress wants to revisit the issue of personal copying at home or at school, it may so choose, but Congress has not done that within the Copyright Office hearing and report recommendations of section 403 of the Digital Millennium Copyright Act. A Title 17 US Code section 110 revision discussion should focus on whether or not amending the law to provide for exemption in digital and other distance environments is consistent with existing law and therefore warranted. In other words, is there a logical reason not to achieve conformity in the law between the treatment of traditional and distance education settings with respect to the performance and display of copyrighted works?

Electronic Reserves and the Creation of Course Anthologies

Problems arise when distance instructors combine preexisting copyrighted material into course reading lists. Creating an electronic reserve or posting material to a course Web site might be interpreted as the creation of a course anthology. However, most electronic reserves still require the student to retrieve articles or other material individually, thus distinguishing it from the classic premade or compiled copy-shop scenario of either *Basic Books, Inc. v. Kinko's Graphics Corporation* (1991) or the recent *Princeton University Press v. Michigan Document Services, Inc.* (1996). Furthermore, current precedent suggests that a "copy" of a print compilation is not made when a user recreates the printed order of the compilation from a digital version if that digital version does not itself reproduce or recreate the print compilation in the same exact order. In *Matthew Bender & Co. v. West Publishing Co.* (1998), a case involving a dispute between publishers in which one publisher created a CD-ROM product of the other's print-based legal reporter, the court commented that

> There is no evidence that Bender and Hyperlaw's case-retrieval systems [the digital version of the compilation] allow a user to browse the cases in the West arrangement [the print compilation] without first taking steps to create that arrangement [downloading or printing every reading from an electronic or Web reserve]. (158 F3d 695)

This suggests that construction of most electronic reserve and Web-based reading lists and the subsequent printing and compilation by students are not the equivalent of an institutionally created course packet or anthology. A different interpretation would be warranted if the entire set of readings, in course reading order, could be downloaded from the electronic reserve under a single print command sequence. However, if students must first access the reserve system and "manually" copy and reconstruct an anthology independently, then it would seem the *Matthew Bender* decision would stand for the proposition that such a reserve system capability is not the equivalent of an infringing print anthology, i.e., a *Kinko's* or *Michigan Document Services* scenario.

New Legislation: Solutions and Concerns

This author suggests consideration of a series of mechanisms, guidelines, and statutory amendments that would allow for the fair use, both in a strict legal sense under Title 17 US Code section 107, and in a general sense, under other sections of the copyright law. This includes the expansion of existing fair use guidelines and principles of library reserve into distance education settings. Such changes would minimize the disparate treatment of distance students with respect to access and use of copyrighted material in instructional settings. The following suggestions are also made to ensure the rights of copyright owners in educational settings.

First, amendment of Title 17 US Code section 110 would allow for the extension of the performance and display right to distance or remote transmissions of live or stored instruction in both traditional broadcast and Web-based instructional transmission settings. The audience permitted to benefit from the reproduction, performance, or display of the copyrighted work would be limited to enrolled members of the class. In Web-based settings (electronic reserve and instruction), this would entail the use of a password mechanism to guarantee that only legitimate users have access to copyrighted material.

Institutions would also be required to post warning notices on Web-based instructional materials and engage in copyright education and compliance programs. This is consistent with the spirit of the copyright warning notice regulations promulgated in conjunction with Title 17 US Code sections 108 and 109 (CFR 1998). In addition, this might include the requirement of student acknowledgment of risk and responsibility for their subsequent misuse of copyrighted material. This might be accomplished through the use of a computer mouse-click acknowledgment prompted by the system each time the student accesses protected material. A warning and acknowledgment would also be part of license mechanisms that attempt to assess a fee based upon a per use or classroom "seat license." This position is reviewed by Keays and Warren (1998) and Street (1998, 397–8). However, a fee would come into play only when a student actually receives a copy of the course work and not merely for viewing the material online.

The author does not suggest that licensing has no place in education or in distance education. Licensing operates for the convenience of both the user and owner. For example, licensing of software does occur on a site or seat basis when those uses are determinable in some way, either by distinct sites (number of terminals in a building) or by users (number of students in a class). An instructor's need to digitize and transfer a copy of a workbook to each of the twenty students in a Web course would, likewise, be a suitable illustration of the benefits of a licensing mechanism.

Assuming that the actual licensing of a variety of materials in different formats could be easily accommodated vis-à-vis a blanket or compulsory license scheme, the problem of a per student or per seat fee remains. Such "compulsory" licensing fails to distinguish a fair use from a licensed "every use" or from an outright purchase of the material. Students should not have to pay for the mere use (viewing on a computer screen) of an item in the same way that patrons or students are not charged for the right to use or view an item in the library. Institutions should not be forced to enter into license agreements based on the false assumption that every viewer will want his or her own copy and that they will subsequently display or perform that copy to others. Moreover, the item itself should not be regarded as an infringing copy. Current law does not make libraries, archives, or nonprofit educational organizations responsible for the potential infringement of patrons, clients, or students if those organizations have taken some measures to ensure user compliance.

One safeguard would be to encourage the use of copyright management information (CMI) technology by institutions in, for example, Web environments. Delta and Matsuura (1999, 5.94–5.106) discuss several methods, including digital watermarking, which allows a person to view the material online but prevents printing without permission, and a tracking technology that records when user downloads have occurred. Using CMI technology would allow students to view videotapes that were part of a Web course vis-à-vis the Title 17 US Code section 110. (This assumes that the law has changed to allow for that use and that a reproduction of the videotape has also been accounted for under Title 17 US Code section 108 or other reproduction provision.) CMI technology, however, would not allow students to make a copy of that videotape or any other material loaded onto the site unless the student has paid the seat fee that allows for the reproduction of the material.

Conclusion

Commentators cannot agree (compare analysis offered by Marke [1998] to that offered by Keays and Warren [1998] of same legislation) whether or not a balance exists in current copyright law schemes and, therefore, whether legislation or other changes would restore balance or skew it. The question is ultimately one of equal treatment of traditional versus distance educational settings and whether a movement toward that equal treatment, as a result of legal change, would also realign the rights of copyright owners and users. The copyright law is asked to arbitrate society's need to reward and encourage new knowledge creation and dissemination and the reality that the knowledge so created is hollow if it cannot be accessed and used by the public at large. Obviously, publishers and owners might not want any use of material to go uncompensated. Likewise, educational entities might want a blanket exception for all uses deemed related to "education." However, neither owners nor users live in a perfect world.

Note

In February 1999 the author testified before the United States Copyright Office during its Field Hearings on Promotion of Distance Education through Digital Technologies (Docket No. 98-12) (Request for Comments and Notice of Public Hearing, 63 Federal Register 71167 [December 23, 1998]). The hearings were held pursuant to authorization contained in the Digital Millennium Copyright Act (US Congress 1998b). This article is based upon the prepared testimony and written comments presented as a part of that process.

In May of 1999, since this article was submitted for publication, the United States Copyright Office delivered its report (US Copyright Office 1999) on distance education to Congress. The report recommended several changes to sections 110 (2) and 112, as well as clarification of aspects of the law in legislative history and further discussion and review of issues. The changes recommended include amending section 110 (2) to "allow the same activities to take place using digital delivery mechanisms, while controlling the risks involved" (US Copyright Office 1999, 145). Specific changes would clarify the meaning of "transmission," expand the coverage of rights, emphasize the concept of mediated instruction, eliminate the requirement of a physical classroom, add new safeguards to counteract new risks, maintain existing standards of eligibility, expand categories of works covered, require use of lawful copies, and the addition of a new ephemeral recordings exemption. The Copyright Office also stressed the importance of clarifying in the legislative history of provision enacted that fair use is technology-neutral and that the "fair use" guidelines that have been created are not to be taken as "absolute codes of conduct." The report also suggested that consideration of licensing mechanisms that would allow for the use of so-called "orphan work," as well as considerations of the impact of international distance learning settings on copyright, be pursued in the near future.

References

Basic Books, Inc. v. Kinko's Graphics Corporation, 758 F Supp 1522 (SDNY 1991).

Bielefield, A., and L. Cheeseman. 1997. *Technology and copyright law: A guidebook for the library, research, and teaching professions.* New York: Neal-Schuman.

Code of Federal Regulations (CFR). 1998. *Title 37. Section 201.14. Warnings of copyright for use by certain libraries and archives.*

———. *Section 201.24. Warning of copyright for software lending by nonprofit libraries.*

Delta, G. B., and J. H. Matsuura. 1999. *Law of the Internet.* New York: Aspen Law & Business.

Feist Publications, Inc. v. Rural Telephone Service Co., 499 US 340, 349–50 (1991).

Fogerty v. Fantasy, Inc., 510 US 517, 527 (1994).

Gasaway, L. N. 1996. Universities, libraries and fair use in the digital age. In *Current legal issues in publishing,* ed. A. B. Strauch, 69–87. New York: Haworth.

Grosso, A. 1994. The National Information Infrastructure: Implications of the information superhighway for commerce, security, and law enforcement. *Federal Bar News & Journal* 41: 481–8.

Hugenholtz, P. B. 1996. Adapting copyright to the information superhighway. In *The future of copyright in a digital environment,* ed. P. B. Hugenholtz, 81–102. Boston, MA: Kluwer Law International.

Information Infrastructure Task Force (IITF). 1993. *The National Information Infrastructure: Agenda for action.* Washington, DC: Government Printing Office.

Information Infrastructure Task Force on Intellectual Property Rights (IITFIPR). 1995. *Intellectual property rights and the National Information Infrastructure: The report of the working group on intellectual property rights* [hereinafter White Paper]. Washington, DC: Government Printing Office.

Johnston, D., S. Handa, and C. Morgan. 1997. *Cyberlaw: What you need to know about doing business online.* Toronto: Stoddart.

Kalil, T. 1995. Public policy and the National Information Infrastructure. *Business Economics,* October, 15–20.

Keays, A. C., and A. J. Warren. 1998. Is distance-learning bill balanced? *The National Law Journal* 26 October, B5.

Marke, J. J. 1998. Proposed legislation on digital copyright. *The New York Law Journal* 19 May, 5.

Marobie-FL, Inc. v. National Association of Fire Equipment Distributors and Northwest Nexus, 983 F Supp 1167 (N.D. Ill. 1997).

Matthew Bender & Co. v. West Publishing Co., 158 F3d 674 (2nd Cir 1998).

Playboy Enterprises, Inc. v. Frena, 839 F Supp 1552 (M.D. Fla. 1993).

Princeton University Press v. Michigan Document Services, Inc., 99 F3d 1381 (6th Cir 1996).

Religious Technology Center v. Netcom On-Line Communications Services, Inc., 907 F Supp 1361 (N.D. Cal. 1995).

Rosenor, J. 1997. *Cyberlaw: The law of the Internet.* New York: Springer.

Street, F. L. 1998. *Law of the Internet.* Charlottesville, VA: Lexis Law Publishing.

Stuckey, K. D. 1998. *Internet and online law.* New York: Law Journal/Seminars Press.

United States Advisory Council on the National Information Infrastructure (USACNII). 1996. A nation of opportunity: Realizing the promise of the information superhighway. Washington, DC: Government Printing Office.

US Code. 1998. Title 17. Copyrights. Chapter 1, Section 106. Exclusive rights in copyrighted works. The code can be accessed at http://www4.law.cornell.edu/uscode/17/ch1.text.html

———. *Section 107. Limitations on exclusive rights: Fair use.*

———. *Section 108. Limitations on exclusive rights: Reproduction by libraries and archives.*

———. *Section 109. Limitations on exclusive rights: Effect of transfer of particular copy or phonorecord.*

———. *Section 110. Limitations on exclusive rights: Exemption of certain performances and displays.*

US Congress. 1997. *Digital Era Copyright Enhancement Act.* House Report 3048. 105th Cong., 1st sess., Washington, DC: Government Printing Office.

———. 1998. *Sonny Bono Copyright Term Extension Act.* Public Law Number 105–298, 112 Stat. 2877. 105th Cong., 2d sess., Washington, DC: Government Printing Office.

———. 1998a. *Copyright Term Extension.* House Report 105–452. 105th Cong., 2d sess., Washington, DC: Government Printing Office.

———. 1998b. *Digital Millennium Copyright Act.* Public Law Number 105–304, 112 Stat. 2860. 105th Cong., 2d sess., Washington, DC: Government Printing Office.

———. 1998c. *Conference Report: Digital Millennium Copyright Act.* Senate Report 105–190. 105th Cong., 2d sess., Washington, DC: Government Printing Office.

US Copyright Office. 1999. *Report on copyright and digital distance education: A report of the register of copyrights.* Available at http://www.loc.gov/copyright/

Factors Influencing Interaction in an Online Course

Charalambos Vrasidas and Marina Stock McIsaac

Vol. 13 No. 3 1999

Abstract

This study examines the nature of interaction in an online course from both teacher and student perspectives. Major components of a conceptual framework to identify interaction were identified. Data analysis suggested that the structure of the course, class size, feedback, and prior experience with computer-mediated communication all influenced interaction. Results of the study reconceptualize interaction as a theoretical construct and emphasize the importance of socially constructed meanings from the participants' perspectives.

Introduction

Online education has captured the interest of educators at all levels. Teachers are being asked to adapt their courses for Internet delivery, while students are being promised more flexible learning formats. As a result, both teachers and learners are questioning how they can benefit from education delivered online.

One of the key components of good teaching is the intellectually stimulating exchange of ideas, those meaningful interactions that occur between teachers and students and among students themselves. What do such interactions mean for the students and teacher, and what influences interaction in well-designed learning environments?

Using an interpretivist approach, this study was an attempt to gain a better understanding of the complexities of the online environment and the factors influencing interaction. Our approach was based on a symbolic interactionist framework (Blumer 1969) and Erickson's (1986) methodological ideas. The purpose of this study was to examine face-to-face and online interaction in a graduate course and to uncover the factors that influence interaction.

Conceptual Framework for Studying Interaction

A pilot study (Vrasidas 1999) examined the conceptual framework underlying interaction in an online course. The results of that study led to the identification of a group of interrelated contextual categories within which major factors operate to influence interaction. These factors do not stand alone. They must be viewed in the overall context of interaction. Changes in one contextual category affect the rest of the framework. The factors that emerged from the pilot study are learner control, social presence, structure, feedback, and dialogue.

The major categories of the framework were fine-tuned by conducting a review of research on interaction in distance education (Baynton 1992; Gunawardena 1995; Hillman, Willis, and Gunawardena 1994; Moore 1989; Parker 1995; Ross 1996; Saba and Shearer 1994). In this conceptual framework, all of the categories are connected via a web of interrelated relationships. Changes in one of the categories influence the other categories and, therefore, the broader context of interaction.

Learning, knowledge, and human activity can be situated within specific contexts (Brown, Collins, and Duguid 1989; Suchman 1987). In order to examine a complex construct such as interaction, researchers benefit from carefully examining the context within which interaction is taking place. Interaction in an online course may consist of institutional and departmental policies, technologies employed, teacher philosophy, course content, and the context in which the instruction takes place. The central bin of this conceptual framework is interaction. Interaction is one of the most important components of any learning experience (Dewey 1938; Vygotsky 1978), and it has been identified as one of the major constructs in distance education research (McIsaac and Gunawardena 1996; Moore 1989; Wagner 1994). Moore (1989) made the distinction between three types of interaction: learner-content, learner-teacher, and learner-learner. Hillman, Willis, and Gunawardena (1994) argued that past discussions of interaction failed to acknowledge the fact that, for any of the three types of interaction to take place, the learner has to interact with the medium. Consequently, they proposed a learner-interface interaction.

Several studies have examined interaction as it relates to technology. Comeaux (1995) found that, in an interactive television course, awareness of technology, such as microphones and cameras, hampered interaction. Ross (1996) found that, during interaction, learners who do not have the skills to communicate using computers are more aware of technology than of the content of communication. Tsui and Ki (1996) found that frequency of interaction increased over time as participants became more comfortable using technology. Levin, Kim, and Riel (1990) argued that successful network communities must meet at least four of the following five criteria. First, members of the group are people that cannot meet face-to-face because of place and time constraints; consequently, they work online on a shared task. Second, the task on which the group works is clearly defined. Third, there is easy access to technology, and participants have the skills to use it effectively. Fourth, there is a common sense of responsibility toward the assigned task and the group process. Fifth, there is good leadership, coordination, and evaluation of the completed activities.

The framework within which interaction occurs consists of many factors. Those factors that directly influence interaction within the contextual categories of the framework in our pilot study were identified as learner control, transactional distance (composed of structure and dialogue), feedback, and social presence. Learner control is central to the notion of interaction. Garrison and Baynton (1987) argued that the concept of control consists of three major components: independence, power, and support. Therefore, control should be examined as the balancing result among these three factors. Independence is defined as the degree to which the learner is free to make choices. Power refers to the abilities and competencies of the learner to engage in a learning experience. Support indicates the resources available that will enable the learner to successfully participate in the distance education course.

Structure and dialogue are components of an online transaction that can reduce the distance between students and teachers. Moore (1973) postulated that transactional distance is the psychological and communication gap that results from the geographical separation between the learners and the teacher. Structure refers to the overall design of the course. Dialogue can be described as the learner-teacher interaction in a distance course. Saba and Shearer (1994) conducted a study to empirically verify the concepts of transactional distance, dialogue, and structure. The authors constructed a model based on mathematical formulas that would predict the amount of transactional distance depending on a set of variables. The variables used in this formula were learner control, teacher control, dialogue, and structure. The results indicated that transactional distance depends on the rate of dialogue and structure. When dialogue increases and structure decreases, transactional distance decreases. When structure increases, transactional distance increases and dialogue decreases.

The third factor of the interaction framework is feedback. Feedback is associated with types of responses that provide information to students about the correctness of their assignments, homework, and class contributions (Mory 1996). In face-to-face situations, nonverbal gestures are exchanged constantly, providing both the teacher and learners with feedback. However, (depending on the technology used) students at a distance usually cannot see nonverbal cues and must rely on verbal feedback. In distance education, feedback is more important than just as a mechanism for informing students of how well they did on an assignment. Stevenson, Sander, and Naylor (1996) found that timely and encouraging feedback on their assignments directly affected students' general sense of satisfaction with the course.

The last factor in the framework is social presence, which can be defined as the degree to which a medium allows the user to feel socially present in a mediated situation (Short, Williams, and Christie 1976). Gunawardena (1995) found that social presence could be promoted in a computer-mediated communication (CMC) setting by employing strategies that encourage interaction.

Taking into account the major factors mentioned above, there is a need to examine the nature of interaction in an online classroom.

Methodology

Theoretical Basis. This study followed Erickson's (1986) methods of interpretive research, which are based on the three premises of symbolic interactionism posed by Blumer (1969). First, human beings act upon the world on the basis of the meanings that the world has for them. Second, the meaning of the world is socially constructed through one's interactions with members of the community. And third, the meaning of the world is processed again through interpretation. The traditional approach to research tends to ignore the importance of meaning and interpretation of the actors in shaping behavior. Interpretive research focuses on the perspectives of the actors involved and attempts to understand the multiple layers of meaning represented by human action.

For this study, we define interaction as *the process consisting of the reciprocal actions of two or more actors within a given context.* Therefore, the learner-content and learner-interface interactions were not examined. The minimum interactional sequence consists of at least two reciprocal actions. Interaction always takes place in response to others' actions or in relation to others. Actors constantly fit their actions to those of their peers. How others act with regard to the world influences the meanings of the world for the individual.

Setting. The unit of study was a graduate online course in the use of telecommunications for instruction at a major southwestern university. There were eight students and one professor. After seven weeks, one of the students dropped the course.

The class was supported with the computer conferencing software FirstClass and a Web site that contained information about the class assignments, schedule, and resources. For the first five weeks, the class met face-to-face in a computer lab. Afterward, the class met two weeks online, one face-to-face, one online, one face-to-face, four online, and two face-to-face.

Students were graded on five areas: assignments, discussions, midterm, final research paper, and presentation of the paper. There were eight scheduled discussions during the course, each of which was moderated by a pair of students. Four discussions took place face-to-face and four took place online. The moderators of the discussions posted questions online and students were asked to respond at least once. After the asynchronous discussion, members of the class discussed the topic in a synchronous chat.

Data Collection and Analysis. The authors observed the scheduled face-to-face meetings in person. All observations were tape-recorded and transcribed. During the last three weeks of the semester, semistructured interviews were conducted with the teacher and all the students. The main purpose of the interviews was to obtain the participants' points of view on interaction. In addition, student work and all the messages from the teacher's mailbox were collected, providing information on how often each student interacted with the teacher and how often the teacher sent messages to the students. The total number of emoticons used by each participant during the online chats was also tallied. Furthermore, the authors kept detailed memos throughout the research process to document notes and reflections on the setting.

During data analysis the authors followed the inductive and deductive stages as proposed by Erickson (1986). Assertions were generated during the inductive stage of data analysis. Assertions are propositional statements that indicate relationships and generalizations in the data (Erickson 1986). First, all the data was collected and organized. Then, the data was read three times to gain an overall understanding of what was happening in the course. Upon reading through the data, questions came to mind, which were recorded in notes and memos containing those issues and events that emerged as important. From these, assertions were generated.

Once assertions were generated from the data as a whole, the analysis entered the deductive stage. This stage involved a detailed examination of the data and the identification of evidence that supported or disconfirmed the initial assertions. These instances were carefully examined to determine whether to keep each assertion, refine it, or drop it. Assertions were warranted using a variety of methods, including interviews, observations, and collection of online messages. The goal was not to identify the convergence of data during triangulation, but rather to identify a variety of sources that would back up the claims. Some explanations and interpretations of events were stronger than others because there was more evidence to support them.

Standards of Rigor. For Erickson (1986), the fundamental validity criterion for interpretive research is defined by the attention paid to "the immediate and local meanings of actions, as defined from the actor's point of view" (119). After closely examining the particulars, researchers reach concrete universals and then begin to make claims about their meanings, in this case, interaction in online courses. Generalization begins with the case at hand. This study attempted to find instances that illustrated recurring themes in the setting examined. This allows the reader to compare these findings with other studies and to judge whether the results found here generalize to other similar settings.

The validity of the account depends on the comprehensiveness of the study and the description of the procedures followed. The use of a variety of sources for data collection is more likely to increase the plausibility of the account. This study should be judged for coherence and not for correspondence of the findings with the "objective" world. The Erickson approach suggests that accounts are valid to the degree that they are plausible. By presenting a detailed, comprehensive, and coherent account, the reader can act as a coanalyst of the study and make judgments about the strength of the assertions presented.

Results and Analysis

Data analysis showed that the four major factors influencing interaction in this course were structure, class size, feedback provided to the students, and participants' prior experience with CMC.

Structure. Careful examination of the data indicated that structure influenced interaction. Some elements of structure, such as required activities, led to more interactions, while other aspects of structure led to fewer interactions. Interactions such as discussing the final paper outline with the teacher, collaborating on peer editing of students' papers, and participating in online discussions were required and were included in the grade. Consequently, these aspects of the course structure increased interaction among participants. Three students indicated that their desire to achieve good grades was an important factor that led to frequent participation and interaction in the course.

The evidence that structure influenced interaction is also indicated by the lack of interaction in certain aspects of the course. An example of this is the lack of interaction in the asynchronous discussions. Table 1 shows how many participants contributed to the asynchronous discussions and the total number of messages posted every week. For example, during the fourth week of the semester, only three students other than the moderators participated in the discussion.

Table 1. Messages Posted by Participants in Each Asynchronous Discussion

Week	Students participating	Student messages	Moderator messages	Teacher messages	Total messages
4	3	4	2	–	6
5	2	2	2	1	5
6	3	3	2	1	6
7	4	4	3	–	7
8	5	5	2	–	7
10	4	6	1	–	7
11	4	4	1	1	6
12	2	2	1	–	3

From the students' perspective, participation in the asynchronous discussions was "busy work." Students felt that there was no need to participate in a discussion that dealt with a topic on which they had already written a paper and would again discuss face-to-face or in an online chat. During her interview, one of the students explained the lack of participation in the asynchronous discussions:

> First of all, you are having us read all this material (uses hands to enumerate things). And then, we have to write a reaction paper on it. And then, we have to answer somebody else's questions. So...What's the point of doing this, just to show that we can upload an answer to a question?" So, it was kind of frustrating.

Expression of disappointment and frustration with the workload was a typical response pattern. Six students attributed the lack of participation in the asynchronous discussions to the course's heavy workload. Students were required to write a 1,000-word essay for each topic and contribute at least one message in the asynchronous weekly discussions. In addition, students had to collaborate with a peer to moderate one face-to-face and one online discussion. They were also required to complete a midterm examination, write an annotated bibliography, submit a research paper outline, peer-edit one of their classmates' final papers, write a ten-page research paper, and give a presentation of the paper on the last day of class.

The teacher admitted that the workload might have been one of the reasons that students did not engage in the asynchronous discussions. In his own words: "...I think that it was a lot of work. It seemed to overwhelm some of them and it ended up turning out to be, I think, something like busy work rather than thoughtful experiences for them." There was only one student who did not complain about the amount of work. She had prior experience with CMC and online courses and was very interested in the course topic. Overall, however, the data suggested that the demanding amount of course work led to fewer interactions in the asynchronous discussions.

Another possible explanation for the lack of interaction in the asynchronous discussions is the fact that the course was based on a combination of face-to-face and online meetings. Students viewed the online meetings as a break instead of as an opportunity to engage in online discussion. Meeting interchangeably between face-to-face and online platforms seemed to influence the online discussions. It may be that the students' needs for socializing, learning, and discussing were met during the face-to-face meetings. Consequently, participants did not feel the need to engage in the asynchronous online component of the course. As one student admitted during the interview, "the online discussions seemed less important than the face-to-face meetings." Another student indicated that, if the course had been completely online, there would have been much more online interaction because "there would be no other option."

Class Size. The small class size also influenced interaction. Of the seven students who remained registered in the course, two took on the role of moderator, leaving five students to participate in the discussion. One of the students never participated in the asynchronous discussions because, according to her, the only reason she was enrolled in the class was to acquire the three credits she needed for graduation. Participants felt that four students were not enough to engage in a productive asynchronous discussion. One of the students explained it in the following way: "Let's say you have five people, and two are not in the mood, then you have only three left. That's all, nothing else. If you have fifteen, if three are not in the mood, you still have twelve." The teacher agreed that class size might have been a reason for the lack of interaction in the asynchronous discussions. During the interview, he commented on the lack of participation, saying that, "It may have something to do with the size of the class in general....The community was never built because it was too small; a bunch of people doing their own thing."

When asked to comment on the class-size issue, two students disagreed and felt that it was not the class size but, rather, the workload. One of them commented:

> I don't think that was it [a little reluctantly]. I think that we were tabbed. I mean...we only had that much time for the class, and because we were doing the paper every week, we were concentrating on that.

However, by examining the data carefully, it became apparent that, had there been more students enrolled in the course, there would have been more interactions during the asynchronous online discussions. The issue of critical mass for such conferences is something that needs to be examined in further research.

Feedback. Another issue that influenced interaction was feedback. Several indicators suggested that students did not receive adequate feedback either from the teacher or their peers in the online portion of the course. A typical comment from a student regarding feedback on class assignments follows:

> I think I would've liked more feedback on each individual paper....Each week...I really spent a lot of time on that...so, it would've been nice to get more individualized feedback on that.

Another student mentioned that, "We wrote quite a few essays, but we didn't get much response on those." By the sixth week of class, during the second online chat, students had not received feedback on any of their assignments. The teacher admitted that, due to time constraints, he did not provide much feedback in the online portion of the course.

Students also felt that their peers were not providing them with enough input and feedback in the discussions. One student stated: "I would've liked more asynchronous conversation amongst my peers about the topic. Feedback from them, bringing in their expertise." The moderators rarely commented on their peers' contributions in the asynchronous discussions. In addition, it was rare that participants in the discussions commented on another participant's contribution. Students felt that responses to the moderators' questions were just postings that met the requirement.

Prior Experience. Experience with CMC was the final factor influencing participation in the online discussions. Students who were new to CMC were not comfortable participating in the online synchronous chats. They felt more comfortable with the asynchronous communication because there they could take time to think and reflect on their ideas. One of the novice students stated that the online chats were "nerve-racking" and it was hard for her to keep up. She was reluctant to post messages. Students who had more than eight years of CMC experience enjoyed participating in chats and asynchronous online discussions. One such student argued that practice is crucial for succeeding in online courses. The importance of prior experience with computers, proficiency in using the conferencing system, participating in chats, and moderating online discussions were all issues that emerged from the data.

In addition, participants who were experienced in the medium used emoticons more frequently. When a student communicates online, there is no body language or voice intonation that indicates humor or sarcasm. Experienced users used emoticons to compensate for the lack of those contextual cues. For example, a smiley face, ":)", might indicate a student who was joking or being sarcastic. Continuous dots, "...", were used to indicate an interruption in speech and signal that something else would follow. The letter *k* was used as an abbreviation for "okay" and "lol" as an abbreviation for "laughing out loud."

In this course, four students and the teacher were experienced users who frequently used emoticons in their online interactions. Three students never used emoticons during their interactions in the synchronous chats. Nonexperienced users felt overwhelmed and ignorant for not knowing what emoticons meant and how to use them appropriately in their interactions.

Another indication that the more experienced students benefited from previous CMC experience was in the number of asynchronous messages exchanged between each student and the teacher. One more experienced student sent a total of eleven messages to the teacher and received seven. In her interview, she stated that she also engaged in four private chats with the teacher in which they discussed course issues and her final project. A less experienced student sent only five messages to the teacher and received four throughout the semester. She never engaged in a private chat with the teacher or with any of her peers.

Discussion and Implications for Practice

The suggestions included in this section are neither prescriptions nor a practice manual. The findings of this study do not attempt to dictate how online courses should be structured, nor do they attempt to explain everything that might have influenced interaction in the course. Rather, they are suggestions based on detailed observation and analysis of this particular course. Researchers and practitioners should judge whether the findings relate and are applicable to their cases.

Careful examination of the data and the interactions identified in the study indicated that structure influenced interaction. Elements of structure such as required activities led to more interactions and increased dialogue among the participants. This finding contradicts the hypothesis that increasing structure decreases dialogue and increases transactional distance (Moore 1991; Saba and Shearer 1994). Several of the interactions identified in this course were a class requirement and part of structure. For example, the participation and moderation of discussions was required and included in the grade. Requiring students to engage in discussions and collaborate on projects increased interaction in the course. Therefore, increased structure led to more dialogue and interaction. Perhaps the development of more seamless conferencing systems in the last six years has eliminated some of the earlier restrictions that technology placed on the delicate structure-dialogue balance. Current conferencing systems allow synchronous chats and asynchronous threaded discussions that were not common previously. This issue is an important one and should be investigated further.

Moore's (1973) original definition of transactional distance was based on the idea that dialogue and transactional distance were primarily influenced by the teacher-learner interaction. New media, such as computer conferencing, now allow for increased collaboration and learner-learner interaction, which may influence transactional distance in the online classroom. Saba and Shearer (1994) worked to empirically verify transactional distance by following a systems model that did not take into consideration the reciprocal nature of interaction and the importance of context.

Cookson and Chang (1995) also suggested that Saba and Shearer's analysis of interaction was incomplete because they focused more on the teacher and ignored learner-learner and group interactions.

The present study suggests that educators can structure for dialogue and interaction and that learner-learner interaction is an important component of dialogue. Other aspects of structure, such as workload and the schedule of face-to-face and online meetings, led to fewer interactions. The fact that students met interchangeably between face-to-face and online platforms influenced their degree of interaction. Perhaps students met their need for socializing, learning, and discussing during the face-to-face meetings and the synchronous chats. Consequently, participants may not have felt the need to engage in the asynchronous online component of the course. This corroborates Levin, Kim, and Riel's (1990) finding that successful network communities consist of participants who cannot meet face-to-face because of place and time constraints. When students cannot meet face-to-face, they are more likely to participate in the online portion of the course since that is their only option.

Prior experience with CMC also influenced interaction. Participants with limited prior experience used CMC less frequently and felt intimidated when others used emoticons during their interactions. These findings are in agreement with several other studies (Anderson and Lee 1995; Comeaux 1995; Ritchie 1993). Training students early in the course to use emoticons, to use the conferencing system, and to employ appropriate etiquette should be mandatory in all online courses. A simple survey or a needs assessment at the beginning of the course can help determine which students need training. The teacher can provide remedial work to those students and help them successfully use the conferencing software. Another suggestion is to assign students to pairs with a mixed range of skills. For example, pairing experienced CMC users with those less experienced can ensure that students with limited skills receive help from their partners.

The other issue that seemed to influence interaction in the course is feedback. Students felt that the lack of immediate feedback in the online portion of the course was discouraging and contributed to their limited participation in the online discussions. When students do not receive feedback, they do not continue to post messages. Unless students receive immediate feedback, they feel they are posting to the network without any response. The teacher should provide timely feedback to students' contributions in all aspects of the course. Furthermore, the teacher should emphasize the necessity for moderators to provide feedback and encourage their peers' participation.

Conclusion

The findings of the study indicated that the structure of the course, class size, feedback, and prior experience with CMC all influenced interaction. This study presents the perspectives of the students and teacher of one class regarding what it is like to participate in an online course. An interesting aspect of online interaction is that it is solely constructed through language. Further analysis of the data transcripts following a discourse analysis approach could shed light on how the ideas of power and control operate in online and face-to-face encounters. It would be useful to explore what discourse says about power and to examine how interaction shapes power in an online environment. In addition, there is a need to further examine the other categories of the conceptual framework developed here to determine ways in which these factors may influence each other and the overall construct of interaction. This study has only scratched the surface of the complex construct we call interaction. Further detailed exploration of factors within multiple contexts may allow researchers to revisit concepts we take for granted and gain an understanding of the meanings of interaction found in the everyday life of online environments.

References

Anderson, J., and A. Lee. 1995. Literacy teachers learning a new literacy: A study of the use of electronic mail in a reading education class. *Reading Research and Instruction* 34 (3): 222–38.

Baynton, M. 1992. Dimensions of "control" in distance education: A factor analysis. *The American Journal of Distance Education* 6 (2): 17–31.

Blumer, H. 1969. *Symbolic interactionism: Perspective and method.* Englewood Cliffs, NJ: Prentice-Hall.

Brown, J. S., A. Collins, and P. Duguid. 1989. Situated cognition and the culture of learning. *Educational Researcher* 18 (1): 32–42.

Comeaux, P. 1995. The impact of an interactive distance learning network on classroom communication. *Communication Education* 44 (4): 353–61.

Cookson, P. S., and Y. Chang. 1995. The multidimensional audioconferencing classification system (MACS). *The American Journal of Distance Education* 9 (3): 18–36.

Dewey, J. 1938. *Experience and education.* New York: Collier Macmillan.

Erickson, F. 1986. Qualitative methods in research on teaching. In *Handbook of research on teaching,* ed. M. C. Wittrock, 119–61. New York: Macmillan.

Garrison, D. R., and M. Baynton. 1987. Beyond independence in distance education: The concept of control. *The American Journal of Distance Education* 1 (3): 3–15.

Gunawardena, C. N. 1995. Social presence theory and implications for interaction and collaborative learning in computer conferences. *International Journal of Educational Telecommunications* 1 (2/3): 147–66.

Hillman, D. C., D. J. Willis, and C. N. Gunawardena. 1994. Learner-interface interaction in distance education: An extension of contemporary models and strategies for practitioners. *The American Journal of Distance Education* 8 (2): 30–42.

Levin, L. A., H. Kim, and M. M. Riel. 1990. Analyzing instructional interactions on electronic message networks. In *Online education: Perspectives on a new environment,* ed. L. M. Harasim, 185–214. New York: Praeger.

McIsaac, M. S., and C. N. Gunawardena. 1996. Distance education. In *Handbook of research for educational communications and technology,* ed. D. H. Jonassen, 403–437. New York: Macmillan Library Reference USA.

Moore, M. G. 1973. Towards a theory of independent learning. *Journal of Higher Education* 44 (9): 661–79.

———. 1989. Editorial. Three types of interaction. *The American Journal of Distance Education* 3 (2): 1–6.

———. 1991. Editorial. Distance education theory. *The American Journal of Distance Education* 5 (3): 1–6.

Mory, E. H. 1996. Feedback research. In *Handbook of research for educational communications and technology,* ed. D. H. Jonassen, 919–56. New York: Macmillan Library Reference USA.

Parker, A. 1995. Distance education attrition. *International Journal of Educational Telecommunications* 1 (4): 389–406.

Ritchie, H. 1993. The effects of interaction mode on participation and interaction frequency during televised instruction with two-way audio. *Journal of Education for Library and Information Science* 34 (3): 218–27.

Ross, A. R. 1996. The influence of computer communication skills on participation in a computer conferencing course. *Journal of Educational Computing Research* 15 (1): 37–52.

Saba, F., and R. L. Shearer. 1994. Verifying key theoretical concepts in a dynamic model of distance education. *The American Journal of Distance Education* 8 (1): 36–57.

Short, J., E. Williams, and B. Christie. 1976. *The social psychology of telecommunications.* London: John Wiley & Sons.

Stevenson, K., P. Sander, and P. Naylor. 1996. Student perceptions of the tutor's role in distance learning. *Open Learning* 11 (1): 22–30.

Suchman, L. A. 1987. *Plans and situated actions.* New York: Cambridge University Press.

Tsui, A. B. M., and W. W. Ki. 1996. An analysis of conference interactions on Telenex—A computer network for ESL teachers. *Educational Technology Research and Development* 44 (4): 23–44.

Vrasidas, C. 1999. Meanings of online and face-to-face interactions in a graduate course. Ph.D. diss., Arizona State University.

Vygotsky, L. S. 1978. *Mind in society.* Cambridge, MA: Harvard University Press.

Wagner, E. D. 1994. In support of a functional definition of interaction. *The American Journal of Distance Education* 8 (2): 6–29.

Perceptions and Effects of Image Transmissions during Internet-Based Training

Robert A. Wisher and Christina K. Curnow

Vol. 13 No. 3 1999

Abstract

This article reports on a study that examined the influence of a student's visual access to the instructor during Internet-based audiographics training. A four-day factual course on information operations was taught through lecture and slides over the Internet to $n = 110$ students situated at seven remote sites. The availability of instructor video was manipulated. For two instructional modules, the transmission of the instructor video was disabled for half of the students, while the other half could view the instructor; this procedure was reversed for two other modules. The results showed that increasing the video capability of an Internet-based course does not necessarily improve the learning of factual information.

Introduction

According to the International Data Corporation (1999), the market for training over the Internet or intranets is expected to grow to over $5 billion by 2003. Internet tools available in the training marketplace include Internet relay chat, application sharing, computer telephony, and multiuser simulation environments. More recently, the development of video streaming via the Internet, which can display the image of an instructor to a student on a time-buffered basis, has sparked interest in offering low-cost video teletraining over the desktop, further tempting developers to imitate the traditional classroom. A prominent question for Internet learning environments, then, is, What training value does a video image of the instructor offer? A secondary question is, What effects do lags in the transmission of static instructional images, such as graphics, over the Internet have on student learning?

The purpose of the present research is to explore these issues empirically. This study examines the effect of manipulating (on vs. off) the video image of an instructor on students' perceptions of both their ability to learn and the instructor's effectiveness. These perceptions were then compared to multisource evaluation data that included an objective final exam. Perceptions of the effect of transmission lags of text and graphic images were also compared to the learning measure. The research was conducted during a course on information operations taught to army reservists. The training was delivered through audiographics over the Internet while manipulating the transmission of instructor video across sites for certain instructional modules.

Audiographics and Instruction. Audiographics is a distance learning application that transmits a visual image accompanied by an instructor's voice, usually through audioconferencing, to students at remote sites. Audiographics is a natural partner for Internet delivery, although it has been in use with direct modem connections for over twenty-five years (Chute, Thompson, and Hancock 1999). The transmitted visual image displays instructional content, such as a text slide, a graphic, or a picture. The instructor can annotate, manipulate, and point to information on the visual image while lecturing or responding to student questions through two-way audio. In some audiographics systems, students and instructors can share application programs, creating a collaborative environment in which any individual can interact to input by others. In an audiographics application the students do not see the instructor but, rather, attend to the content—the visual image and the instructor's presentation. Of the three types of interaction occurring in distance learning as described by Moore (1989), the interaction between student and content—viewing the image and listening to the instructor—is most important.

Audiographic applications differ from video teletraining in that the latter allows students to see the instructor and, in the case of two-way video, the instructor to see the students. The Internet and other technologies, however, offer the capability for the visual presence of an instructor alongside the display of instructional content, thereby creating a hybrid audiographic system.

Effects of Video. From a training perspective, there are categories of learning for which there is apparently little need to see the instructor, such as learning declarative knowledge or facts. Indeed, audio accompanied by static print materials has been demonstrated to be as effective as face-to-face classroom instruction for step-by-step procedural tasks (Wisher and Priest 1998) as well as for graduate education (Burge and Howard 1990). However, there are surely categories of learning in which the student depends on the instructor for visual cues. For example, training in first aid procedures such as cardiopulmonary resuscitation or communication skills such as sign language depends on visual motion cues during instruction. The cases in which video motion can be beneficial to learning are governed by several factors. These factors include (1) attention being directed to relevant features that change, (2) motion allowing discriminations to be made, and (3) tasks that are difficult to express verbally (Wetzel, Radtke, and Stern 1994). From the perspective of return on investment, however, there should be a convincing reason for the added costs of transmitting instructor video during a distance learning program, particularly when the training objectives do not require the categories of learning that can benefit from video motion. The proverbial talking head is not necessarily important for learning.

Student Perceptions and Preferences. How do student perceptions and preferences pertaining to video capability relate to learning? The historical findings from instructional television demonstrate that there are generally no significant relationships. For example, in a study by Greenhill, Rich, and Carpenter (1962) that examined preferences for screen size, students were divided into two groups and assigned to a large or small screen. The results showed that the large majority of students preferred the large screen; however, this preference was unrelated to achievement in the course. In a study by VanderMeer (1954) that examined preferences for color versus black-and-white films, half of the students saw two instructional films in color then two in black and white, while the other half saw the films in the opposite rendition. Although students preferred the color films, there was no relationship between preference and learning. On the basis of these and many other studies, it is generally not necessary to use a higher-quality video presentation to achieve efficient learning, even though there is a preference for the higher quality. As Chu and Schramm (1967) observed in a comprehensive review of learning from television, satisfaction with instructional television is not always correlated with learning from it. This observation parallels research outcomes on the training effectiveness of maintenance and flight simulators that demonstrate higher fidelity simulations (e.g., high-quality graphics, audio, or motion) do not necessarily improve learning or transfer to actual equipment operation (Hays and Singer 1989). Similarly, in more recent research on training in virtual environments, Johnson and Stewart (1999) report data indicating that more immersive and costly visual display environments do not improve visual-spatial learning. In the broader context of distance learning, Moore and Kearsley (1996) noted that the analysis of student satisfaction surveys generally shows no significant relationship between attitude and achievement.

Method

Information Operations Course. The course focused on information security and was introductory in nature. It covered definitions, the nature of the threat, the military and civilian organizations involved, the function of computer emergency response teams, and national strategies related to computer security incidents, such as the vulnerability of computers and networks to cyberattacks. The four-day course was divided into eleven instructional modules oriented to declarative knowledge and facts. The comparison group consisted of three iterations of traditional, face-to-face classroom instruction taught on consecutive days by three different instructors. The training method involved lectures accompanied by 375 PowerPoint slides. The distance learning version used audiographics and was taught over two weekends using the same content and the same three instructors as the face-to-face courses. There were no additional costs related to the conversion of the course to the distance learning format. For both course formats, students had a workbook that contained copies of the slides with space for notes.

Participants. Participants in the audiographics version of the course were personnel ($n = 110$) from various army reserve and National Guard units. The number of participants per remote site ranged from seven to twenty-eight. Participants in the three face-to-face classroom versions were personnel ($n = 108$) from similar military units. The number of students per classroom iteration ranged from twenty-seven to fifty-three.

Conduct of Training. The face-to-face version was taught in the Washington, DC, area, requiring most participants to travel to a central training facility. The distance learning version originated from the Army Reserve Readiness Training Center, Fort McCoy, Wisconsin. Seven remote sites in Massachusetts, Vermont, Virginia, Iowa, Oklahoma, Texas, and the state of Washington were connected through the following:

1. A projection screen displaying visual images. These were transmitted with application controls over the Internet through a DataBeam T.120 audiographics multipoint conferencing unit server located in Atlanta. Microsoft NetMeeting was the client application software.
2. A twenty-five-inch or larger monitor displaying a real-time video image of the instructor. This was transmitted through a standard telephone line using H.324 data compression.
3. An audioconferencing system enabling full-duplex, two-way voice communication between all sites connected through an audiobridge.

To avoid problems arising from any delay in the transmission of slides during training, a separate computer connected to the server through the Internet allowed the instructor to observe when the next slide was fully available to the remote sites. A facilitator was available at each remote site for testing connectivity and administering tests and evaluation forms.

Throughout the training, the instructor controlled the presentation of slide images transmitted over the Internet. The slides were available at the remote sites on CD-ROM as a backup in the event of network problems. For each module, every remote site was able to display the slides and hear the instructor. The sites were also able to view an image of the instructor on an adjacent monitor. A toggle switch permitted the instructor video image to be disabled temporarily at certain remote sites.

Measures. Three survey forms were developed for the audiographics group. The precourse form collected demographic information and a self-assessment of prior knowledge on the eleven instructional modules. The midcourse survey measured perceived ability to learn with or without the instructor video being transmitted, perceived distraction of any lags in slide transmission time, and a self-assessment of learning on the eight modules taught up to that point. The final survey asked participants to rate the technical and administrative aspects of the program and included a self-assessment of learning on the final three topics. A comprehensive fifty-item knowledge test was administered to both groups. The reliability of the knowledge test was moderate ($r = .67$).

The transmission times of 110 slides, sampled during the four intermediate modules, were recorded with a stopwatch. Each slide's immediate appearance on a dedicated monitor was compared to its delayed appearance on an adjacent Internet monitor. The T.120 transmission error correction code used during the course worked in a manner such that the slides appeared concurrently to all sites through a hub-and-spoke network arrangement.

Procedure. For the distance learning group, eight instructional modules were covered during the first weekend; the second weekend included the final three modules along with a general review and the written knowledge test. The three initial modules were taught through audiographics with accompanying instructor video. The instructor video was manipulated during the four intermediate modules, each approximately one hour in duration. Participants were informed of the change in advance. The instructor video transmission was disabled at three remote sites ($n = 59$) for modules 4 and 5, while the video remained on at the other four sites ($n = 51$). This manipulation was reversed for modules 6 and 7; transmission to the three remote sites was reenabled while transmission to the other four sites was disabled. The audiographics portion was active for all sites throughout the training. Thus, a counterbalanced, within-subjects experimental design was attained.

The final survey was administered upon completion of training but before the written knowledge test. Scores from the same knowledge test, along with demographic information, were collected on a post hoc basis for participants in the three face-to-face classes, which served as a comparison group. No further evaluation of the comparison group was conducted.

Results

Demographics. The median age of participants in the audiographics group was thirty-six years, compared to a median age of thirty-five years for the comparison group. The military rank of personnel between the two groups was comparable, with about half enlisted and half officers. Also, 76% of the audiographics group had experience with PowerPoint, the presentation software package used to present the slides throughout the course.

Learning Outcomes. Overall, the results of the final written test indicated that there was no difference in learning outcome between the distance learning and face-to-face groups. The test results were 88.2% correct for the audiographics group and 87.5% correct for the face-to-face group [t (208) = .60, *n.s.*; p = .55]. Within the audiographics group, a secondary source of data was available through the self-assessment of knowledge before and after the training. The results of this measure will be described below followed by a refined analysis that more closely examines the effects of instructor video on learning.

Since objective pretesting of knowledge was not feasible, a surrogate measure of prior knowledge was added to the precourse survey. Participants were asked to rate "how well they knew" each of the eleven modules on a 5-point scale, with a rating of 1 indicating "not at all" and a rating of 5 indicating "very well." The mean ratings for the modules ranged from 1.3 to 2.7, with an average rating of 2.0 indicating that the material was largely unfamiliar prior to training. The highest rating was for the module on the widely used Army Operations Field Manual.

After training, but just before the written test, participants rated the amount learned on each module on a 5-point scale, a rating of 1 indicating that "nothing" more was learned and a rating of 5 indicating that "a lot more" was learned. The overall results revealed a mean rating of 3.6 (range 3.1 to 4.0). To examine the validity of the ratings, the data were then analyzed contingent upon ratings of prior knowledge. For each module, ratings by participants were segmented into a Low Prior Knowledge category (a rating of 1 or 2) or a High Prior Knowledge category (a rating of 4 or 5). Those who rated in the middle (about 22% of all cases) were excluded from this particular analysis, resulting in a clearer comparison between low and high categories. The two categories were then contrasted for learning patterns as measured by the reported amount learned. This resulted in the pattern displayed in Figure 1.

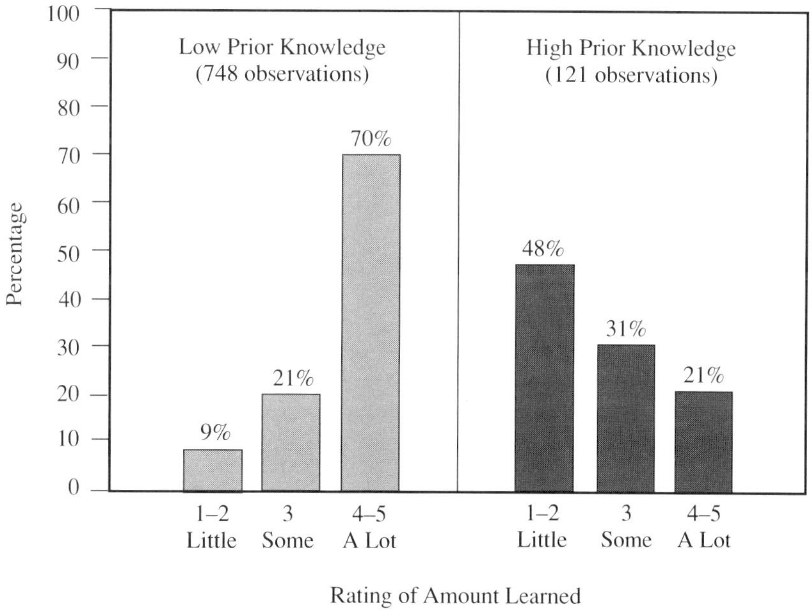

Figure 1. Breakout of Self-Assessment of Prior Knowledge by Amount Learned for All Modules.

The learning patterns for those with low prior knowledge showed a distinctly upward trend in contrast to the pattern for those with high prior knowledge, which showed a distinctly downward trend. As would be expected in an introductory course, those entering a module with a low level of prior knowledge learned more on average than those entering with a high level of knowledge. This supports the construct-related validity of the measure.

Perceptions of Instructor Video. On the midcourse survey, participants were asked to respond to the following question: "The TV monitor [instructor video] was turned off on purpose for a few topics. How did this affect your ability to learn the material?" The responses indicated that 23% of participants perceived it as decreasing their ability to learn, 74% said it made no difference, and 3% said it increased their learning ability. Another pair of items asked the participants to rate, on a 5-point scale with 1 being "poor" and 5 being "excellent," the overall effectiveness of instruction with the instructor video turned either on or off. The results indicated that the students perceived the audiographics instruction to be significantly more effective with the presence of instructor video; effectiveness was rated at 3.7 with the monitor turned on compared to 3.3 with the monitor turned off [t (98) = 5.25, $p < .001$].

Effects of Instructor Video. For the four modules subject to the experimental manipulation of instructor-video transmission, an item analysis was conducted on the corresponding nineteen items from the written test. Also, the self-assessment ratings of amount learned for these same modules were analyzed. The findings are presented in Table 1, which shows agreement across the two measures. Despite participant perceptions, being able to see or not see the instructor appears to have had no effect on learning.

Table 1. Mean Performance on Learning Measures with Instructor Video On or Off

	Written Test*		Rating of Amount Learned*	
Module	**Video On (%)**	**Video Off (%)**	**Video On**	**Video Off**
4	90	85	3.9	4.0
5	96	95	2.9	3.2
6	85	85	3.9	3.6
7	79	80	3.8	3.8
Overall Mean	87.2	86.6	3.64	3.64

*There was no significant difference between video on or video off for any module.

A refined analysis of the relationship between instructor video and learning was then conducted. The learning assessment data for the same four modules were further analyzed using the previously described procedure of dividing participants into categories of prior knowledge. Within each category, comparisons were made between cases with the instructor video on and off. If instructor video had no impact on learning, then we would expect this to hold regardless of the categorical level of prior knowledge. The results are displayed in Figure 2 for those reporting low prior knowledge and in Figure 3 for those reporting high prior knowledge.

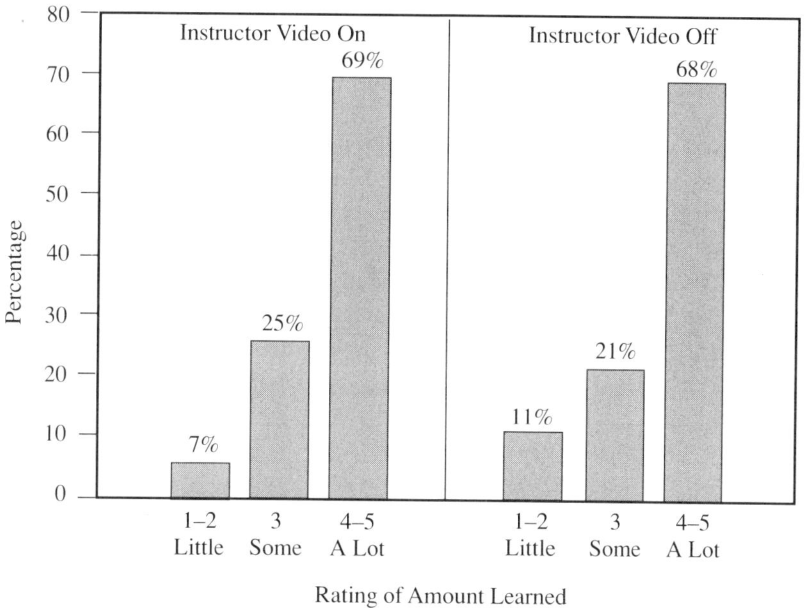

Figure 2. Reported Learning between Video Conditions for Those with Low Prior Knowledge: Four Modules with Video Manipulation.

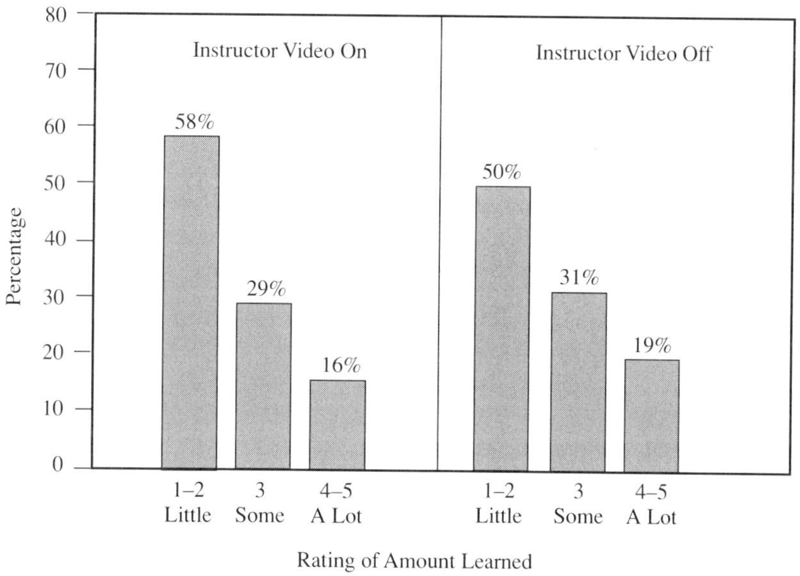

Figure 3. Reported Learning between Video Conditions for Those with High Prior Knowledge: Four Modules with Video Manipulation.

Mean differences in the amount learned for video on or off and the category of prior knowledge were tested with four separate ANOVA procedures.[1] As expected, those with a low level of prior knowledge reported learning more than those with a high level of prior knowledge: $F\,(1{,}99) = 16.17, p < .001$; $F\,(1{,}79) = 24.51, p < .001$; $F\,(1{,}89) = 7.96, p = .006$; $F\,(1{,}86) = 5.37, p = .023$ for modules 4 through 7, respectively. The learning patterns within each category, however, did not differ between the experimental conditions of instructor video on or off. Results indicated no significant differences in reported learning between the video on or off conditions: $F\,(1{,}99) = .03$, $p = .87$; $F\,(1{,}79) = .43, p = .51$; $F\,(1{,}89) = .47, p = .50$; and $F\,(1{,}86) = .08, p = .77$ for modules 4 through 7, respectively. Overall, these analyses converge with the results from the written test. Regardless of prior knowledge, these results further indicate that the presence of instructor video did not improve learning.

Transmission Delay. System administrators reported a 97.6% up time for the T.120 connection. With packet-based networks, variable delays can cause latency problems in the receipt of information. For example, the slide images might appear to be filling in through a series of visual chunks. The 110 slides that were sampled for transmission delays from the originating site to the remote sites were categorized on the basis of amount of information: those having a small amount of text (one-half page or less), those having full text, those with a graphic, and those containing a table. Also, a category was created for progressive disclosure slides. These were slides that had two or more customized frames and were composed frame by frame using individual keyboard strokes with the average time reported being the time to display the first frame. The results are presented in Table 2.

Table 2. Average Internet Lag Time for Transmitting Course Slides

Slide Type	Average Latency (sec.)	% > 2 sec.	Number
Small amount of text	1.17	7	15
Large amount of text	1.59	25	22
Table	1.92	63	29
Graphic	2.35	79	36
Progressive disclosure	3.15	100	8
Total	1.98	41	110

The average delay was 1.98 seconds. Participants were asked whether any delays in slide transmission were distracting through the following question: "Sometimes there was a transmission lag in creating new slides. When this occurred was it a distraction?" Fifty percent responded that there was "no distraction," 48% reported it was a "minor distraction," and 2% claimed it was a "major distraction." In terms of the objective learning measure, those who felt the transmission delay was not distracting scored higher (90%) on the written test than those who felt the delay was a minor distraction (87%) [$t\,(83) = 2.02, p = .046$].

Discussion

The use of more than one evaluation measure can provide a deeper understanding of a phenomenon under investigation (Denizen and Lincoln 1994). Furthermore, a state of convergence across measures can increase confidence in the internal and construct validity of data (Cook and Campbell 1979). In the present research, the convergence between the learning measures strengthens the validity of the principal finding regarding the transmission of instructor video. Although participants perceived the absence of the instructor video as reducing instructional effectiveness, the objective and self-assessment measures of learning showed no difference in learning between video conditions. A secondary finding showed that participants who were distracted by delays in the slide transmissions scored slightly, but significantly, lower on the objective test.

The validity of the self-assessment variable has been questioned as being a reaction measure rather than a learning measure (Meyer 1980). This might depend on the population under investigation. Personnel within the military training culture are accustomed to frequent performance feedback, receiving "Go" or "No-Go" scores on myriad tasks from first aid to complex skill performance. In the present research, individual ratings were guarded by the Privacy Act, so there was no incentive for an individual to inflate an assessment. These assessments may have behaved more like a surrogate between a reaction and the learning measure due to the nonaffective nature of the questions on prior knowledge and amount learned.

Some researchers distinguish reaction measures as falling into two categories: affective reactions and reactions as utility judgments (Alliger et al. 1997). Affective reactions refer to how much students enjoyed the training in contrast to utility judgments, which identify the perceived usefulness of a training program for later job performance. In a metanalysis of thirty-four studies, Alliger et al. (1997) found that affective reactions correlated "just about zero" with immediate learning, whereas utility judgments correlated positively with immediate learning. This might help explain why the present results from the multisource measures converged so well; the self-assessment of amount learned was not an affective reaction, but, rather, a utility judgment of learning.

As was the case with other investigations of student perceptions and preferences, especially in the area of instructional television, the present results support the lack of association between student perceptions and learning. Although students rated the effectiveness of instruction as lower when the instructor video transmission was disabled, there was no difference in learning as measured by either the written test or the self-assessment ratings. Instructor video during audiographics training appears to have no instructional value for the acquisition of declarative and factual knowledge.

During the training, the mode of interaction was primarily between student and content. There were few questions asked during the presentation, as the protocol was to poll sites for questions at the end of a module or before a break. During the training, the students could concentrate on the content displayed on the screen or seen in the workbooks and passively listen to the instructor explain and elaborate. The fact that the transmission delay, averaging 1.98 seconds, distracted approximately one-half of the students supports the importance of the student-content interaction. This view is underscored by the finding that those participants who considered the delay to be a distraction scored slightly, but significantly, lower on the written test. In research on computer-based training, it has been noted that response times of two seconds or less are considered acceptable (Kearsley and Hillelsohn 1982). Since most of the participants were familiar with the

PowerPoint® application, they may have anticipated an immediate display rather than the slower composition of slides with graphic and tabular formats, most requiring more than two seconds to display. In circumstances that use the Internet for audiographics training, then, it is important for instructors to manage the delay inherent in the transmission of slide images.

The use of the audiographics version of the information operations course increased the number of students able to enroll in a single course and succeeded in achieving learning outcomes comparable to the face-to-face classroom versions. Although the cost savings were not computed, there was clearly a strong advantage for avoiding travel and lodging costs for over 100 participants. The distance learning alternative of three instructors traveling to the training studio and several facilitators being dispatched to the remote sites is, instead, a much more cost-effective approach.

Conclusion

Just as with instructional television, training simulators, and virtual reality environments, it is not always necessary to increase the video capability of a distance learning program to increase training effectiveness. Too often, developers and designers become captivated by technical capabilities rather than examining the influence of media on the underlying learning process (Sherry 1996). The results of the present research clearly show no training advantage in having a video presence of the instructor. Future applications of training over the Internet should determine whether the program of instruction includes the categories of learning for which the student depends on the instructor for visual cues. If not, transmitting video to accompany audiographics is of questionable value to the learning process.

Notes

1. Four ANOVA procedures were used rather than one ANOVA due to the four separate pairings of prior knowledge and amount learned for each participant, which would have violated the assumption of independence of observations.

Author's Note: The authors would like to thank Lt. Col. Paul Brady and Maj. Ken Morris for their willingness to experiment and Maj. Michael Freeman, Ralf Zielinski, and James Pritchert for their technical assistance.

References

Alliger, G. M., S. I. Tannenbaum, W. Bennett, H. Traver, and A. Shotland. 1997. A meta-analysis of the relations among training criteria. *Personnel Psychology* 50: 341–58.

Burge, E., and J. L. Howard. 1990. Audio-conferencing in graduate education: A case study. *The American Journal of Distance Education* 4 (2): 3–13.

Chu, G. C., and W. Schramm. 1967. *Learning from television: What the research says.* Stanford, CA: Institute for Communication Research. ERIC, ED 014900.

Chute, A. G., M. M. Thompson, and B.W. Hancock. 1999. *The McGraw-Hill handbook of distance learning*. New York: McGraw-Hill.

Cook, T. D., and D. T. Campbell. 1979. *Quasi-experimentation: Design and analysis issues for field settings*. Chicago: Rand McNally.

Denizen, N. K., and Y. S. Lincoln. 1994. Introduction: Entering the field of qualitative research. In *Handbook of qualitative research*, ed. N. K. Denizen and Y. S. Lincoln, 1–17. Thousand Oaks, CA: Sage Publications.

Greenhill, L. P., O. S. Rich, and C. R. Carpenter. 1962. *The educational effectiveness, acceptability, and feasibility of the Eidophor large-screen television projector.* University Park, PA: The Pennsylvania State University, Division of Academic Research and Sciences. ERIC, ED 030306.

Hays, R. T., and M. J. Singer. 1989. *Simulation fidelity in training system design: Bridging the gap between reality and training*. New York: Springer-Verlag.

International Data Corporation. 1999. *Worldwide and U.S. IT education and training markets, 1998–2003.* Report #19144. Framingham, MA: International Data Corporation.

Johnson, D. M., and J. E. Stewart. 1999. Use of virtual environments for the acquisition of spatial knowledge: Comparison among different visual displays. *Military Psychology* 11 (2): 129–48.

Kearsley, G. P., and M. J. Hillelsohn. 1982. Human factors considerations for computer-based training. *Journal of Computer-Based Instruction* 8 (4): 74–84.

Meyer, H. 1980. Self-appraisal of job performance. *Personnel Psychology* 33: 291–5.

Moore, M. G. 1989. Editorial. Three types of interaction. *The American Journal of Distance Education* 3 (2): 1–6.

Moore, M. G., and G. Kearsley. 1996. *Distance education: A systems view*. Belmont, CA: Wadsworth Publishing.

Sherry, L. 1996. Issues in distance learning. *International Journal of Educational Telecommunications* 1 (4): 337–65.

VanderMeer, A. W. 1954. Color vs. black-and-white in instructional films. *Audio-Visual Communication Review* 2: 121–34.

Wetzel, C. D., P. H. Radtke, and H. W. Stern. 1994. *Review of the effectiveness of video media in instruction*. Hillsdale, NJ: Erlbaum.

Wisher, R. A., and A. N. Priest. 1998. Cost-effectiveness of audio teletraining for the U.S. Army National Guard. *The American Journal of Distance Education* 12 (1): 38–51.

Methodology for Cost-Benefit Analysis of Web-Based Telelearning: Case Study of the Bell Online Institute

Tammy Whalen and David Wright

Vol. 13 No. 1 1999

Abstract

Educators, trainers, and business people need to be able to evaluate the cost-effectiveness of Web-based training in order to make informed decisions about the extent to which this new medium should be used in their organizations. The present study hypothesizes that there are several key design elements that should be considered in costing Web-based training projects. The relative importance of these elements is examined using a case-study approach. The methodology used in this case study can be employed in future cost-benefit studies of Web-based training. This case study also provides a detailed cost-benefit analysis, including the break-even number of students required to recover Web-based course development costs and the return on investment over a five-year period.

Introduction

Web-based training is receiving a great deal of interest in academia and private industry, and cost analysis has become increasingly important. Many universities, such as the University of Phoenix, the University of Maryland, and Athabasca University, to name a few, have multimillion-dollar budgets for Web-based teaching of part-time students. In private industry, Bell Canada is a good example of how companies are using Web-based learning both for in-house employee training and as a service product offered to customers who want to apply distance learning to their own organizations. In both cases, the cost benefit of Web-based training must be established.

Internally, Bell Canada is interested in using Web-based training because it is a cost-effective and convenient alternative to classroom training. Since Web-based training is also a customer product, it is necessary to demonstrate its value in order to interest customers in using this type of training model. For these reasons, Bell Canada undertook a pilot project to examine the cost-effectiveness of Web-based training.

The literature in the area of cost-benefit analysis of Web-based distance learning is sparse; the objective of this paper is to fill the gap in the literature. The costing methodology discussed in this paper was developed by the authors and tested in the Bell Canada case study. The results of the cost-benefit analysis provide further information about the economic benefits of Web-based training.

Measurements of Financial Performance

Although few cost-benefit analyses for Web-based training are available, standard measures of financial performance apply to this type of study. Two common measures are the break-even point—the point at which costs are recovered—and return on investment (ROI)—which illustrates the economic gain or loss from having undertaken a project.

Break-Even Number of Students. To offset the high fixed costs of Web-based courses, a certain number of students must be trained at a delivery cost per student of less than that of the delivery cost per student for classroom training. The number of students that offsets the fixed costs of Web-based training is the break-even point. In Figure 1, the total fixed costs for classroom and Web-based courses are represented by the intercepts of the vertical axis. The cost of course delivery per student is represented by the slope of each line. Since Web-based courses cost more to develop, the line meets the vertical axis at a higher point than for classroom costs. However, since Web-based courses cost less to deliver per student, the slope of the line is more gradual. The point at which the lines cross is the break-even number of students needed to recover the higher fixed costs of Web-based delivery.

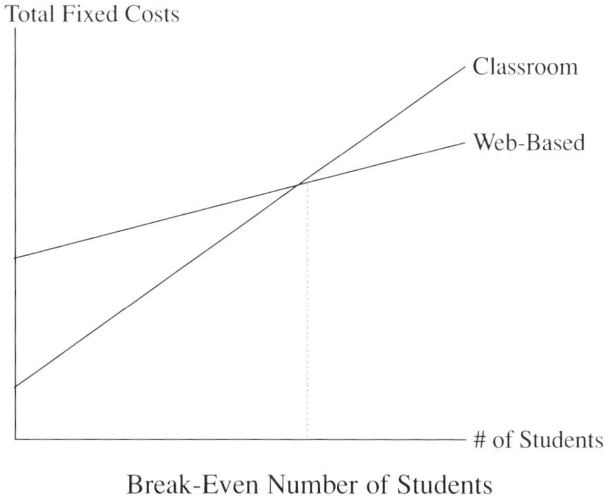

Figure 1. Break-Even Number of Students

Return on Investment. The ROI is a percentage that represents the net gain or loss of using Web-based training instead of classroom delivery. For example, an ROI of 300% means that $3 was saved in reduced delivery costs for every $1 spent on Web-based training.

Cost Comparison: A Background

In comparing Web-based distance education and classroom course delivery, there must be a clear basis for measuring output. It can be argued that the true measure of training output is the information and skills acquired by students. However, many studies in the literature report that there is no significant difference in the amount of learning that students acquire through classroom training and distance learning (Russell 1998). For the present costing analysis, the basis for comparison will be the costs of development and delivery of the courses themselves. In analyzing the costs of Web-based courses, the basis for comparison is the cost of delivering an equivalent course in the classroom. It was assumed that the learning outcomes for the Web-based courses in this study would have been the same if the courses had been delivered in a classroom.

Costs are divided into fixed and variable costs in order to compare technology-enabled learning to traditional classroom delivery. Fixed costs are defined as costs that remain the same regardless of the output. Variable costs are those that vary directly with the amount of output. Thus, variable costs increase with the number of students, while fixed costs are incurred before a course is even offered. Clearly, costs that would be incurred even if a course were delivered in a classroom (i.e., sunk costs) should be ignored in costing Web-based training. For example, if a course were previously offered in the classroom and no further research and development for course materials were needed, the cost of creating the intellectual property for the course would be a sunk cost. Likewise, the cost of feasibility studies should not be included as a costing element.

In an analysis of distance education using videoconferencing-based delivery at the University of Ottawa, Aubé, Chilibeck, and Wright (1996) established the fixed costs for videoconferencing as videoconferencing equipment, technicians' salaries for running the equipment, installation costs, and fees for basic telephone lines. Variable costs for videoconferencing in distance courses included fees for long-distance network usage, shipping charges for supplementary print materials, honoraria for professors, and salaries paid for the preparation of course materials. The break-even point, which was found to be twenty-two courses with the videoconferencing configuration used at the University of Ottawa, is the financial measure used in the analysis.

Trevor-Deutsch and Baker (1997) reported on the costing of a course with multimedia elements delivered via videoconferencing in an academic setting. They considered the following costs for traditional classroom delivery: the instructor's salary and benefits; the number of courses taught by the instructor; and the costs of course development, course materials, administrative support, classroom overhead, and any additional time the instructor spent on the course for activities such as grading and meeting with students. Costs for the same course delivered at a distance included equipment costs and course development costs. The break-even point was calculated at 331 students. Future courses using existing equipment and some of the development features of the pilot course were estimated to have a break-even point of eighty-two students—a 75% reduction in the break-even point of the pilot.

Another study compared CD-ROM-based learning to classroom learning in a high-tech industry setting (Hall 1997). Costs for traditional classroom delivery included development time, classroom overhead costs, instructor costs, and travel costs for the participants. The CD-ROM training costs included equipment and course development time. Development time was high for the CD-ROM course, totaling $1,205,394 over three years. However, the classroom delivery costs were also high, primarily due to high travel costs for the students and the length of time spent away from the job. Costs over the three-year pilot period for the CD-ROM-based course were 47% less than those for the classroom-based course. The payback period was fifteen months, and the internal rate of return—the discount rate that makes the net present value of the investment equal to zero—was 61%. The break-even number of students needed to recover development costs was not calculated. The course material was compressed by 60%, from four days in the classroom to 11.2 hours for the CD-ROM version. The reduction in training time was attributed to improved instructional design; the ability of students to test their knowledge and then omit some sections of the course; and the variety of instructional models, such as text and animation, available to students, which contributed to more effective learning.

Several other publications are relevant to the discussion of Web-based costing analysis. In a recent article, Hall (1998) itemizes the current contractor rates for the types of experts required for Web-based course production. Bates (1995) also discusses the costing of distance education courses, although the Web is not included in his analysis. Several bibliographies on both ROI and evaluation have been compiled by the American Society for Training and Development (1998) and are available on their Web site at http://www.astd.org/ Another report by the Higher Education Information Resources Alliance (1994) primarily examines the noneconomic benefits of using information technology in an academic setting. While all of these studies are useful in providing a comparative look at methods of determining the costs and benefits of distance education, few reports deal specifically with the economic analysis of Web-based courses. This study takes a new approach to looking at cost-benefit analyses for the new delivery method of the Web.

Costing Methodology

Web-based training has become a widely explored topic in the education and training literature, but there are still few comprehensive, tested costing methodologies available for use by educators, trainers, and business people who need to make decisions about the cost-effectiveness of Web-based training for their own organizations. This study hypothesizes that there are several key design elements that must be costed in a majority of Web-based training projects. These costs are divided into fixed capital costs and variable operating costs.

Capital costs include the server platform shared by all courses mounted on that server as well as the cost of the content development shared by all students taking that course. Content development includes six items: (1) instructional and multimedia design; (2) the production of text, audio, video, graphics, and photographs; (3) the development of authoring and delivery software or the cost of licensing commercial software; (4) the integration, modification, and testing of course content; (5) student and instructor training; and (6) course testing. Operating costs represent the costs for the time students and instructors spend using the courses.

These costs are analyzed to determine the costs per course, the costs per phase of development, the costs per student, and the costs per mode of delivery (i.e., synchronous or asynchronous). The Ratio Analysis section of this article provides an evaluation of the break-even number of students required to recover course development costs and the ROI over five years. The costs of producing future courses using the same instructional design or the same mode of delivery can be estimated from the results of this study.

To verify the costing methodology, it is necessary to determine whether some of these costing elements are more important than others. In other words, do some elements dominate others? Or, are some elements insignificant? To test the hypothesis that all these elements are critical to costing analysis for Web-based course design and delivery, the costing methodology is applied to the following case study.

Bell Online Institute Case Study

The Bell Online Institute (BOLI) is the Bell Canada business unit that delivers Web-based training to Bell Canada employees. BOLI also functions as a testing ground for various Internet-based learning platforms used for delivery of training at Bell Canada. A separate business unit, the

Bell Institute for Professional Development (BIPD), provides traditional classroom course delivery and oversees all internal training.

The BOLI case study was undertaken to measure the cost and evaluate the effectiveness of training delivered on four different Web-based learning platforms:

- WebCT (http://www.webct.com/), developed at The University of British Columbia, for asynchronous training;
- Mentys (http://www.globalknowledge.com/), obtained from Global Knowledge Network, for asynchronous training;
- Pebblesoft (http://www.pebblesoft.com/), for asynchronous training;
- Centra Symposium (http://www.centra.com/), for synchronous training.

Three courses designed for delivery on these learning platforms were produced by three independent vendors. All of the courses were on telecommunications topics: TCP/IP (using the WebCT and Mentys platforms), frame relay (using the Pebblesoft platform), and routing (using the Centra Symposium platform). The courses were estimated to be equivalent to two-day classroom courses. The pilot courses were delivered to engineers working in Bell Canada's Advanced Communication Systems group.

Three of the learning platforms—WebCT, Mentys, and Pebblesoft—present course materials asynchronously. That is, course materials reside on a server on an ongoing basis and may be accessed at the student's convenience. The frame relay course on the Pebblesoft learning platform was authored in French. The fourth platform, Centra Symposium, is a synchronous learning platform using 28.8 Kbps delivery over the Internet or an intranet. The system supports text, graphics, and animation to present course materials. Shared features for system users of Symposium include audio communication among the course participants and the instructor, an electronic whiteboard, an Internet browser, and a live text chat room.

Cost Analysis: Fixed Costs

This portion of the analysis helps determine whether the high fixed costs associated with providing learning in a technology-enabled format are justified in comparison to the costs of traditional classroom delivery already provided through BIPD. The actual billed rates reported by the vendors are used in the cost charts found throughout the paper. All costs are reported in Canadian dollars.

Capital Costs. License Fees for Learning Platform Software. The price of a learning platform depends on the number of people who will be using the software and ranges widely from vendor to vendor. An upgrade cost of 10% per year is assumed. Using 10% of the costs as an annuity, the present value of the upgrades and the original purchase price are shown in column three of Table 1. The cost of the platform must be amortized over the total number of courses that will use the platform. BIPD presently has 150 independent study courses on CD-ROM or diskettes. It is assumed that all of these courses could potentially be taught using any of the asynchronous platforms. There are presently 700 classroom-based courses offered through BIPD. It is estimated that 10% of these could potentially be offered using the Centra Symposium synchronous platform. Table 1 summarizes the costs associated with learning platforms.

Table 1. Learning Platform Costs

Platform	License	Upgrade Cost	Cost per Course
WebCT (asynchronous)	$3,000	$4,103 ($3,000 + $1,103)	$27 per course ($4,103 / 150 courses)
Mentys (asynchronous)	$150,000	$205,161 ($150,000 + $55,161)	$1,368 per course ($205,161 / 150 courses)
Pebblesoft (asynchronous)	$175,000	$239,348 ($175,000 + $64,348)	$1,596 per course ($239,348 / 150 courses)
Symposium (synchronous)	$35,000	$47,871 ($35,000 + $12,871)	$684 per course ($47,871 / 70 courses)

Hardware. In this study, it is assumed that a server must be purchased to offer the course but that client computers are already available on the desktops of the employees participating in the course. The purchase price of the server was estimated at $15,000. The total number of courses, as established previously, is 220 (150 asynchronous + 70 synchronous). It is assumed that not all courses would need to run on the server at one time. By amortizing the cost of the server over the number of courses, the cost of the server per course equals $68 ($15,000 / 220 courses).

On average, it is estimated that each asynchronous course requires 100 megabytes of memory. A synchronous course would typically require less interactivity with the course material because of the presence of a live instructor. Therefore, the course would include less multimedia and require only twenty-five megabytes of memory per course.

During the pilot study, staff time was required to set up desktop machines—for example, the installation of browser plug-ins—to take advantage of the multimedia aspects of the courses. However, this cost was not included in the study since newer versions of the learning platforms will automatically install the software needed for the desktop computers.

Total Capital Costs per Course. The capital cost per course is equal to a server cost of $68 ($15,000 / 220 courses) plus the platform costs per course for each different platform.

- Synchronous routing course using Symposium: $752 ($68 + $684)
- Asynchronous TCP/IP course using WebCT: $95 ($68 + $27)
- Asynchronous TCP/IP course using Mentys: $1,436 ($68 + $1,368)
- Asynchronous frame relay course using Pebblesoft: $1,664 ($68 + $1,596)

Phase 1: Content Development. Content development variables include instructional design; multimedia design; the production of text, audio, motion video, graphics, and photos in a machine-readable format; course authoring; software development; integration of content and testing; modification/adjustment; training; and course testing. Only one of the courses, TCP/IP, included motion video elements.

Developer Salaries. The billed hourly rates for the independent contractors were used in the analyses found throughout this paper. These are the rates that customers of these companies were willing to pay for Web-based course development.

Differences in Synchronous and Asynchronous Course Development. Significant differences were found between the asynchronous courses and the synchronous course regarding course development costs. The asynchronous courses were similar in the types of tasks performed by developers and the total amount of time spent on course development. The synchronous course, however, required far less development time, primarily due to less use of multimedia. For example, the synchronous course contained no audio, video, or photographic elements and also had fewer graphics. An average of 1,321 development hours were spent on the asynchronous courses, while only 144 development hours (89% fewer) were required for the synchronous course. Since development costs depend on the number of hours required, the synchronous course cost much less to develop.

Cost Analysis: Variable Costs

Phase 2: Usability Testing. Phase 2 of the BOLI pilot project involved course testing in which Bell Canada employees participated in training using the Web-based courses. This represented the total variable costs for the project. Since Bell Canada must pay employees for the time they spend in training, student salary costs are a significant factor in this costing analysis. More time spent in course delivery translates into higher student salary costs and less cost savings. The salary costs of students and, for the synchronous course, of both students and the instructor were analyzed to compare the delivery costs per student. Figure 2 gives an overview of the delivery costs for all courses. These costs are described in more detail in the following section.

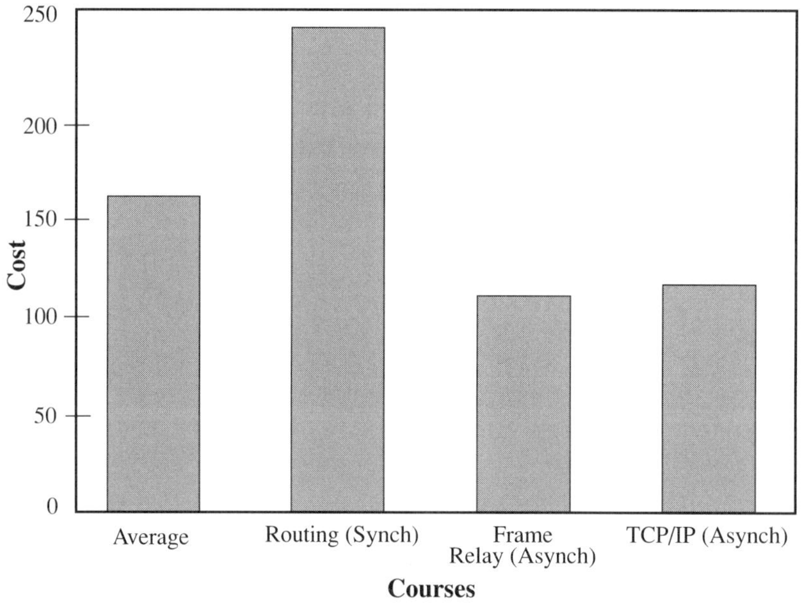

Figure 2. Delivery (Salary) Costs per Student for Each Course

Table 2 gives a summary of the fixed and variable costs for each Web-based course in the study, as well as the baseline classroom course costs. A detailed analysis discussing how these numbers were derived is found in the following section.

Table 2. Fixed and Variable Costs for Web-Based Courses

Course	Total Fixed Costs	Total Variable Costs
Classroom	$28,600	$1,284 ($600 + $614 + $70)
Routing	$24,332 ($23,580 + $752)	$242 ($176 + $66)
Frame Relay	$88,364 ($86,700 + $1,664)	$110
TCP/IP on WebCT	$158,708 ($158,613 + $95)	$110
TCP/IP on Mentys	$160,049 ($158,613 + $1,436)	$110

Cost Analysis of Courses

Classroom Courses. Life Span and Duration of Courses. The life span of a classroom course is five years, meaning that no upgrade of course material is expected within a five-year period. The duration of classroom courses is fourteen hours. Although the actual time spent in the classroom is approximately twelve hours, the course participants are paid for two normal seven-and-a-half-hour workdays.

Costs of Classroom Training. Although none of the Web-based courses in this pilot project had been offered previously in the classroom, it was estimated that the courses were equivalent to two-day classroom courses. Therefore, the costs of delivering these courses in a classroom setting can be calculated by using the figures for delivering a typical two-day classroom course at BIPD.

Course Development Costs. For each day of classroom training, BIPD requires twenty days of development (20:1). BIPD charges two different development rates depending on whether or not BIPD will deliver the courses and have the opportunity to recover some development costs from future delivery. If BIPD delivers the course, there is a charge of $715 per day for course development to the business unit requesting the course. If BIPD does not deliver the course, there is a charge of $995 per day for course development. Therefore, the development of a two-day classroom course similar to the ones in the pilot project would cost the customer a total of $28,600 ($715 * 40 days).

Tuition Fees. In-house tuition fees are also charged to the participants' department to recover BIPD's normal operating costs. Classroom courses at BIPD have, on average, ten participants. Each participant is charged $250 for tuition and another $50 per person to cover such costs as the instructor, course materials, and refreshments. This totals $300 per day for each participant. Therefore, for a two-day course similar to those in the pilot, a cost of $600 per participant would be charged by BIPD to the business unit in which the participant works.

BOLI did not charge tuition to participants in the pilot. However, tuition charges for Web-based courses are anticipated with the full implementation of Web-based training to Bell employees. The costing information in this study will be taken into account to determine an appropriate price to charge business units in the company.

Salary Costs for Course Participants. Twenty Bell Canada engineers were enrolled in the synchronous course, each earning an average annual salary of $57,700. The loaded annual salary, including vacation, pensions, and benefits; a portion of a supervisor's salary; office space; and office supplies and services, is $85,500 per year, or $44 per hour.

Each of the three pilot courses was equivalent to a two-day classroom course. Each participant was paid for fourteen hours of work for this period, at an average loaded hourly rate of $44. Therefore, the salary cost of offering classroom courses is $614 per participant.

Travel Costs. Approximately 10% of employees taking courses at BIPD travel to a different city to take the course. At a typical travel cost of $350 per day, which includes airfare, one night in a hotel, and travel allowances, a two-day course costs Bell Canada $700 per student who travels. If 10% of the students travel, the travel cost per student is $70.

Web-Based Courses. Life Span and Duration of Courses. The life span of Web-based courses is also five years. The duration of Web-based courses is two and a half hours for asynchronous courses and four hours for synchronous courses.

Course Compression. Compression ratios for Web-based courses are 79% for asynchronous courses and 67% for synchronous courses. Hall (1997) points out that there is strong evidence that CD-ROM-based multimedia training requires less time than classroom training. Reported course compression ratios range from 20% to 80%, with 40%to 60% being most common for CD-ROM training. In the BOLI pilot, course compression ratios were at the high end of the reported ranges in the Hall study for both synchronous and asynchronous courses. The Web-based asynchronous courses lasted two and a half hours, while comparable classroom versions would have lasted twelve instruction hours. Course compression was, therefore, 79% for both asynchronous courses. The synchronous course lasted four hours, while a comparable course offered in a classroom would have lasted twelve instruction hours. This equaled a compression ratio of 67% for the synchronous course.

Salary Costs for Course Participants. Synchronous Course. For one engineer to complete the four-hour synchronous course, salary costs totaled $176 ($44 × 4 hours). There was also an instructor present during the full four hours of the synchronous course. Theoretically, the Centra Symposium system can accommodate fifty participants at one time. However, this large number of concurrent participants would seriously limit the opportunities for interaction among the students and the instructor. For this study, it was assumed that the synchronous routing course would be taught in groups of ten. To calculate the cost of the instructor's salary per student, an hourly rate of $164 was used—the billed rate reported by the course vendor. This equaled a cost of $66 per student ($164 × 4 hours / 10 students).

Asynchronous Courses. The asynchronous courses each had twenty-nine participants, who were also Bell Canada engineers. Based on the average loaded rate of pay, the salary cost for one engineer to complete a two and a half hour asynchronous course was $110 ($44 × 2.5 hours).

There are also opportunity costs involved in having employees spend time away from their work to take courses. For example, the completion of a project may be delayed due to time spent in training, and that delay may have unforeseen consequences for the organization's business. One advantage of asynchronous Web-based training, as opposed to either synchronous or classroom training, is that these problems are alleviated due to greater flexibility in scheduling students' time.

However, although student salary costs are one measure of opportunity costs, total opportunity costs are almost impossible to determine and, therefore, have not been included here.

Web-Based Course Development Costs

Asynchronous Courses. Frame Relay Course. The frame relay course was one of two courses delivered on an asynchronous platform. The course vendor had difficulty using Pebblesoft because the initial software was delivered without French character support. This caused an estimated 24% increase in development time. If the project had been completed without the software problem, the hours spent on course development would have equaled 932 hours, and development costs, at $562.50 per day, would have totaled $69,900. Table 3 gives the total cost of each developer task at the billed rates reported by the course vendors and also summarizes the number of hours spent on each task, including the percentage of the total that this represents.

Table 3. Frame Relay Course (Asynchronous): Cost and Time per Developer Task

Developer Task	Cost	Percentage of Time
Training	$1,200	1.4% (16 hours)
Tests	$9,975	11.5% (133 hours)
Instructional Design	$18,525	21.4% (247 hours)
Multimedia Design	$13,125	15.1% (175 hours)
Text Production	$6,225	11.5% (133 hours)
Audio Production	$1,875	2.2% (25 hours)
Graphics Production	$12,300	14.2% (164 hours)
Photo Production	$1,575	1.8% (21 hours)
Authoring/Software Development	$6,075	7% (81 hours)
Content Integration	$7,800	9% (104 hours)
Testing Integration	$2,550	2.9% (34 hours)
Modification/Adjustment Integration	$5,475	6.3% (73 hours)

Total cost at $562.50 per day = $86,700. (All costs are reported in Canadian dollars.) Total of 1,156 hours.

TCP/IP Course. Another vendor produced an asynchronous course on the topic of TCP/IP. Two different platforms were used to deliver the course: Global Knowledge Network's Mentys system and WebCT, developed at The University of British Columbia. A staff member of BIPD also participated in course development by designing the content architecture for the instructional design plan. The TCP/IP course included a five-minute video segment and was the only course that included video. Table 4 gives the total cost for each developer task as well as the number of hours spent on each task and the percentage of the total time spent.

Table 4. TCP/IP Course (Asynchronous): Cost and Time per Developer Task

Developer Task	Cost	Percentage of Time
Training	$7,893	5% (74 hours)
Video Production	$26,667	16.8% (250 hours)
Instructional Design	$36,800	23.2% (345 hours)
Multimedia Design	$9,173	5.8% (86 hours)
Text Production	$747	0.1% (7 hours)
Audio Production	$4,053	2.6% (38 hours)
Graphics Production	$31,253	19.7% (293 hours)
Authoring/Software Development	$12,907	8.1% (121 hours)
Content Integration	$19,093	12% (179 hours)
Testing Integration	$3,733	2.4% (35 hours)
Modification/Adjustment Integration	$6,293	4% (59 hours)

Total cost at $800 per day = $158,612. (All costs are reported in Canadian dollars.) Total of 1,487 hours.

Synchronous Course. Routing Course. The routing course was delivered on the Centra Symposium platform. The pilot course was delivered to twenty Bell Canada engineers from Quebec City, Montreal, Ottawa, Toronto, and Hamilton. The course was offered in two parts, one in the morning and one in the afternoon. The morning session lasted two and a half hours and the afternoon session lasted one and a half hours, for a total of four hours. All of the engineers were present for the entire course.

Staff from the BIPD assisted the independent course vendor in developing the routing course and cofacilitated the pilot course delivery. Table 5 summarizes the cost, the number of hours, and the percentage of the total time for each developer task.

Table 5. Routing Course (Synchronous): Cost and Time per Developer Task

Developer Task	Cost	Percentage of Time
Training	$2,620	11.1% (16 hours)
Tests	$655	2.8% (4 hours)
Instructional Design	$17,849	75.7% (109 hours)
Multimedia Production	$491	2.1% (3 hours)
Text Production	$1,310	5.6% (8 hours)
Graphics Production	$655	2.8% (4 hours)

Total cost at $1,228 per day = $23,580. (All costs are reported in Canadian dollars.) Total of 144 hours.

Ratio Analysis

Break-Even Number of Students. The break-even number of students for each course is listed below.

- Routing course: 4 students [($28,600 - $24,332) / ($1,284 - $242)]
- Frame relay course: 51 students [($88,364 - $28,600) / ($1,284 - $110)]
- TCP/IP course on WebCT: 111 students [($158,708 - $28,600) / ($1,284 - $110)]
- TCP/IP course on Mentys: 112 students [($160,049 - $28,600) / ($1,284 - $110)]

Return on Investment. Expected Number of Students per Year. To calculate the ROI, an assumption must be made concerning the number of students that will be trained per year with a course. The number of students trained per year is used to calculate the fixed costs per student so that these costs can be amortized over all students who will use the course. Otherwise, we would be trying to recover all fixed costs with the first student, which clearly cannot be done and which fails to take into consideration the reusability of both the course itself and the hardware and software used to deliver it. In the present study, it was expected that 30% to 40% of Bell Canada's 300 Wide Area Network engineers would take this course, equaling 125 participants. Another seventy-five participants from other Bell Canada departments are also expected to take each of these courses. Thus, the expected number of students per year was 200 students per course.

Platform Costs per Student.

- WebCT: $0.14 per student ($27 / 200 students)
- Mentys: $7 per student ($1,368 / 200 students)
- Pebblesoft: $8 per student ($1,596 / 200 students)
- Symposium: $3.50 per student ($684 / 200 students)

Salary Costs per Student for Classroom Training. To calculate the ROI, it is necessary to know the savings per student for Web-based delivery over classroom delivery. Therefore, the delivery cost per student in a classroom must be determined. The cost of offering these three courses in a classroom to 200 participants per course annually would be $122,769 per course, or $368,308 for all three courses. Assuming a classroom course would be offered to 200 students per year, the classroom course development costs per student would equal $143 ($28,600 / 200 students). Table 6 presents an analysis of the savings per student for each course. The ROI for each course in the expected case of 200 students trained per course per year is found in Table 7.

Table 6. Savings per Student

Classroom Course Costs	
Course Development	$143
Tuition	$600
Travel	$70
Salary of Students	$614
Total	$1,427

Web-Based Course Costs

	TCP/IP Course on WebCT	TCP/IP Course on Mentys	Frame Relay Course on Pebblesoft	Routing Course on Symposium
Course Development	$660	$660	$434	$53
Server ($15,000 / 3 courses / 200 students)	$25	$25	$25	$25
Learning Platform	$0.14	$7	$8	$3.50
Salary of Students	$110	$110	$110	$176
Salary of Instructor	—	—	—	$66
Total	$795	$802	$577	$324
Savings per Student over Classroom Delivery	$632	$625	$850	$1,103

Table 7. Course ROIs

Course	ROI	Dollars Saved for Every $1 Spent
Routing (synchronous)	3283%	$33
Frame Relay (asynchronous)	697%	$7
TCP/IP (asynchronous using WebCT)	228%	$3
TCP/IP (asynchronous using Mentys)	283%	$3

The present value of the cost savings was estimated to be 3.621, an amount that takes into account the five-year life span of the courses and a discount rate that reflects a moderate investment risk. The ROI was positive in all cases, although the courses with the least amount of multimedia content—the synchronous routing course and the asynchronous frame relay course—had the best ROIs. The TCP/IP courses had the highest percentage of multimedia content as well as the highest break-even points.

Table 8 summarizes the number of multimedia development hours per course, the corresponding break-even number of students, and the ROI over five years. The results indicate that all courses will break even within the first year if 200 students per year take each course.

Table 8. Multimedia Development Hours, Break-Even Points, and Five-Year ROIs of Courses

Course	Multimedia Development Hours	Break-Even Number of Students	ROI Over 5 Years
Routing	144 hours	4 students	3283%
Frame Relay	1,156 hours	51 students	697%
TCP/IP on WebCT	1,487 hours	111 students	288%
TCP/IP on Mentys	1,487 hours	112 students	283%

Discussion

Comparison of Multimedia Content per Course. There was a significant difference in the amount of multimedia content in the courses and, therefore, in the amount of time spent on multimedia development. The synchronous routing course contained only a few graphics, while the asynchronous courses contained a higher percentage of graphics as well as audio and photographs. The TCP/IP course had the largest percentage of multimedia because it included a five-minute video segment. The percentage of development time spent in multimedia production and design for each course is listed on the following page.

- Synchronous routing course: 5%
- Asynchronous frame relay course: 33%
- Asynchronous TCP/IP courses: 45%

Importance of Each Costing Element. While this is just one case study, there still appears to be evidence that the costing elements chosen for this study are all important. There was some variation in the use of any particular element among the courses, although the variations were small and some elements were consistently used more or less frequently for all of the courses. None of the costing elements could be discounted as unimportant, and none of the costing elements clearly dominated the others in importance. More research needs to be done in the area of costing analysis for Web-based course design and delivery, but practitioners working in the field may still find the conclusions of this study useful for their own cost-benefit projects.

Conclusion

Web-based training has higher fixed costs than classroom-based training; however, these higher course development costs are offset by lower variable costs in course delivery. This is primarily due to the reduction in course delivery time (course compression) and the potential to deliver courses to a larger number of students than is possible in a traditional classroom without incurring significant incremental costs. Realizing savings for Web-based courses requires a sufficient number of students in order to recover course development costs. Since employees must be paid for time they spend taking a course, student salaries are an important consideration in this costing study.

While all of the measures of financial performance indicated that there is a strong business case for Web-based training, financial indicators suggest that the amount of multimedia content in a course is the most significant factor in cost. The TCP/IP course, which had the least cost savings and a breakeven of 112 students, contained a five-minute video segment. As a result, the number of hours spent in multimedia production was far higher than for the other courses. With a breakeven of four students, the synchronous routing course, which was the most cost-effective course in the pilot, contained only live audio and a few graphics. The limited amount of multimedia content in the synchronous course offset the higher costs of course delivery resulting from the cost of having a live instructor present during delivery and the greater student salary costs due to the extra time required to deliver the course.

In comparing the number of hours spent on multimedia development across all courses, the variations are relatively small. This indicates that all of the elements discussed previously are important to consider when costing Web-based course development. The methodology used in this case study can, therefore, be used in future cost-benefit studies of Web-based training.

Note

The research for this paper was supported in part by Industry Canada's Network of Centres of Excellence in Telelearning. The authors wish to express their appreciation for the comments of the anonymous reviewers on the first draft of this paper.

References

American Society for Training and Development (ASTD). 1998. Bibliography: Evaluation. Alexandria, VA: ASTD. Available online at http://www.astd.org/

American Society for Training and Development (ASTD). 1998. Bibliography: Return-on-investment. Alexandria, VA: ASTD. Available online at http://www.astd.org/

Aubé, S., M. Chilibeck, and D. Wright. 1996. Cost analysis of video conferencing for distance education at the University of Ottawa. Working Paper, 96-45. Ottawa, Canada: Faculty of Administration, University of Ottawa.

Bates, A. W. 1995. *Technology, open learning and distance education.* London: Routledge.

Hall, B. 1997. *Web-based training: A cookbook.* New York: John Wiley & Sons.

———. 1998. The cost of custom WBT. *Inside Technology Training,* July–August, 46–7.

Higher Education Information Resources Alliance. 1994. What presidents need to know about the payoff on the information technology investment. Background papers for HEIRAlliance, Executive Strategies Report #4. Boulder, CO: CAUSE.

Russell, T. 1998. *The "No Significant Difference" phenomenon as reported in 248 research reports, summaries, and papers.* 4th ed. Raleigh, NC: North Carolina State University.

Trevor-Deutsch, L., and W. Baker. 1997. Cost/benefit review of the interactive learning connection, University Space Network Pilot. Ottawa, Canada: Strathmere Associates International Ltd.

Being Unreal: Epistemology, Ontology, and Phenomenology in a Virtual Educational World

Roy Lundin

Vol. 12 No. 3 1998

Abstract

This paper addresses new flexibility in educational programs and delivery in terms of the possibilities now available for extending the body and the mind through electronic communications. Issues are raised regarding what is true and the nature of reality in the virtual world of the Internet. Finally, the article discusses the ability of people to cope with these issues in terms of the education required, the development of 'information literacy', and the implications of personal responses to them. These ideas are developed within the context of the "World Brain/World Mind" concept first set forth by H. G. Wells in 1938.

Being Unreal

Education was the key focus of the original "World Brain/World Mind" concept put forward by H. G. Wells in 1938. He interpreted this concept as a hard copy, published "World Encyclopedia" because, at that time, few of the present day options for open learning/flexible delivery and online databases were even remotely anticipated. Wells's original concept involved combining the best thinking and best information in one place—a published World Encyclopedia—to provide access for informed decision making. Then, this knowledge and wisdom would be diffused throughout the general populace. Such mass education would have indeed required some form of distance education and flexible delivery.

Since the 1970s, a World Brain/World Mind special interest group of the American Society of Information Science has existed. It meets and writes to discuss the natural implications of Wells's concept for the information industry and education generally. In 1997, this group held a conference at the University of Calgary organized by a major authority and writer on the topic, Dr. Abe Goodman. Subsequently, a network group was established to address the implications of a new concept of the World Brain (see http://ksi.cpsc.ucalgary.ca/WB/).

Since the publication of Wells's book and particularly during the last fifteen years or so, the development of a global Virtual World Brain via the Internet has developed. Although this is significantly different from Wells's original concept, much of his original thinking still applies. In this Virtual World Brain, it is now possible to experience new levels of unreality. 'Being Unreal' can constitute a major portion of a person's life, and this can have significant implications for teaching and learning. Educators should, however, view this concept in terms of some rather old philosophical questions.

- What is true?
- What is real?
- What kind of learning will take place through technologies?

- What is the teacher's role?
- How will information transform itself into knowledge?
- How will learners determine the quality and authenticity of the information?

This paper attempts to address these questions, drawing upon the traditional methodologies of epistemology, ontology, and phenomenology. Supported by illustrations from experiences and information relating to the Virtual World Brain, these methodologies will be used to analyze the current state of education in this virtual educational world. It might be suggested that these methodologies should now form a part of all levels of education and training curricula, thus leading to new forms of 'information literacy' as we enter a new era of global distance education.

Distance Education Evolution

Daniel (1996, 47–55) describes three stages in the history of distance learning.

- St. Paul sent hand-written letters to individual churches and asked the local elders to read them to their congregations. The churches were, therefore, like remote classrooms or study centers—asynchronous communication.
- Two technologies, the printing press and universal postal services, enabled distance learning to move into people's homes and workplaces. These options were employed in correspondence education from the midcentury—again, asynchronous communication.
- Telecommunications and the development of a range of 'knowledge media' from the mid–twentieth century have introduced a new set of options for educational delivery both on and off campus—options for both asynchronous and synchronous audio, visual, and graphics communication have become possible through single function technologies.

In a similar vein, higher education is entering its "third generation" according to Moore (1993). The first generation, which lasted for centuries, was based on bricks-and-mortar technology in which students received degrees from a university based in a specific place. The second generation has been only partially place-free and has involved various forms of open learning universities and agencies that use a range of distance delivery modes and technologies, such as the United Kingdom's Open University. Daniel (1996) refers to these as "mega-universities." Moore (1993, 4) explains the third generation as follows:

> Such restrictions are no longer necessary. With the development of the communications technologies of the 1990s—the electronic highways to our homes and workplaces—we are rapidly approaching technical readiness for the Virtual University, the third generation of higher distance education.

At the 1993 North American Free Trade Area symposium on higher education and strategic partnerships, it was proposed that a "North American University"—a mega virtual university—be established, but there did not seem to be a readiness for such a concept. There is, however, increasing interest in the notion of emerging mega-universities with staff and students drawn from global networks (Daniel 1996). When John Tiffin launched his Global Virtual University in Hawaii in

January 1998, a search of the World Wide Web found in excess of 850 virtual universities listed online (see http://206.154.197.130:80/VU/). The globalization of virtual universities or the international virtual education marketplace has exciting potential; however, several issues must be considered in making such educational delivery effective. In addition to the philosophical questions listed previously, there are several other questions that should be asked, including

- How will credit be obtained for subjects taken from another country?
- Where will the teaching staff belong if they are teaching through another institution?
- Where will the students belong?
- What are the regulatory and cultural implications of the globalization of education?

The Internet has become the most recent focus for education. As indicated previously, it represents a Virtual World Brain/World Mind; not only can it comprise the information, knowledge, and wisdom of the great thinkers of the world, past and present, but also it can contain information from literally anyone from anywhere. Herein lies the dilemma of the modern learner. If the learner attends a virtual educational institution, uses virtual libraries and virtual textbooks, communicates with virtual teachers and students in a virtual class, and obtains a virtual academic award, how real and valid is the learning experience?

Philosophical and practical questions like those posed earlier have, of course, pervaded education for centuries, particularly with regard to distance education. However, the virtual world is different from hard copy; it is now possible to lie with impunity. At this stage, there are far more questions than answers with regard to the educational implications of the Virtual World Brain/World Mind. This paper will limit itself to two basic questions: What is true? and What is real?

What Is True?

Epistemology is essentially the study of knowledge and what true belief is. The origin, processes, and validity of knowledge in the modern Virtual World Brain present serious issues for learners. Some people are highly skeptical of the contents of the Internet, labeling most of it rubbish. On the other hand, it is possible to 'play genius' and find answers and information on literally any topic available, whether it be adult learning principles, Shih-tzus (a breed of dog), or a recipe for making mead. The electronic networking of what now constitutes the Virtual World Brain presents, therefore, an incredible resource for learning. But...what is true? The following stories illustrate this problem.

High School E-mail List. A high school teacher and his class of students in a northern suburb of Brisbane, Australia, were involved in regular use of e-mail and the Internet for their studies. This included memberships in various lists and newsgroups. One day, a news flash came through one of the lists stating that there had been a massacre in a particular city in a Latin American country. It requested that people contact their foreign affairs department to urge that assistance be given to the victims. After a day or two of deliberations, the teacher and students decided they should contact the originator of the message with a query as to the state of affairs. The response came back saying: "Is that message still up on the Net? I thought it had been scrapped ages ago!" The message was simply not true.

Check Your E-mail. When a former girlfriend of Oracle chief Larry Ellison sued the billionaire tycoon for wrongful termination, the company settled the case out of court for $100,000. Still, Mr. Ellison's lawyers, who were not quite convinced of the validity of the claim, continued to investigate. They found that an e-mail message used by prosecutors to win the case was forged by Ellison's ex-paramour, Adelyn Lee. The message, sent five days after Ms. Lee was terminated, came from the computer system of her immediate supervisor, Craig Ramsey. It read, "I have terminated Lee per your request" (Savarnejad 1997).

Hanson "War Hero" Exposed. The following article appeared in the Brisbane, Australia, daily newspaper in early 1998 in connection with a new political party that had been established just prior to a state government election:

> The way Pauline Hanson's One Nation Party tells the story, supporter Ron Hardy is a hero. According to the Hanson Internet site, Mr. Hardy's war-time exploits earned him the nation's highest military honor—the Victoria Cross—handed to him by the King of England. The website claims Mr. Hardy, who wants One Nation to win seats in the June 13 state election, was a prisoner of war of the Japanese and worked on the Hellfire Pass. He even endured an appendectomy without anesthetic at the hands of legendary war hero Weary Dunlop and then, three hours later, returned to work. Ms. Hanson could not hope for a better endorsement—if it were true. But it isn't. It seems to have no basis in fact. One Nation deleted the endorsement from its website last night after admitting it had no evidence that Mr. Hardy was a VC winner. (Franklin 1998)

Killer Net. In New Zealand, author and television producer Lynda La Plante is planning a series of programs entitled *Killer Net* about a group of students who get drawn into an interactive computer game of virtual reality murder that becomes murder for real. She was inspired by various stories and experiences of the Net, but

> Even more alarming was a story La Plante heard from an American woman about her 11-year-old daughter, who arranged a meeting with a schoolboy friend she had made via one of the Internet chat rooms. Fortunately the girl told her mother what she had done. The police were called, staked out the meeting-place and the "schoolboy" turned out to be a man wanted for murders in three states. (Allen 1998)

In addition to the potential for producing untruths on the Internet, there exists the fragmented nature of the information, which has led some commentators to describe the Internet as "anarchy." Students can use the Internet to find answers to specific questions and use these in their studies. For example, a university lecturer was grading her students' assignments and noted several references to literature by prominent specialists in the field that she had not yet read. When she asked the students for the sources of these references, their reply was "The Internet." She labeled this "feral learning."

A serious question arises, particularly for young people, concerning the possibility of actually developing frameworks or constructs of knowledge through this type of learning process. Will this kind of fragmentation of the curriculum and, therefore, of the knowledge gained result in individuals whose minds are a reflection of the Virtual World Mind—essentially a collection of unconnected information that may not be able to be converted into useful knowledge?

On the other hand, given the potential for very powerful learning design models and processes available through the emerging media, there may be even greater possibilities for positive, integrated learning. In a time when students increasingly assume control of the processes and content of learning through the Internet, questions regarding the nature of learning should be researched as they relate to the implications for educators and their role in the professional act of teaching.

Harris (1996, 11) sums up the problem of learning as follows:

> The belief that 'global connectivity' can bring knowledge to students and teachers is mistaken. The Internet provides only information. Students must learn how to manage, analyze, critique, cross-reference, and transform information into usable knowledge. One approach to teaching these constructivist processes is to think of students as free-range 'infoseekers' and to provide exploration in authentic contexts.

The accumulation of an encyclopedia of information, whether in hard copy or electronic form, still begs the question of information's becoming true knowledge. Gaining knowledge is a much lengthier and more complex process than simply getting online.

The best scenario that educators can hope for is one in which true and valid knowledge will become increasingly valued and such knowledge will entail the need for wide access to information that can be used to make informed decisions (Jakupec and Nicholl 1994). Major reports on education describe a rapid move in all countries toward a knowledge economy, sometimes erroneously called the "information economy." For example, a major report in Australia (Tinkler, Lepani, and Mitchell 1996, 67) states

> Like other industries before it, such as manufacturing and financial services, the education industry is being fundamentally transformed by three linked factors:
>
> - Globalization and increasing international competition for market share;
> - Changing market requirements for services and products with the move from an industrial economy to a knowledge economy; and
> - The transformative impact of information technologies on the structure and organization of the industry in responding to these imperatives.

Given these considerations, serious discussion within global education circles must address the use of the Virtual World Brain/World Mind to develop and promote this "education industry" in an equitable and authentic manner through the presentation of truthful information that can be validated.

What Is Real?

In the chat rooms, palaces, moos, and MUDs of the Internet, it is possible to break all bounds of physical and social reality. One can have a virtual home, or several homes, a mansion, a castle, a basic brick house, or a box, each with its own address. It is possible to have cybersex with one or multiple partners; to be virtually married—even polygamously; to get divorced; to acquire virtual pets that hatch, grow up, learn tricks, and die; and to make virtual money and gamble. All this can be done anonymously, under an assumed persona, or as an animal or nondescript entity without obligation, without inhibition, and without risk.

The general term for an assumed persona is 'avatar', which can be any image, be it drawn or scanned, that participants use to depict themselves. My first experience with this was in meeting a penguin in The Palace. One then wonders how to begin the conversation. Is this a five-year-old girl or a sixty-year-old professor? It is essentially genderless, ageless, and raceless.

Ontology is the traditional study of what constitutes 'being' and the nature of reality. Such questions as "What is real?" face new challenges when applied to a virtual world. Many who consider the grasp on reality already tenuous may wonder about the psychological and social effects of the possibility of entering an unreal world. The distinction between what is real (ontology) and what is apparent (phenomenology) then arises, posing a very complex, multidimensional environment for learners. If reality is based on unreal experiences, what, then, is the basis of reality?

Carole Parker was married with three children and worked from home in suburban Australia when she discovered online chatting. In her book, *The Joy of Cybersex,* she explains how her online experiences destroyed her marriage and her life. One quote is particularly relevant here.

> I felt my online identity was quite separate from my day-to-day existence. I treated Worlds Chat as a game, and enjoyed the theatrics of donning my avatar. Online, I could be who I wanted to be: young, beautiful, tough, witty, the all-round party girl, almost like stepping back in time to my single days.
>
> I believed I was having fun, and that was all; the actions and words that happened in cyberspace were separate from my real life. (Parker 1997)

Another illustration of unreality is the use of 'bots' to sell goods and services in the Internet relay chat rooms. For example:

> **Meet Dusty, History's First Cyber Robot**
>
> Chat-room visitors beware: in the near future that friendly person you've been talking to may not be a person at all. It may be a Bot.
>
> As if the world of online chat isn't dicey enough, we are about to come face to face with talking computers. The first will be Dusty the SpokesBot. Black Sun Interactive (http://www.blacksun.com) has created SpokesBots that go into chat rooms to spread the word of their masters. (Copilevitz 1997)

'Virtual' has become the specific term used to describe the various worlds, locations, and processes on the Internet. Tiffin and Rajasingham (1996) talk about being "in search of the virtual class"; Moore (1993) and Daniel (1996) describe the nature of "the virtual university," and so on. Online, there are virtual educational enterprises, virtual campuses and classrooms, virtual learning programs, and virtual textbooks. Assessment of learning outcomes through the virtual networks also becomes problematic for several reasons. Teachers may find it impossible to determine if students have actually created a piece of original work now that electronic forms of information can be cut, pasted, and edited seamlessly into new 'essays'.

The implications for education are, to say the least, puzzling. Will a virtual degree from a virtual university have any validity in the 'real world'? What will be an institution's response to someone who applies for entry and requests recognition for prior 'virtual' learning? More particularly, what will become of the role of the teacher, and how will teaching occur?

The convergence and rapid developments of technology make it increasingly possible for learners to become independent from educational institutions in their acquisition of information and, perhaps, learning. For example, the "wearable computer" can now take the form of clothes; the Philips vest has memory and solar cells woven into fabric and a Velcro belt for the different communication devices, including various types of headsets and sunglasses (see http://lcs.www.media.mit.edu/projects/wearables/ and http://www.wearcam.org/personaltechnologies/index.html). The use of these devices may lead to a shift from the idea of the university or school as bricks and mortar in a specific geographic location to one in which the learner is his or her own university. The whole notion of what constitutes an educational institution, versus a community of scholars, must be addressed in light of the implications of an environment in which the learner can now draw on multiple sources for course work, request recognition for prior learning, and demonstrate competencies through private assessment agencies. What will be your institution's response when such a student approaches with a request for accreditation for such learning? One might conclude that, at best, this globalization may provide new opportunities and access to learning where little or none previously existed; at worst, however, it could result in educational 'invasion'.

Parker (1998, 43) expands the notion of "being unreal" in terms of the emerging forms of communication and information technologies.

> When you have no keyboards, no screens, no mice and your phone, television, shopping and even a lover are integrated into a single communication device that connects you wirelessly to the rest of the world via low orbiting satellites, the distinction between virtual and real life will be almost impossible to discern.

It is this kind of possible educational future that leads to the need for educators to address with their students the issue of developing information literacy skills.

Information Literacy

A major difference between H. G. Wells's vision and the present-day phenomenon of the Virtual World Brain/World Mind is that the former was based on the notion of an elite group of thinkers contributing to an authoritative collection of best knowledge, "unifying, and so implementing and making more effective, the general intelligence services of the world" (Wells [1938] 1994, 77). The Virtual World Brain, on the other hand, can potentially include everyone. Five-year-old children are now online publishers with the same capacity as heavyweight thinkers. There are no gatekeepers of the information put into the Virtual World Brain/World Mind.

Information literacy is emphasized both online and offline to assist learners in addressing the problematic nature of information authenticity and overload from the Virtual World Brain/World Mind. Constructivism views knowledge as only a construction of one's mind and information as merely a representation of some potentially useful data headed somewhere. Davis (1992, 1) has described information as a hierarchy of "mind stuff"; "Information is low on the totem pole of consciousness, just a notch up from raw data and a leg up from total noise." In the same way that educators have abandoned the notion of learners as empty vessels waiting to be filled with knowledge imparted to them by teachers, so too is it fallacious to think that learners need merely to 'access' a vast store of information in order for learning to occur. The methodologies inherent in the philosophical processes of epistemology, ontology, and phenomenology must become mainstream in education...again.

In addition to access, learners need to have the skills of literacy—the ability to read, evaluate, and use information from a range of text, graphic, and audiovisual sources and, in turn, to create text, graphic, and audiovisual messages in a range of contexts. More important, literacy is the ability to determine the authenticity and quality of information by assessing the authority of the source, validating this through other sources, and critically analyzing the content of messages. This all involves high-order thinking skills and a stability of personality grounded in a strong sense of reality, as opposed to one influenced by fantasy and unreal explanations.

Online sources of criteria for evaluating information and courses on the Internet are available. For example, Tillman (1998) sets forth the following basic criteria of trustworthy sources of information:

- ease of determining the scope and criteria for inclusion, allowing the user to see if there is a match with his or her needs;
- ease of identifying
    - authority of authors,
    - currency,
    - last update,
    - what was updated;
- stability of information (will it stay there?);
- ease of use in terms of both convenience or organization and speed of connection, as well as ease of access for the user (for example, if someone has put up a huge graphic or QuickTime movie, it must be worth the user's time to wait while it downloads).

Similarly, the Milton S. Eisenhower Library of Johns Hopkins University (http://milton.mse.jhu.edu:8001/research/education/net.html) provides criteria and guidelines for evaluating information found on the Internet, including

- authorship,
- publishing body,
- point of view or bias,
- referral to other sources,
- verifiability,
- currency.

The Internet as a Virtual World Brain/World Mind can be a tool for powerful educational models of delivery. It can also be a tool for social engineering through processes such as campaigning or stirring mob or mass mentality or a tool of 'spin doctors', shifting public opinion and initiating social changes much more quickly than ever before in history and in possibly dysfunctional directions. An educated public, therefore, should be critical. However, given the present lack of external controls or regulations, learners must develop their own discriminating skills in order to determine authenticity, quality, validity, authority, and reliability of information.

The ultimate question is, perhaps, whether the mental health of the Virtual World Brain/World Mind can be maintained or whether it will degenerate into a morass of delusion.

References

Allen, C. 1998. Terrors of the Internet. *The Dominion* (Wellington, NZ), 23 May, 27.

Copilevitz, T. 1997. Meet Dusty, history's first cyber robot. *Courier Mail* (Brisbane, Australia), 17 May, 34.

Daniel, J. S. 1996. *Mega-universities and knowledge media: Technology strategies for higher education.* London: Kogan Page.

Davis, E. 1992. Tongues of fire, whirlwinds of noise: Images of spiritual information. *Gnosis* 23. Also available online at http://www.levity.com/figments/whirlwinds.html

Franklin, M. 1998 Hanson "war hero" exposed. *Courier Mail* (Brisbane, Australia), 13 March, 1.

Harris, J. B. 1996. Information is forever in formation, knowledge is the knower: Global connectivity in K–12 classrooms. *Computers in Schools* 12 (1–2): 11–22.

Jakupec, V., and K. Nicholl. 1994. Open learning: Politics or pedagogy? *Distance Education* 15 (2): 217–33.

Moore, M. G. 1993. Editorial. Free trade in higher education. *The American Journal of Distance Education* 7 (3): 1–7.

Parker, C. 1997. *The joy of cybersex.* Sydney, Australia: Reed Books.

———. 1998. Getting it online. *The Australian Magazine,* 30–31 May, 43–5.

Savarnejad, A. 1997. Check your e-mail. *The Australian,* 6 May, 56.

Tiffin, J., and L. Rajasingham. 1996. *In search of the virtual class.* London: Routledge.

Tillman, H. N. 1988. *Evaluating quality on the Net.* Available online at http://www.tiac.net/users/hope/findqual.html

Tinkler, D., B. Lepani, and J. Mitchell. 1996. *Education and technology convergence: A survey of technological infrastructure in education and the professional development and support of educators and trainers in information and communication technologies.* Commissioned Report No. 43, National Board of Employment, Education and Training, Employment and Skills Council. Canberra, Australia: Australian Government Publishing Service.

Wells, H. G. [1938] 1994. *World brain: H. G. Wells on the future of education.* Reprint, with an introduction by Alan Mayne, London: Adamantine Press.

Copyright Law, the Internet, and Distance Education

Anita Colyer[1]

Vol. 11 No. 3 1997

Abstract

This article examines copyright issues related to online course development and delivery. An overview and brief history of copyright law is presented with attention to the ways in which various technologies have shaped modern interpretations of copyright law. Examples of recent lawsuits and several case studies provide a context for examination of fair use issues and liability for online copyright infringement. Finally, some helpful questions are presented on topics such as process issues, institutional policies, software and licensing, copyright issues, and other alternatives. These questions should provide a basis to help online course providers think through issues related to copyright, the Internet, and distance education.

Introduction: Promises and Risks

For distance educators, the Internet is a land of infinite possibility. It provides the opportunity to connect learners, resources, and teachers in ways about which our predecessors may have only dreamed. It is now possible to make entire courses, programs, and degrees available for the distant learner through computer technology. The promises this new environment holds are extraordinary. One of the most amazing features of the Internet is the way in which it facilitates the proliferation of information. The user can download more information in a few minutes than was contained in entire libraries during medieval times, and the Internet is growing by leaps and bounds.

These changing times yield both opportunity and crisis. The biggest problem businesses and service providers faced in the past was the hurdle of disseminating information. These days, the struggle is very different in nature; the Internet contains a myriad of miscellaneous tidbits of information at the cost of context, content control, and ownership. The resulting disorganization is compounded by yet another logistical headache: the Internet, for many practical reasons, renders obsolete most existing copyright and royalty systems. Once information is made available electronically, it is virtually impossible to control; it can be downloaded, duplicated, given away, or otherwise saved, altered, or sold. One of the biggest challenges facing the further growth of a stable electronic information environment, for economic and other reasons, is that of devising a way to manage user access and address the surrounding copyright and intellectual property issues that confront anyone placing information on the Internet.

The goal of this article is to provide some guidance on copyright and intellectual property issues in the electronic environment. The article will present a brief overview of copyright law, examine case studies and recent litigation in an attempt to clarify issues related to fair use and other copyright issues, and suggest some questions that may help to direct others' efforts in resolving copyright issues in online course environments.

Background

Copyright Protection: The Intent of the Law. Copyright law is grounded in the age of print, and its ideologies are rooted firmly in the philosophical tenets of capitalism and democracy. In the early eighteenth century, beginning with the 1710 Statute of Anne (considered by some to be the first copyright law), knowledge was cut free of control by the church and state and established as "an item of trade in an open marketplace" (Bennett 1993, 87). Later in the eighteenth century, the US Constitution established a copyright clause (article 1, section 8, clause 8), which states that the goal of copyright protection should be to "Promote the progress of science and the useful arts." The purpose of this copyright law was not to provide the creator of a publication with an unending monopoly, but to provide a "limited grant" of protection to the creator in order to allow him or her to reap some reward, financial or otherwise, for his or her labors and, at the same time, to safeguard the free flow of ideas in the public interest (Lehman 1995).

At the time of its inception, copyright law was relatively easy to enforce. Copying was an unwieldy affair involving the operation of numerous complex pieces of heavy and costly equipment followed by the dissemination of hard copies through assorted logistical processes. The printing process was slow, and it was controlled by those who owned the machinery of production—people who became the publishers of textbooks and other printed information. Certainly there was little, if any, concern that the general citizenry, possessing neither the equipment nor the know-how, might print, give away, or even sell unauthorized copies of copyrighted materials.

Changing Assumptions about the Nature of Information. The production and distribution issues affecting copyright in today's society have changed radically. In the 1970s, the widespread use of the photocopier became the first copyright crisis of the electronic age; the general public no longer needed to own the machinery of production or master the printing process to be able to produce and distribute multiple copies of copyrighted materials. These technological advances prodded the government to revise its copyright law with the implementation of the 1976 Copyright Act, which outlined acceptable and unacceptable uses of copyrighted materials. Wincor (1994, 87) rightly observes that "our copyright approach began, and has largely remained, a series of reflexes to the development of new technology, not a declaration of natural law or some other principle supporting the protection of intellectual productions."

As the physical processes of the printing press and the photocopier have given way to the conduits of network proliferation, the electronic revolution in publishing has forced us to confront some very fundamental changes in the established assumptions about the nature of information. The first change relates to the increasing accessibility of information. Bennett notes the more promising egalitarian aspects of the digital environment.

> In some regards electronic scholarly communication more nearly approximates a phone system or a broadcasting environment than a conventional publishing environment. This environment involves and empowers individuals in unprecedented ways in the creation and distribution of information. For that reason, it is an environment that particularly favors the promotion of learning and the democratic uses of knowledge, which are the constitutional underpinnings of U.S. copyright law. (1993, 88)

The second change concerns the nature of the publishing process. Publishing has become more "democratic" in the digital age; anyone with a computer can become a desktop publisher, and through the proliferation of electronic networks, those created materials can be dispersed to thousands of people. With computers becoming increasingly prevalent in the modern home and workplace, the machinery of production truly lies in the hands of the people. But an electronic environment that democratizes the publishing process has both benefits and drawbacks, one which encompasses both being that there are fewer keepers at the gates of knowledge. Consequently, there are no standards for what does and does not get published and no central organizing system to help locate the information. One critic offers the following recommendation: "Information users do not need more, less well-organized information. They need less, better-organized information" (Duranceau 1995, 85). Organization and context are two of the missing girders of what politicians have called the National Information Infrastructure; without these supports, the structure may very well collapse under its own weight.

The third major aspect of information that has changed is its increasing mutability. While a publication was previously recognizable by certain parameters of its own physicality, the electronic environment has removed many of the defining features of "publications." When is an electronic item a publication? How can it be determined whether an electronic publication enjoys the benefits of copyright protection? Is a work in progress a publication or a fragment of a publication? Does each draft of an electronic publication—which may be modified daily or even hourly—receive the benefits of full copyright protection that individual drafts (published or unpublished) of a scholarly article currently enjoy?

Fourth, there exists the issue of control of ownership. When information was published primarily in books, it was difficult and time consuming to alter an author's work. But there is no corresponding physical mechanism to prevent today's computer user from downloading and altering an article and then claiming authorship of it.

What are the implications of these changes for distance educators and other information creators and users as traditional controls on information relax and virtually disappear? This article will examine some specific situations, beginning with several cases involving lawsuits related to the electronic distribution of information and then moving into a discussion of some more hypothetical examples, where issues related to ensuring copyright protection and information integrity in the electronic environment can be explored.

Copyright: The Letter of the Law (Examples)

Recent Litigation. The following are a few of the cases involving the electronic distribution of copyrighted materials that have been addressed by the courts.

Case 1. In the 1993 case of *Playboy Enterprises, Inc. v. Frena,* a federal court ruled that a computer user who posted copies of Playboy photos to an electronic bulletin board was guilty of "public display" of copyrighted materials and, therefore, guilty of copyright violation. "Since Playboy's trademarks were used to identify the photo files, the Court found that Playboy's trademark rights were also infringed" (Bovet 1995, 48).

Case 2. In the case of *Sega Enterprises, Ltd. v. MAPHIA,* a court ruled that a bulletin board operator to whose bulletin board users posted and accessed Sega video games was contributing to copyright infringement (Tickle 1995, 400).

Case 3. In a 1994 case, MIT student David LaMacchia was charged by a federal grand jury with "using university computers to distribute more than $1 million worth of pirated software over the Internet." The student used two MIT computers as electronic bulletin boards where "Internet users could place copies of commercial programs, allowing other users to receive illegal copies" (Lewis 1994). The student's lawyer, Harvey Silvergate, argued that LaMacchia, acting in his capacity as owner of the bulletin board, was merely responsible for the maintenance of the technological conduit and not for the content that it contained and that LaMacchia should, therefore, not be held accountable for information that was placed there by other users. Silvergate argued,

> Can AT&T be held liable for criminal conversations held on their phone lines?...Can the *New York Times* be held liable because gamblers use the information published in its sports section? Of course not. I don't see how you can make distinctions between people who run newspapers, phone lines and computer bulletin board systems. (Lewis 1994, A9)

Case 4. A 1995 case involved litigation between the Church of Scientology and Arnaldo Lerma, a computer user who posted several of the church's top secret, copyrighted documents to an Internet newsgroup. Lerma's computer and disks were seized by the courts pending review of Lerma's alleged infringement. His comments were,

> You have to jump through a lot of expensive hoops to get access to this....This is the big secret at the end of the rainbow, and you could go to the court clerk and get it for 50 cents a page. The Internet is the First Amendment in silicon. (Allen 1995, A12)

Case 5. In the article "Copycats on the Superhighway," Coleman (1995) describes the following situation in which a publisher unwittingly committed copyright violation. Pacific Hitech, a publisher located in Utah, downloaded a large number of literary works off the Internet. The works, which did not contain a copyright notice, were all literary classics that are currently in the public domain. After downloading them, the publisher, seizing the opportunity to make a profit, put the works on CD-ROMs and began selling them to the general public. Imagine the publisher's surprise when it turned out that "someone had transferred more than 800 works from a CD-ROM published by World Library on its 'Library of the Future,' removed the copyright notice to that electronic version, and launched it into the Internet" (Coleman 1995, 68). Pacific Hitech, the infringing publisher, was forced to "stop selling its version of the works, to destroy its master copies, and to give all unsold CD-ROMs to World Library for recycling or destruction." The attorney for World Library issued the following caveat:

> Uploading or taking material off of the Internet might be an infringement of that copyright, even though the underlying work may be in the public domain. Unlike trademark law, copyright law has no exemption for innocent infringement. (Coleman 1995, 68–9)

The issues related to the definition of liability for Internet users, bulletin board owners, and service providers are only now being clarified. For example, several bills limiting the liability of online service providers for third-party copyright infringements occurring over their networks (S 1146, HR 3209, and HR 2180) are pending in the 105th Congress.

Assumptions of Fair Use. All of the previous examples demonstrate that copyright law is one of the more confusing aspects of placing information on electronic networks. But some help is available. Section 107 of the 1976 Copyright Act sets forth guidelines for assessing fair use of a copyrighted work, many of which can be applied to the use of copyrighted materials in a digital environment. The criteria listed in this section have traditionally been used in court cases where copyright infringement is charged. The four considerations for fair use are as follows:

1. the purpose of the use (commercial or nonprofit);
2. the nature of the work itself;
3. the amount or substantiality of the segment used in relation to the whole;
4. the effect of the use on the potential market for the work.

Some of these criteria, which were already cloudy during the print age, have become even more nebulous during the electronic age. These criteria will now be applied to some example situations in an attempt to clarify the boundaries of copyright infringement.

Example 1. Joanne Chopak, a professor teaching an online distance course in literary history at a large research university, wishes to assign her thirty students several poems by an obscure American writer to analyze for next week's class. Instead of requiring the students to purchase the costly anthology in which the poems appear (which the students will probably not use for any other aspect of the class), she reprints the poems on her class home page on the World Wide Web (WWW). Is Professor Chopak's position defensible through the doctrine of fair use?

Applying the criteria of fair use described in Section 107, the following can be ascertained:

1. The use is for a nonprofit educational purpose.
2. The copyrighted work is a work of literature.
3. The poems are reprinted in their entirety.
4. The effect of the use is such that Professor Chopak's students, who have access to the poems on the Web, will not purchase the anthology from the educational publishing company that produced it. Therefore, placing the poems on the Web could potentially preclude the purchase of the anthology not only by the thirty students in Professor Chopak's section of literary history, but also by the hundreds, or even thousands, of other people who may stumble across the poems on the Web.

It is fairly clear to see that the use, while not aimed at obtaining any personal financial gain, has violated two of the primary aspects of fair use: the professor has used several works in their entirety (one poem is defined as a complete literary work), and the professor's decision has deprived the educational publishing company of the revenue commensurate with the items' use.

Example 2. John, a clerical employee at a small university, has been charged by the marketing director with the task of creating a "presence" on the WWW for his distance education department. John's friends have assured him that it is very easy to create a new home page on the Web simply by using his Web browser to view the source of any document he likes and then copying the HTML (hypertext mark-up language) code that has programmed the document to appear in a certain format on his computer screen. John browses through the Web for several days, copying and downloading some formatting and several images he has located on other people's home pages. He has not copied items from any pages that contain copyright notices and believes that everything else is fair game. John is especially proud of an ornate and unique symbol he borrowed from one of the home pages he came across on the Web. When he is finished, John has put together a very attractive home page for his department using a minimum of effort and a very minor outlay of his university's financial resources. Has John violated the copyright doctrine of fair use? Here are his assumptions.

1. The work has been created for the academic department for which John works.
2. The works he borrowed were from electronic works created by other users of the WWW. None of these works contained copyright notices, and so John assumed they were available for free use.
3. The portions of the individual pages that he copied were relatively minute—a photo here, a symbol there—and nowhere did he violate the 10 percent rule of fair use.
4. None of the home pages from which John borrowed contained any indication that a fee was required for the viewing or use of the information they contained.

What are the copyright issues that John has failed to consider in his pursuit of creating the perfect Web page?

- According to the 1989 amendment of the copyright law, a publication does not need to contain a copyright notice in order to be copyrighted by its creator; therefore, any publication that has been published is a legally copyrighted publication (even original works that have not yet been published are protected), whether it bears the standard copyright notice or not.
- John's employer, a university, could derive some monetary benefit from the presence of the promotional information contained on the Web page that John put together; therefore, his department could benefit financially from work published and owned by other private individuals without their consent. The producers of this information have not received a fair share of any of the profit derived from their work.
- Although the amount of information that John copied from each page was very slight, there is no hard and fast "10 percent rule" of fair use. The three criteria of "copyrightability" as defined by the courts are "originality, creativity, and fixation" (Lehman 1995). The information that John copied from each page may have been small in amount, but any one of those portions, especially the highly original, creative symbol John located, may have been at the heart of the identity, design, or content of the page from which it came. John may, therefore, have unwittingly violated copyright law.

In the cases described above, lack of awareness of copyright law may have made unwitting violators of the professor and the clerical worker. In both cases, since the potential violation of copyright occurred during the work hours of someone employed by a university, the employers, as well as the individuals involved, are implicated if liability should occur: "The copyright in a work prepared by an employee within the scope of employment vests in the employer, and the employer is the author" (Lehman 1995). In these cases, both employers and employees would be well advised to move cautiously when copying and placing copyrighted materials on the Internet.

Questions to Ask and Issues to Consider

Following are some questions that may help a distance learning organization think through many of the issues related to copyright, the Internet, and distance education. These items can be divided into the following categories: process issues, institutional policies regarding copyright and intellectual property, software and licensing issues, common copyright issues, other alternatives, and several miscellaneous issues (including ethical issues and the need for faculty development).

Process Issues: Playing It Safe. Does the organization employ someone who ensures that all written course content is free of plagiarized material and that all copyrighted items are adequately identified and cleared? Many people are not fully aware of the intricacies of copyright law and may unwittingly use material without properly quoting or identifying a source. At Penn State's Department of Distance Education, for example, it is part of the instructional design staff's responsibility to lay out the rules related to copyright up front, before course development begins. On occasion, designers have come across unidentified copyrighted items imbedded in course materials. In such cases, the designer is instructed to return the material to the faculty member, requesting that sources be identified so that permission can be obtained or that the faculty member reword those sections, perhaps summarizing key points of the original work.

Does someone in the organization track permissions requested against actual numbers of copies printed or students accessing the materials? It may be surprising to discover that, in the most popular courses, permissions need to be recleared more often than expected in order to be within legal compliance. A revised course could be considered a "new work," in which case all permissions should be recleared for use. Information that should be documented includes the title and author of the work, its original copyright date, the publisher, the date of clearance, the terms of clearance, and the credit line as the publisher wishes it to appear.

Institutional Copyright and Intellectual Property Policies. Is a copyright notice placed on all materials, indicating that they are owned by the department or university? Many users wrongly assume, especially with regard to Internet-delivered resources, that, if there is no prominent copyright notice on an item, then the item is not copyrighted. A notice should be placed on all materials for the sake of clarity. A typical copyright statement might be "Copyright © 1998, [the institution]."

Were any of the course materials produced with the help of an external grant or funding of any kind? If so, the university's copyright and intellectual property issues related to that particular grant or funding arrangement should be examined. Does the university own the copyright on the product? Or does the organization that funded the project own it? Do any of the terms of the grant limit the use, sale, or distribution of any of the content that has been produced? If unsure, a grant officer or office of sponsored programs should be consulted up front concerning the particular terms of the grant or funding.

To prevent misunderstandings, are the copyright arrangements regarding distance-delivered materials spelled out for the content experts (and design teams) in clear language? Significant resources are often devoted to the development and delivery of distance and technology-based course resources. For this reason, many universities copyright materials developed in these formats. For example, all of Penn State's distance education materials are copyrighted by the university. Course content experts sign a contract at the beginning of the development process indicating that they understand that they are developing a course that will enter into the copyright domain of the university (a copyright that is then registered with the Library of Congress). The copyright agreement specifies the percentage of material from the copyrighted "work" (or course) that authors are permitted to use elsewhere and specifies when that ownership expires. Such agreements also specify royalty percentages and terms of disbursement. Policy manuals should be reviewed carefully.

Does the university lump "Web-delivered materials" into the same category as "software" or "courseware"? If so, the university's policies may state that these materials (as opposed to faculty "publications" such as articles or textbooks) are owned by the university. Or, it may be discovered that the university has not yet addressed intellectual property issues related to online course materials. Likewise, it would be wise for employees working on the creation of distance materials to understand the legalities related to the ownership of those materials. For example, what if a designer uses personal photographs, taken on his or her own time, to enhance a course Web site? Do those items enter into copyright? Or should the designer provide, in writing, permission for the use of those materials, thus retaining individual ownership of the items? If the organization's position regarding these or other issues is uncertain, it should be investigated immediately. Copyright and intellectual property lawyers should be consulted, and any and all copyright-related training sessions should be attended.

Software and Licensing Issues. Will any of the copyrighted items (including software) be distributed internationally? If so, it should be clearly indicated in any and all permissions correspondence that the materials may be supplied to an international audience. Publishers sometimes have different rates and different rules related to the distribution of materials within a country as opposed to materials that may be distributed internationally. Web-based materials have the potential to be accessed by an international audience. If software is being distributed—either by selling it with a course package or by including software applications, viewers, or installers on a course Web site or CD—it must be ensured that the licensing issues related to such software have been investigated. For example, some software makers require that international purchasers of their product buy a "copy-protected" version of the software to prevent easy duplication of such software on the international black market. Copy-protected versions of software usually cost more and are often not as readily available as the standard versions, so these issues should be explored before making software available to students at the time of enrollment. Another option would be to require that students purchase any required software on their own, using contact information provided to them at the time of registration. In any case, time must be budgeted into the process to ensure that the student has adequate time to order, purchase, install, and troubleshoot the software before a course begins.

Have the legalities (copyright, licenses, etc.) related to making online resources accessible for distance students been explored in partnership with the university library? One of the hottest items discussed at a recent copyright event was the growth in the use of online reserves for resident instruction students. Although enthusiasm for online reserves runs high, many copyright issues related to such systems remain unclear and are currently being debated between the libraries and the copyright owners. Additional questions are also being raised: if a library places documents on an electronic server, what clearances must be obtained, and what system is in place for tracking usage and passing costs on to the end user? Such systems may present logistical headaches as well. Many such systems are protected by domain screens or Internet protocol (IP) screens that would render the resources inaccessible to distant students without some kind of user authentication process. These issues should be explored with the institution's library, and it should be determined how such systems might best be modified to address the needs of distance students.

Common Copyright Issues. Do content experts provide articles or portions of textbooks they have written, claiming that these items can be used freely because they themselves are the author(s)? In many cases, once an article or textbook has been published, the copyright of that item is taken on, owned, and protected by the publisher, not the author(s). Often, faculty who write articles or books have sold (or signed over) their copyright to the publisher of that item and may be bound by a publisher's agreement limiting the author's ability to redistribute that material freely. Most contracts define a date upon which rights revert to the author. The safest policy would be to request permission rather than to automatically assume that the item in question can be used.

Is "educational use," in residence or distance instruction, considered to be the primary defining criterion of "fair use"? It is wrong to assume that copyrighted items can be used in courses because the courses are designed for an educational purpose. Educational publishers make their living on the profits they earn from the public's book purchases and journal subscriptions. Violation of a publisher's copyright is a serious legal infringement whether it occurs in the educational or business arena. Distance learning, perhaps more so than most other types of instruction, is generally a premeditated affair. Because distance education relies heavily on resources that have been created by a design team, course development can span weeks, months, or even years of materials preparation. Once created, those materials may have a shelf life of several years (in many programs, a course is offered until a newer textbook edition renders the current course version obsolete). In taking the safest and most conservative approach possible, these aspects of the distance education course design process place resource-based distance courses largely outside the realm of "fair use," although several current bills are attempting to address digital transmission issues related to distance learning (see, for example, section 5 of HR 3048, pending). Adequate time to obtain permissions should be built into the course planning process. Content experts should be advised, in no uncertain terms, that, if the publisher of an item cannot be tracked down and permission obtained, the item will not be used. In general, a recommended policy (again, a very conservative approach) is that it is better to be safe than sorry: permission should be requested if the legality of "fair use" in the educational environment is at all uncertain. When in doubt, legal experts should be consulted; the boundaries of fair use, most practically defined, lie at the edges of whatever an organization's lawyers are prepared to defend.

Other Alternatives. Was permission to use an article denied? Or, was a fee requested that is considered to be prohibitive? The faculty member can summarize key points of the article and include appropriate citations. If the quoted material is substantial enough, the students can be required to purchase copies of the book or reprints of the article, if available.

Are students provided with the most cost-effective and learning-efficient educational resources, even if that means providing the materials in an alternative medium? In the race to make the quickest, most effective, and most profitable use of the Internet, some distance educators assume that the best way to provide all distance course materials is through the Internet. Many faculty members also assume that their course readings packets can be made "cheaper" or "more accessible" for students if readings are provided on the Web instead of in print. This is not always the case, and, in fact, many publishers are reluctant to allow copyrighted materials to be stored in any kind of electronic environment, even a seemingly secure environment such as a Web site that is screened and password protected. Furthermore, other, more practical problems are raised by such an approach. The first of these is access. Many students still do not have access to the Internet, and some of the students who do claim to be online use the Internet at their workplace, where access and printing privileges may be circumscribed. Is it really effective to ask students to print out text-heavy documents (because we all know that nobody reads text-dense materials on-screen; they hit the "print" button every time)? Further, neither can it be assumed that resident instruction students have unlimited access to computer resources and printers. Perhaps the inclusion of copyrighted articles scanned into a Web site is not the most effective way to deliver such materials. Placing these materials on the Web shifts the burden of printing to the consumer, which, in the end, may or may not provide the most effective and most efficient course package for the student.

Did a content expert provide an overabundance of items that require permissions clearance, without regard to the impact of those items on the course development timeline and total course cost to the end user? If an institution processes copyright permissions in such a manner as to pass the costs of permission fees along to students, the cost of such packets can be astounding. Simply making the faculty member aware of the consequences of including so many items (increased cost to student, increased time in the development process due to permissions) may be all that is needed to get him or her to pare down the list of copyright permissions to a more manageable few. It can be suggested that the faculty member select only crucial items for inclusion, listing the rest of the items as "optional" or "recommended" readings on the course syllabus.

Does the course require that students refer to current articles in certain, subject-specific journals? Rather than asking for permission to reprint items or place them on the Web, it might be worthwhile to explore requiring students to subscribe to a particular journal for the duration of their course work. Some newspapers, magazines, and journals are willing to make their publications available at "student" subscription rates that are significantly lower than regular prices if they are aware that the items are being used in an educational setting.

Is another medium going to be included on the Web site—for example, film or video footage spliced into a QuickTime movie or Shockwave animation? Copyright rules can be different for different media. While tracking down permission to include the famous Bikini Atoll bomb footage on a Physics CD, we discovered the intricacies of film and video copyright—chasing down ownership of footage from PBS to the federal government to the camera operator, and then ascertaining whether or not the camera operator was employed by the government at the time or whether the shoot was a "work for hire" done by another company. We also learned firsthand that, even if a musical work is ancient and, therefore, within the public domain, an individual group's performance of that work is protected by copyright. Tracking and clearing such items can be resource-intensive and can slow down the design and development process. Also, there are very practical issues to consider: placing such items on a Web site has the potential to raise the technology bar for the student. Instead of using just a regular browser, the student may now need to locate and install several helper applications and plug-ins. Who will provide technical support and guidance to students unfamiliar with that process? And, in the end, is the instructional benefit provided to the student by such technology worth the costs? Would the student be better served by simply asking him or her to go to the nearest video store and rent the item in question?

Was it decided, against all good advice to the contrary, to use a copyrighted item whose owner could not be found, after making every reasonable effort to obtain copyright permission? Those efforts should be documented, and any evidence that can be provided to that effect (canceled envelopes, referral letters, etc.) should be kept on file in case a question should ever arise.

Miscellaneous Issues: Ethical Compliance and Faculty Training. Are all other legal and ethical issues covered—for example, in regard to use and display of student work and student participation in research projects (either as researcher or as research subject)? To use examples of "good" student projects in a current or subsequent edition of a course, students' permission should be requested before displaying or reprinting such items. If students are required to conduct research projects that involve the use of human subjects, or if the content experts who author and/or teach the courses plan to use student performances, feedback, or anecdotes in any research or public presentations, those projects should be submitted to the university's regulatory compliance office, which governs the ethical treatment of human research subjects. Students involved in any such projects should sign release forms, as should any other research participants.

Does the distance education organization provide faculty development events where legal and ethical issues, such as copyright and regulatory compliance, are discussed alongside technology and pedagogy issues? One of the most important steps in the copyright compliance process is educating all parties concerned, from designers to graphic artists to programmers to faculty to editors to administrators to invested others, about the ideological, legal, ethical, and practical issues related to copyright law. One of the best ways to reach a wide audience at one time is to provide a faculty development event where participants—for example, a panel—are invited to provide a clear discussion of the pertinent issues. Copyright law is a hotly debated issue in academia, and panelists with divergent backgrounds—perhaps a university copyright lawyer, a leading faculty member or two known for their technology innovation, a librarian, several administrators with a stake in the issue, and representatives from academic publishing—might create a lively debate.

Conclusions

This article began our discussion of electronic copyright issues by examining the promises and risks of the Internet. It concludes with the following brief summary. The Internet has the potential to become a force of great change in our society, but all of the hype and hope must be tempered with a healthy dose of realism. As we move into an increasingly information-based world economy, one premise is true above all others: an information network is valuable only as long as we can ensure the integrity of the information that it contains. In the electronic publishing environment, information integrity is tied in many ways to issues of information production, ownership, and control. The good news is that all can become both creators and consumers; all can help to shape what the Internet becomes. This is a tremendous opportunity, one that brings great responsibility.

We must be reminded that the original intention of copyright law was not to thwart information usage, but to protect the free flow of information in the public interest. To enable that principle to guide us, we must reaffirm our commitment to safeguarding the rights of both the producers and the consumers of that information, and indeed, in the online course delivery environment, we may often find ourselves playing both roles simultaneously. Although the electronic environment offers new challenges to existing copyright law, many of those challenges could be met by providing public education on the appropriate uses of information. Many people who violate copyright law in the electronic environment do so simply out of ignorance. As responsible users of the Internet, we need to educate both ourselves and others about the spirit and the practice of copyright law, which, in the end, is based on mutual respect, respect for both producers and consumers of information and respect for the value of information itself as a private and a public "good."

Note

1. Ms. Colyer wishes to make the following disclaimer: I do not hold a law degree and make no pretense of being a copyright lawyer. The advice contained in this article is, however, based on more than ten years of experience with the instructional design unit of The Pennsylvania State University's Department of Distance Education. A significant portion of that time has been devoted to overseeing permissions procurement activities and policing copyright/intellectual property issues to ensure that the instructional design unit is in compliance with university policy. The approach taken in this article is, admittedly, an extremely conservative one, a stance with which more liberal proponents of "fair use" will likely take issue. If you have specific questions on copyright or intellectual property issues, I urge you to consult your own organization's lawyers, copyright clearance unit, and/or intellectual property office.

References

Allen, M. 1995. Dissidents use computer network to rile Scientology. *New York Times,* 14 August, A12.

Bennett, S. 1993. Copyright and innovation in electronic publishing: A commentary. *The Journal of Academic Librarianship* 19 (2): 87–91.

Bovet, S. F. 1995. Legal issues in cyberspace. *Public Relations Journal,* May, 48.

Coleman, R. 1995. Copycats on the superhighway. *ABA Journal* 81: 68–71.

Duranceau, E. F., ed. 1995. The economics of electronic publishing. *Serials Review* 21 (1): 77–90.

Lehman, B., committee chair. 1995. Intellectual property and the National Information Infrastructure. The report of the working group on intellectual property rights, Information Infrastructure Task Force, September. Available from http://www.uspto.gov/veb/offices/com/doc/ipnii/ipnii.doc

Lewis, P. H. 1994. Student accused of running network for pirated software. *New York Times,* 9 April, A1.

Tickle, K. 1995. The vicarious liability of electronic bulletin board operators for the copyright infringement occurring on their bulletin boards. *Iowa Law Review* 80 (2): 391–418.

Wincor, R. 1994. Unrest on the frontiers of copyright. *Communications and the Law* 16 (3): 83–9.

Online Graduate Degrees: A Review of Three Internet-Based Master's Degree Offerings

Robert W. Strong and E. Glynn Harmon

Vol. 11 No. 3 1997

Abstract

This article briefly reviews and compares three offerings of graduate degrees via the Internet—two master's programs in the field of management and one master's program in the area of library and information science. Three different management degrees offered by the University of Phoenix, the master of arts in management offered by The Graduate School of America, and the master of science in library and information science offered by the University of Illinois at Urbana-Champaign are described according to each program's online and printed prospecti. Based on this information, the three programs are compared and evaluated. The article concludes with a consumer's guide that formulates some key questions that any potential student of these types of programs should ask before enrolling in such a program.

Introduction

The Internet and the World Wide Web (WWW) have become pervasive in the academic realm, particularly in the course work required to achieve success in higher education. The Internet has been extended far beyond its original scope as a highly specialized scientific communications network for the defense establishment and major research universities possessing high-capacity computers; in the view of many, it is becoming the meat and bones of much that takes place in all the academic disciplines from physics to the classics. Distance and independent education available on the Internet and the WWW are the current buzzwords of higher education, and the hottest topic on many campuses is the coming of the "virtual university."

Articles about the phenomenon of the virtual university have appeared in a wide range of magazines and newspapers, including *Forbes* (Gubernick and Ebeling 1997), the *Wall Street Journal* (Lublin 1996), *Information Week* (McCartney 1996), and *U.S. News & World Report* (Lord 1995); and the *Wall Street Journal* publishes a regular advertising section called "Education Online." Articles and publications, many of which are available only on the Internet, abound on the subject. In 1994, Sunny J. Baker published one of the earliest of this type of piece on the Web entitled "A (Very) Preliminary Review of Online Degree Programs in the United States: Models of Instruction, Participant Roles, and Research" as part of her research for a Ph.D. degree in educational media and computers from Arizona State University. The WWW of 1998 is full of sites containing reports on the topic, including Rick Kauffman's "Assessing the Virtual University" (1996) and Shin Yamasaki's recent University of Colorado master's thesis, *Distance Education through the Internet* (1996).

Many large universities have recently established major research or study committees to explore the realm of the virtual university and online degree programs. The University of Texas

System's Information Technology Initiative can be reviewed simply by accessing its Web site (http://www.utsystem.edu/TIF/), and the Distance Education (DE) Committee at The University of Texas at Austin recently circulated a draft of its policy recommendations report to the university's president declaring that "DE employs a set of technologies that will enable a fundamental change in pedagogy to focus more on the learning process. This change is a desirable goal even in the traditional academic setting" (1997, 1). Furthermore, legislation (HR 1404) was recently introduced in the Texas House of Representatives that would permit all state universities to make any already-approved course offering available via the Internet without additional approval from the state's coordinating board of higher education.

The WWW is replete with sites that offer themselves as guides to online higher education courses and to online degree programs. Higher education sources as diverse as the Northwestern Michigan College University Center (http://www.nmc.edu/~ucenter/institution.html) and the Indiana Higher Education Telecommunication System (http://www.ihets.org/IPSE/) and commercial sources such as the Electronic University Network (http://www.wcc-eun.com/eun/) and PonyExpress.Net (http://www.ponyexpress.net/~saleh/mdegrees.htm) are putting up Web sites that both list and provide hotlinks to dozens of sites that offer online degree programs as well as certification programs and individualized study programs. These guides to Internet courses have become such big business that they are now available in printed versions that sell at a premium and are in high demand in library reference collections. The foremost among these is Dan Corrigan's *The Internet University* (1996), a best-seller in the genre.

From among this abundance of resources and information, this article examines three graduate-level online degree offerings, two in management and one in library and information science (LIS). The programs will be described based on the prospecti, both online and printed, available for each program, and a brief comparison will be made of these degree offerings. Finally, a consumer's guide for online degree programs will be proposed based on what has been found in these offerings and other material available on evaluating online courses.

In describing the actual degree programs, the following information for each program will be discussed: the number of credit hours and/or courses in the program and the approximate length of time required to complete it; resident study requirements, if any; synchronicity of course work; admission requirements for the program; program costs, if published; hardware and connectivity requirements, if specified and costed; and, finally, accreditation status. The URL for each program's Web site is also provided.

Program Descriptions

University of Phoenix (Arizona). This program (http://www.uophx.edu/online/) offers several online master's degrees in management, each with a different emphasis but all sharing a core of courses centered in the traditional master of business administration (MBA) curriculum. The Professional MBA program is designed to teach managers how to manage. This degree requires fifty-one credits and can be accomplished in twenty-seven months according to published material. The individual courses are of five- or six-week durations for two or three credits respectively. The MBA in technology management (MBA-TM) focuses on managing, developing, and marketing technology. This degree also requires fifty-one credits and twenty-seven months to complete. While many of the core courses are the same as the Professional MBA, other required courses are technology-oriented. Additionally, the MBA-TM program has some special admission requirements concerning the technology background of its applicants.

A third degree offered by the University of Phoenix is the master of arts in organization management (MAOM), which focuses on the human aspects of management science. This program requires only forty-one credits and, according to the prospectus, can be completed in twenty-four months. Again, this degree is based on the same core MBA courses as the other two degrees described.

There are no published requirements for resident courses or even an in-residence orientation for completion of any of these degree programs. Under certain conditions, students in the MBA programs may transfer in up to twelve graduate credits (four courses), while the MAOM students are limited to nine credits (three courses); California residents may transfer in only six credits to either program. The program materials indicate that the online course work is a combination of synchronous and asynchronous modes, with heavy emphasis on synchronous class "meetings" involving all students and the professor. Recent news reports indicate that the school keeps virtually no full-time faculty, as "most of its classes involve working professionals teaching other working professionals…" (Bronner 1997).

The general admission requirements for these three programs are a bachelor's degree with a 2.5 GPA (on a 4.0 scale) from an accredited college or university (any graduate study already completed must show a GPA of at least 3.0) and a minimum of three years of work experience in a capacity which provides exposure to organizational systems and management processes. To be eligible for the technology management program, the experience must have been within organizations in which technology is key to the business. Further, if the MBA-TM candidate does not have an undergraduate degree in an applied science, such as engineering, then he or she must have a minimum of four years applicable experience.

Computer hardware, software, and connectivity requirements to participate successfully in the University of Phoenix program are clearly specified in their Web site but are less clear in the printed program materials. The costs of the computer-related items are not discussed except for a $117 piece of proprietary software called "Alexware" required to participate in the programs. The published material does encourage prospective students to contact the online campus staff to discuss these issues.

Until recently, the University of Phoenix's only published statement about the costs of its programs was that tuition was "...comparable to that at other private universities and colleges throughout the country." The university's Web site now includes a page on "Tuition and Fees" that lists graduate tuition at $460 per credit, plus miscellaneous fees (including the required connectivity software) of $225. Assuming that a student completed these programs with the minimum required credits (exclusive of any transferred credits and related fees), the estimated direct costs of either of the MBAs would be $23,685 and the MAOM would cost $19,085. These costs do not include books, supplies, computer-related expenses (except the Alexware), or other costs.

The University of Phoenix does, however, point out that, unlike most schools, payment for a full semester at a time is not required; instead, tuition is collected as each course is taken. Financial assistance is "available for qualified individuals," and there is strong encouragement for students to take advantage of employer tuition-reimbursement programs. The University of Phoenix's degree programs are fully accredited under the university's accreditation by the North Central Association of Colleges and Schools (NCACS).

The Graduate School of America (TGSA). TGSA (http://www.tgsa.com) is located in Minneapolis, Minnesota, and offers master of science and doctor of philosophy degrees in management, education, human services, and interdisciplinary studies as a "distance learning graduate school." All of these offerings are Internet based. TGSA's online master of science in management will be described here as most comparable to the other programs examined. The master of science in management requires forty-eight quarter credits (each course is four credit hours) and completion time is estimated to be in the range of eighteen to thirty-six months. The program consists of twenty required credits, twenty-four elective credits, and a four-credit "Integrative Management Project." A student may transfer in up to twelve quarter credits of outside graduate course work with a grade of B or better from a regionally accredited institution.

From the Web site and printed brochure, it appears that the online instruction is all asynchronous; participation in class work and assignments is "at the time you choose." Until recently, this program had some requirements for "resident" courses. There were two "focused seminars" of two and a half days each at various regional locations on different topics. The student was permitted to choose both the topic and the site (locations and topics are not given in the prospectus). There was also a two-week "extended seminar" in St. Paul, Minnesota, during the summer. On May 15, 1997, TGSA announced that all residency requirements for their online master's program were being dropped and that attendance at the focused seminars and the two-week summer session were no longer required (Larson 1997).

The admission requirements for the TGSA master of science in management are a bachelor's degree from an accredited institution, an undergraduate GPA of at least 2.7 (on a 4.0 scale), and a Test of English as a Foreign Language (TOEFL) score of at least 550 for international applicants whose native language is not English. The admissions committee can waive one criterion for an applicant with demonstrated strengths in the other areas.

Computer equipment and connectivity requirements are described in very general terms but are not costed. The TGSA Web site states that, "If you have access to the World Wide Web, you already have all the equipment you need. No special software is needed." However, the site also mentions that, for optimal access to online course information, TGSA recommends a 28.8 Kbps modem (or better) and the use of Netscape Navigator 3.0 or Microsoft Internet Explorer 3.0 (or better) for your Web browser.

TGSA's May 15, 1997, program revision announcement also included a reduction in tuition from $1,000 per course to $795 per course and declares that

> This reduction, combined with the elimination of residency fees, lowers the cost of the Online Master's program by over $3,500. Depending on how many credits you are able to transfer…the total cost of the Online Master's program is now between $7,155 and $9,500 (not including books and materials). (Larson 1997)

However, these figures do not include costs for computer hardware, software, or connectivity. Financial aid is available, with emphasis on TGSA eligibility for veterans' educational benefits. Participation in employer tuition-reimbursement programs is also promoted.

TGSA received accreditation from the NCACS on November 14, 1997, following evaluation and site visits during the summer and early fall of that year. The accreditation is valid for a five-year period.

University of Illinois at Urbana-Champaign (UIUC). The final program examined is the master of science in LIS (MSLIS) offered by UIUC (http://alexia.lis.uiuc.edu/leep3/), which has campuses in central Illinois. The program, known as "LEEP3," is an Internet-based degree offering that is closely tied to the nationally recognized resident degree program in LIS offered by UIUC. The LEEP3 degree requires ten units of credit (forty semester hours of course work). As a full-time student, the program can be completed in one calendar year; completion as a part-time student is estimated to require two to five years. Limited transfer of other graduate credit is permitted, and the LEEP3 program can be combined with either the traditional MSLIS degree program or with a "Fridays Only" MSLIS program offered by UIUC, which permits commuting students to complete an MSLIS degree in two and a half years by attending classes only on Fridays during fall and spring semesters.

The LEEP3 program requires that the students spend two weeks in residence during their first summer in the program for orientation, technical training, and a core course. They are also required to come to campus for at least one three-day weekend during the semester (it is not clear if this applies to part-time students for every semester they are enrolled). There is also a notation that states that students may be required to come to campus for another summer session in the second or later summer. The program prospectus is fairly specific about the amount of time per week required to complete each course, including the amount of time connected to the Internet (up to ten hours per week). It also specifies that some classes will be synchronous, while others will be entirely asynchronous, but it does not give the proportions.

The admission requirements for the UIUC LEEP3 degree program are identical to the traditional MSLIS degree program: graduation from an accredited institution whose requirements for the bachelor's degree are substantially equivalent to those of UIUC; a GPA of 3.0 (on 4.0 scale) for the junior and senior years or last sixty semester hours; three letters of reference; and international applicants must have a TOEFL score of 640 or above. UIUC also requires an official copy of the applicant's scores on the Graduate Record Examinations (GRE) aptitude test taken within the last five years; however, no minimum or desired score is published.

The LEEP3 Web site provides a very detailed set of specifications for all computer equipment, software programs, and network connectivity required to participate in the program, but no estimated cost for these items is included. Another part of the site, the LEEP Cost Fact Sheet, includes a breakdown of the tuition and fee costs for full-time program enrollment, including the differential for non-Illinois residents. The total for Illinois residents is $7,380, and the cost for nonresidents is $18,266. While the current cost fact sheet provides a list of travel requirements for the resident portions of the program, it no longer includes an estimate of the expenses involved. The Web site notes that the final cost of part-time participation will be higher due to increasing costs involved in the extended time element. Financial aid is available under the regular UIUC admissions criteria, but there is no special promotion of employer tuition reimbursement programs.

The UIUC LEEP3 Internet degree program is fully accredited as part of the regular UIUC degree offerings by the NCACS; it is also accredited by the American Library Association. The program prospectus emphasizes that all Internet courses are identical to the traditional and "Fridays Only" MSLIS curriculum and that the same faculty teach them. The degrees awarded are indistinguishable.

Comparison of Programs

The three Web degree programs described here can be examined and evaluated in a number of different ways. Certainly, the most obvious is to attempt to match the differing elements that the various degrees offer with the academic and career objectives of the individual seeking the degree. These three schools offer substantially different paths for achieving potential business and career success, and it must be left to each individual to make the kinds of personal assessment involved in such a goal-oriented approach. However, there are some general elements of these programs that can be evaluated, and some meaningful comparisons can be made regarding certain aspects of each program.

The University of Phoenix MBA programs are clearly oriented to the fast-paced, high-tech corporate world of today, focused as they are on the "hot-button" topics of technology management and organizational development. These programs have become the darlings of the *Wall Street Journal, Information Week,* and similar publications, which have provided them with free publicity and have sold them prime advertising space. Of the three schools examined, these degree programs have the lowest stated admission requirements and the added attraction of no requirement for resident course work. Additionally, they offer the possible attraction of an emphasis on synchronous course work and the prestige of a degree from a university with a good reputation in the academic realm. The major potential drawback to these programs may be their high cost. The published program cost for the MBA degrees is nearly $24,000, while the MAOM degree cost is over $19,000 not including computer equipment and connectivity costs. However, if an applicant has a corporate tuition-reimbursement program available and has access to the company's computers and connectivity with which to accomplish the course work, the University of Phoenix offerings could be a very attractive degree program.

TGSA offers a more generalist approach to a graduate management degree in a program that has only slightly higher admission standards than the University of Phoenix but fairly generous provisions for waivers of those requirements. Some prospective students will find the totally asynchronous course work an attraction, and the recent elimination of the resident seminars requirement could be viewed as a plus by many applicants. The $205 reduction in TGSA's tuition per course has dropped the published "course of instruction" cost range for this program from $10,600–$13,600 to $7,155–$9,500. (Previously published costs for this program were somewhat misleading in that none of the travel and housing costs for resident course work were included in the course of instruction cost.) The cost range does not include the costs for computer, software, and connectivity; the computer and connectivity requirements are only generally outlined in the program's prospectus. While these costs will add to the published course of instruction cost, this program's true cost should be well below those of the University of Phoenix programs. Again, corporate tuition-reimbursement programs and corporate computer access could offset these cost issues for TGSA applicants.

TGSA's recent receipt of full accreditation has removed a major liability from this program and has significantly raised the value of its degrees in the long run. Accreditation significantly improves the marketability of the degrees for students, and it opens this program to full participation in corporate and governmental tuition-reimbursement programs that only permit enrollment in accredited schools.

The Internet MSLIS offered by UIUC is without question the most academically oriented of the programs examined and has the clearest, most explicit prospectus. It is a fully accredited program with the highest admission standards—identical to its traditional resident program—and offers a degree involving curriculum and faculty identical to the resident MSLIS programs. While it does have what some may view as inconvenient resident course requirements, the requirements for synchronicity of course work, Internet time, computer hardware/software, and connectivity are more clearly explained and detailed than in any other program. Unfortunately, the current UIUC prospectus does not spell out in detail the total anticipated cost of the program, including travel, housing, computer, and connectivity expenses.

The large increase in out-of-state tuition for UIUC has raised the direct cost for non-Illinois students into the range of the University of Phoenix's MAOM degree. Further, the travel costs escalate the farther away the student is from central Illinois. These factors are probably the clearest indication that this Internet degree program was designed as a regional offering rather than a national program. Indeed, the entire issue of a state university offering a graduate professional degree in the jurisdictions of other state higher education authorities does not seem to have been addressed in this or any other program.

A Consumer's Guide

Beyond the specifics of the three individual online graduate degree programs that are cursorily examined here, there is a series of general questions that should be raised when considering enrollment in such a program. Some of these questions have been addressed above in terms of a specific program; however, it might be helpful to look at a general set of possible questions. Adapted from the *Consumer's Guide to College Courses on the Internet* (1997), created by Susan McIlheran of Drake University, these questions can be broken into three categories: questions about the institution, questions about the degree program, and questions about costs and cost-benefit (see Table 1).

To assist future consumers of online graduate degree programs, a brief guide of key questions to be asked about these types of programs has been formulated. Questions about the institution include such things as whether the institution is accredited, what its admission standards are, and what the drop-out and completion rates for students in that institution's online degree programs are. Additionally, the student should pose direct and serious questions to the institution concerning whether the institution's learning resources will be available to the online student and what support services will be offered to Internet degree seekers.

Another set of questions that should be posed focuses on the degree program itself and the course work involved in it. The first of these questions is whether the program meets the student's needs and moves the student toward his or her desired goal. Related questions involve whether the degree will be valued by current or potential employers and whether the course work will be transferable if the student should switch to another program or school. Additional questions deal with the credentials and qualifications of the program's faculty, the nature of the interaction between students and faculty (synchronous or asynchronous course work, chat rooms, conferences, etc.), how the course work will be evaluated, and finally, whether there are any requirements for resident instruction or orientations. The potential transferability of courses to other programs or schools is a particularly problematic area of concern: while institutional accreditation implies a certain legitimacy in terms of transferring course credits, each individual situation may be different due to restrictions imposed by a receiving school.

A third issue that must be addressed early on concerns the cost of the program: are these costs completely spelled out and are the institution's estimates realistic and based on concrete experience factors? Beyond these questions, the answers to which should be determinable from the institution, the prospective student (and possibly his or her employer, if a tuition-reimbursement program is to be involved) must carefully assess the cost-benefit ratio involved in embarking on any such program in terms of criteria such as the marketability of learning received (for the student), the usefulness of the courses and learning for applications in the workplace (for the employers), and the time required to recover the costs (for whoever pays those costs). Given the apparent high cost of even the least expensive online graduate degree program, this should be a major consideration in the decision-making process.

Table 1. A Consumer's Guide to Online Degree Programs

Questions about the institution.

1. Is the institution and the program accredited?
2. What are the admission requirements?
3. What are the drop-out and completion rates for students in the program?
4. Will the institution's learning resources be available to the online student?
5. What support services will be offered to online degree seekers?

Questions about the degree program and the course work involved.

1. Will this program meet your needs and move you toward your desired goal?
2. Will this degree be valued by your current or potential employer?
3. Will the course work be transferable if you should switch to another program or school?
4. What are the credentials and qualifications of the program's faculty?
5. What is the nature of the interaction between students and faculty (synchronous or asynchronous course work, chat rooms, conferences, etc.)?
6. How will the course work be evaluated?
7. Are there any resident instruction or orientation requirements?
8. Are courses updated appropriately?

Questions about the cost of the program.

1. Are all costs completely spelled out?
2. Are the institution's estimates realistic and based on concrete experience factors?
3. What is the cost-benefit ratio in terms of criteria such as the marketability of learning received (for the student); the usefulness of the courses and learning for applications in the workplace (for employers); and the time needed to recover costs given potential increased earning or increased productivity?

Summary

For many educators and policymakers, both public and corporate, online degrees appear to be at least a partial answer to the fiscal squeeze of increasing demand for degree programs and diminishing per capita resources available to provide those programs. In such an environment, it is incumbent upon both potential students and their employers, actual or potential, to carefully assess the value of programs in providing useful and marketable learning for their respective needs.

This article has briefly examined the prospectus of each of three graduate degree programs at the master's level that are currently being offered via the Internet and the WWW, two in management and one in LIS. The evaluation of these offerings (not of the degrees themselves) indicates clear and distinct differences in the aims, the quality of information provided, and the potential benefits of the various programs. Some major potential problems identified in considering these programs include issues of cost, accreditation, residency requirements, and synchronicity of course work, all of which should have significant bearing on the prudent individual's decision to enroll in such a program. The questions developed in this article are, of course, of a preliminary nature. The fluidity of the environment and the rapid pace of change that characterize the WWW require that these questions change continually and that new ones be added. However, this article represents a first step in an attempt to inform the educational "consumer" of some online graduate degree offerings as well as some important questions that should be considered in any evaluation of them.

References

Baker, S. J. 1994. A (very) preliminary review of online degree programs in the United States: Models of instruction, participant roles, and research. Available from http://www.virtualschool.edu/mon/Academia/OnLineDegreePrograms/

Bronner, E. 1997. Upstart university hurdles tradition. *Austin American Statesman,* 19 October, A19.

Corrigan, D. 1996. *The Internet university: College courses by computer.* Harwich, MA: Cape Software.

Distance Education Committee, The University of Texas at Austin. 1997. Draft. Report on distance education policy. (Copy in possession of authors.)

Electronic University Network. 1997. Degrees through the EUN. Available from http://www.wcc-eun.com/eun/

Gubernick, L., and A. Ebeling. 1997. I got my degree through e-mail. *Forbes,* 16 June, 84–90.

Indiana Higher Education Telecommunication System. 1997. Indiana partnership for statewide education: Distance education resources for instructors and students. Available from http://www.ihets.org/IPSE/

Kauffman, R. 1996. Assessing the virtual university. *Adult Assessment Forum Archives.* Available from http://www.intered.com/virtual.html

Larson, T. 1997. Important changes to the online M.S. program. (Director of Admission, The Graduate School of America.) (E-mail to authors for further information.)

Lord, M. 1995. Getting a degree by e-mail. *U.S. News & World Report,* 30 October, 91–3.

Lublin, J. S. 1996. Schools boot up to offer on-line M.B.A.s. *Wall Street Journal,* 24 September, B–1.

McCartney, L. 1996. Virtual MBA: Going back to school doesn't mean sitting in a classroom again. *Information Week,* 4 November. Available from http://www.informationweek.com

McIlheran, S. J. 1997. Consumer's guide to college courses on the Internet. Available from http://www.mac.drake.edu/IAICU/consumer_guide.html

NMC University Center. 1997. Links to colleges and universities offering degree programs online. Available from http://www.nmc.edu/~ucenter /institution.html

PonyExpress.Net. 1997. Education via Internet. Available from http://www.ponyexpress.net/~saleh/mdegrees.html (or /ddegrees.html).

Yamasaki, S. 1996. Distance education through the Internet. Master's thesis, University of Colorado, Boulder. Available from http://rintintin.colorado.edu/~yamasaks/thesis/thesis.html

GRASS ROOTS

We receive many reports that describe particular distance education programs and projects, not all of which can be published. However, from time to time, we publish some of these reports in the GRASS ROOTS section. The first article that follows describes the use of an Internet tutorial in Web-based courses. The second article that follows describes an evaluation method for a distance education course delivered in Brazil via the World Wide Web. The third article that follows describes the use of an electronic bulletin board in an off-campus doctoral program.

Implementing an Internet Tutorial for Web-Based Courses

Sherri Smith and Andrea Benscoter

Vol. 13 No. 2 1999

Abstract

The Division of Criminal Justice at the Florida Gulf Coast University offers an entire criminal justice degree program via distance learning, principally through computer-based Internet courses. During the spring 1998 semester, an Internet tutorial was provided during the first week of classes to students in all Internet courses in the program. Its purpose was to familiarize students with basic computer skills and Internet usage. This article focuses on the use of the Internet tutorial in Web-based courses, including an explanation of the tutorial and a discussion of its benefits for students and faculty and its implications for future computer-based Internet courses.

Distance Education via the Internet

The concept of distance learning has evolved over time, and distance learning has relied on various media throughout the years to deliver instruction (Schlosser and Anderson 1994; Willis 1993). Distance education has expanded during the 1990s to include the use of the Internet to offer classes completely online. Faculty and administrators developing and implementing distance learning courses are becoming aware of the advantages that Internet-based instruction can provide to students over other delivery options (Barnard 1992). Some universities are considering the use of Internet courses as a way to increase student enrollments and reduce costs (Phelps et al. 1991). Internet-based instruction is emerging as a viable option for colleges and universities offering distance education.

While Internet-based distance learning courses may provide advantages absent in other delivery options, the development and delivery of these courses involve complex issues and require comprehensive planning to be successful (Barker and Hall 1993; Young, Barnes, and Lowery 1995; Smith, Bradley, and Benscoter In press). Internet courses necessitate changes in the way instructors teach courses. Ingesman (1993) suggests that one of the most challenging features of Internet-based instruction involves overcoming both faculty and student inexperience with computer-based technology. Internet courses require faculty and students to become familiar with computer software and other technologies necessary for course delivery. Instructors offering Internet courses have recognized that this type of course typically requires a considerable amount of time for the users to become familiar with the technological aspects of the course (Geddes 1993; Owston 1997). Other challenges for Internet courses include (1) hardware malfunctions, (2) server connection problems, (3) software installation problems (Owston 1997), (4) software conflicts, and (5) lack of user knowledge. Many of these concerns can be addressed by requiring students to participate in an Internet tutorial prior to engaging in course content activities. While the Internet tutorial does not eliminate the potential for students and faculty to encounter software and/or hardware problems during the course, it potentially decreases the number of basic problems typically encountered with Internet-based distance learning courses.

This article focuses on the use of this Internet tutorial in Web-based courses. Issues for discussion include an explanation of the Internet tutorial and a discussion of its benefits for students and faculty.

Background

Florida Gulf Coast University (FGCU) opened in August 1997, and the university made a commitment through a partnership to deliver an entire criminal justice degree program through distance learning. Faculty and administration decided to offer this distance learning program predominately though computer-based Internet courses. Specific delivery mechanisms utilized by the Division of Criminal Justice include (1) electronic mail (e-mail), (2) e-mail distribution lists (listservs), (3) Web pages, and (4) Web-based bulletin boards (WebBoard).

During the fall semester of 1997, nine Internet courses were offered in the Division of Criminal Justice. "Criminal Justice Systems and Processes" was one of the Internet courses offered. This course provided students with an Internet tutorial during the first few weeks of the semester to familiarize them with basic computer skills and Internet use. Once classes were under way, faculty of the other Internet-based courses began to experience and identify ongoing problems related to students' lack of knowledge regarding basic computer and Internet skills. After evaluating the benefits of providing an Internet tutorial to students in the systems and processes course, faculty and administrators decided that the Internet tutorial would be beneficial for students in all Internet courses offered in the Division of Criminal Justice at FGCU. During the spring 1998 semester, all Internet courses provided an Internet tutorial to students during the first week of classes.

The Internet Tutorial

The Internet tutorial evolved out of a series of exercises (tasks) required of students during the first week of the systems and processes course. The required activities for the first week were designed to familiarize students with the basic technology and computer-related information necessary to participate in the class. The tasks also allowed the instructor to address issues such as (1) student familiarity with computers; (2) status of students subscribed to the course listserv;

(3) functionality of student e-mail; (4) compatibility of student word processing programs with university-supported software; (5) compatibility of student Web browsers with the WebBoard software; and (6) student ability to access the library databases needed for research assignments. Students were required to complete the series of technical exercises prior to being given the password information needed to access the "cyber classroom."

Each Internet course offered in the Division of Criminal Justice currently includes an Internet tutorial. The tutorials are designed specifically for each course according to the Internet delivery mechanisms used for class assignments. The tutorial consists of a Web page containing detailed technical information and specific tasks that students are required to complete during the first week of the semester. Students must successfully complete all tutorial activities in order to obtain the user name and password that allows them to access the cyber classroom. Specific activities include (1) subscribing to the course listserv; (2) creating and attaching a document to an e-mail message and sending the message to the course instructor's e-mail address; (3) accessing and using the WebBoard; (4) exploring the university library's Web site; (5) using a search engine to conduct an Internet search; and (6) sending e-mail to the course instructor to request the user name and password to access the course cyber classroom. Additionally, the Internet tutorial page provides links to other information for students to access if they are unfamiliar with specific tasks, such as how to attach a document to e-mail.

Subscribing to the Course Listserv. A listserv is set up for each Internet course offered in the Division of Criminal Justice. The course listserv allows students and the instructor to communicate with the entire class without sending multiple e-mail messages to multiple addresses. The first tutorial assignment requires students to subscribe to the course listserv. The tutorial Web page provides a link for students to access the listserv subscription page. The student completes and submits the subscription Web form to automatically add his/her e-mail address to the listserv. The listserv generates a welcome message to each subscriber confirming that his/her subscription was successful. Within the welcome message, instructors include an additional assignment requiring students to send a message to the listserv with their name, e-mail address, and a brief biography. This assignment allows students to demonstrate their ability to send e-mail to the listserv. It also introduces the students to their instructor and classmates. Allowing students to complete this assignment during the first week of class eliminates the instructor's task of manually subscribing users. This exercise also ensures that all students are subscribed to the course listserv and will receive all e-mail messages sent to the listserv throughout the semester. Technical assistance is available to address problems regarding student e-mail before the student is required to participate in assignments related to the actual course content.

Attaching a Document to an E-mail. The second tutorial assignment requires that students create and attach a document to an e-mail message and send the document to their professor's e-mail address. The purpose of this activity is to familiarize students with the proper procedures for sending e-mail attachments to the professor, a procedure they will use to submit papers and exams throughout the semester. This exercise also helps determine whether or not the students' word processing programs are compatible with the software supported by the university. Specific instructions for this task are divided into two steps.

In step one, students are instructed to create a new document using a word processing program (e.g., Microsoft Word, Corel WordPerfect, Microsoft Works, etc.). Within the document, students are asked to type "I am learning to attach documents to e-mail." The file is saved using the file name "attach." If students are using a word processing program other than Microsoft Word, they are instructed to use the "Save As" command to save their document as a Word document or in rich text format so that the professor can open the document. A link to step-by-step instructions is provided on the Internet tutorial for students who are unfamiliar with saving a document as a different file type.

Once the document is saved, students are instructed to exit the word processing program in order to perform step two. Step two requires students to attach the document to an e-mail message addressed to the professor. An additional Web page with step-by-step instructions is provided to guide students through this assignment. If a student is unable to send the document as an attachment or if the instructor is unable to open the document, the student is asked to contact the instructor and identify his/her (1) word processing program, (2) computer type (i.e., PC, Mac), (3) operating system (e.g., Windows 95, Windows 3.1), (4) e-mail program, and (5) the problems encountered in the initial attempt to send the attachment. The course instructor and the technical assistant review the information provided by the student and make specific suggestions to remedy the problem. Students are provided with the contact information for the technical assistant so they can obtain individualized assistance via e-mail, office visits, and/or telephone.

Accessing and Using the WebBoard. In addition to e-mail, a Web-based bulletin board (WebBoard) is used in each class to simulate class discussion. The WebBoard software allows the instructor to organize posted messages and monitor students' participation. The third tutorial assignment provides a link to detailed instructions for accessing the course WebBoard. Students must have a user name and password to access the WebBoard. The first part of the assignment requires students to create a WebBoard profile, if they do not already have one for another class. After students access the course WebBoard, they must read and reply to a welcome message posted by the instructor. This assignment helps students become familiar with the functions of the WebBoard prior to being assigned tasks related to course content.

Exploring the University's Library Web Site. Distance learning students have the additional challenge of accessing library materials for research assignments. It is often too far for the student to travel to the campus library to locate books and journal articles. Fortunately, the Internet makes it possible for students to access library material and electronic databases from their homes. As part of the Internet tutorial, students are required to access the university's library Web site and explore library tutorials designed to help them with the process of conducting a library search for books, journals, and full-text articles. This task helps familiarize the students with procedures for using the State University System of Florida's Library User Information Service (LUIS) and other electronic databases. Once students have explored the library tutorials, they are instructed to provide specific information to the instructor regarding search rules for LUIS as well as descriptive information regarding basic screen displays found in LUIS. By providing this information, students demonstrate their knowledge of the basic skills needed to conduct library searches during the semester.

Using an Internet Search Engine. The Internet tutorial also requires students to access and practice using an Internet search engine (e.g., Excite, Infoseek, Yahoo). The assignment instructs students to conduct an Internet search on a specifically identified, course-related subject. For example, students in Criminal Justice Systems and Processes were instructed to conduct an Internet search for Web pages related to the topic of women and crime. After students locate a Web site they find relevant and interesting, they are asked to share the information with the entire class by sending an e-mail message to the course listserv that includes the URL and a description of the site. Once this assignment is completed, students have access to a variety of Web pages identified by their peers. This task introduces students to various Internet search engines available on the Web and encourages them to participate in collaborative activities throughout the course.

Students who have successfully completed the tasks assigned in the Internet tutorial send an e-mail message to the course instructor requesting the user name and password information necessary to access the cyber classroom. The tasks that students perform in the tutorial increase the likelihood of future success with technical tasks throughout the course. These activities help familiarize students with a variety of course tutorials that will be available to them throughout the course and provide them with contact information for future technical assistance. The Internet tutorial is designed to introduce students to various Web-based technologies necessary for success in the course.

Conclusion

Faculty in the Division of Criminal Justice have found that the Internet tutorial benefits both students and faculty engaged in Internet-based courses. The tutorial forces students to become familiar with the basic tasks necessary to communicate in the course prior to allowing them access to the course content in the cyber classroom. Once students have successfully completed the tutorial and are given access to the cyber classroom, they are better prepared to concentrate their efforts on course content.

Faculty and administrators interested in Internet-based course delivery should consider the use of an Internet tutorial to assist students in becoming familiar with basic computer and Internet activities. As colleges and universities begin to offer Internet-based courses in their curriculum, it becomes necessary to consider the level of student proficiency with basic Internet activities. Student knowledge and comfort level with available technologies vary widely. In order for Internet courses to provide a conducive learning environment for students, support systems must be in place to assist those in need of technical education and assistance.

References

Barker, B. O., and R. F. Hall. 1993. A national survey of distance education use in rural school districts of 300 students or less. Unpublished manuscript, Annual Conference of the National Rural Education Association, Burlington, VT.

Barnard, J. 1992. Multimedia and the future of distance learning technology. *Educational Media International* 29:139–44.

Geddes, T. 1993. The higher education distance learner and technology. In *Occasional papers in open and distance learning,* no. 14, ed. Peter Donnan, 14–21. Charles Sturt University, New South Wales: Open Learning Institute.

Ingesman, L. 1993. Training distance teachers. *Educational Media International* 30: 83–7.

Owston, R. 1997. The World Wide Web: A technology to enhance teaching and learning? *Educational Researcher,* March, 27–33.

Phelps, R. H., R. A. Wells, R. L. Ashworth Jr., and H. A. Hahn. 1991. Effectiveness and costs of distance education using computer-mediated communication. *The American Journal of Distance Education* 5 (3): 7–19.

Schlosser, C. A., and M. L. Anderson. 1994. *Distance education: A review of the literature.* Washington, DC: Association of Educational Communications Technology.

Smith, S., P. Bradley, and A. Benscoter. In press. Providing distance education in a criminal justice degree program: A team approach. *Journal of Criminal Justice Education.*

Willis, B. 1993. *Distance education: A practical guide.* Englewood Cliffs, NJ: Educational Technology Publications.

Young, D. B., F. M. Barnes, and B. R. Lowery. 1995. Distance education: How to begin. *Journal of Criminal Justice Education* 6 (2): 299–309.

A Method for Evaluation of a Course Delivered via the World Wide Web in Brazil

Mônica G. M. Magalhães and Dietrich Schiel

Vol. 11 No. 2 1997

Abstract

This paper describes the application of evaluation methods to a distance course and discusses the need for ongoing evaluation to control the quality of distance education courses. During the last quadrimester of 1996, a course in graphic mechanics was offered in Brazil via the World Wide Web through a distance education program entitled "Programa Educ@r." Evaluation methods and data analysis were developed and applied during the period of the course, and results of the evaluation are discussed.

Introduction

Distance education programs are increasing in number and becoming one of the most important new trends in education. These programs, delivered using current technologies, provide new ways for students to learn and a variety of methods for facilitating interaction between students and teachers. Developing program materials for delivery through new technologies, such as the World Wide Web (WWW), are new initiatives in São Carlos, State of São Paulo, Brazil, and it is difficult to find information on and methods for evaluating these programs. With the objective of filling this gap, an evaluation of the distance course in graphic mechanics was conducted through an ongoing evaluation system of data collection and analysis.

In Brazil, twenty-three science centers are connected via the Internet to the Center of Scientific and Cultural Divulgation at the University of São Paulo. Twenty schools are also connected to the same network. The graphic mechanics course is among several programs developed for the project entitled "Programa Educ@r"[1]. Still in the beginning stage, the following programs are also being developed for the project: environmental education, mathematical training for primary school teachers, and physics for high school students. This paper describes an evaluation of the graphic mechanics course in the Programa Educ@r project.

A Graphic Mechanics Course via the WWW

The basic experimental equipment for the physics program consists of an air puck (Hessel 1982). This specially designed puck enables the user to register its position on the table with an oscillating pen. Similar to using a strobe photo (Huggins 1979), the student can obtain specific positions at a defined time. The principal objective is to interpret movements and write programs in Logo (Papert 1980) in order to simulate the experimental data obtained. By beginning with a constant velocity and passing through one-dimensional and two-dimensional accelerated movement, the student simulates central movement in a circle and central movement with the puck being pulled by a centrally fixed spring. All of these movements are replicated by simulation in Logo. The last step of the process consists of instructing the student to replace the central force of the spring with an attraction force that is proportional to the inverse square of the distance. The student will obtain an elliptic gravitational orbit that clearly shows a higher velocity near the attracting center in accordance with Kepler's second law. The student can also replicate the gravitational movement of a satellite attracted by a planet that is, in turn, attracted by a star, and can test what will occur if the inverse square attraction law is altered. All of these calculations are performed without reference to differential and integral calculus.

This physics program is used in distance education courses delivered via the WWW. The student executes the experiments described above directed solely by instructions presented on a home page (http://www.ifqsc.sc.usp.br/educar/fisica/fisica.html—in Portuguese). The student registers the results obtained from experiments onto this same Web page, thus completing an interactive table. The results of acceleration and velocity obtained by the student are verified automatically through the main server, and the results are returned to the student. At the same time, these results are sent to a staff member who is able to comment and give additional instructions to students who have difficulties. The programs written in Logo are sent to the staff using a special browser on the home page. This enables the staff to guide the student through difficulties such as missing spaces in commands, which, while they may seem minor, can seriously hinder the work. The student spends a great deal of time on experimental work, calculations, and programming and relatively little time sending messages. Because of the small amount of time spent on the Internet, this program can function well even in places such as Brazil, where a fast data highway does not yet exist.

Evaluating the Distance Course

Apart from the reliance on well-defined programs, the success of distance education depends on appropriate didactic material, suitable resources to deliver instruction to the students, and qualified human resources. When coupled with a complete diagnosis of the students' needs and the needs of the region, evaluations performed during and after the course can produce highly positive results. At this time in Brazil, there are very few programs that consider all of these factors in their evaluations (Alves 1996).

The evaluation process is fundamental to achieving quality control in distance education. It facilitates the identification of possible flaws in the instructional system and guides the changes needed to improve distance education programs.

The lack of quality control in distance and traditional systems is one of the shortcomings of the educational process. To avoid this problem, one must have an ongoing evaluation system for distance education courses. Data gathered through student and teacher questionnaires can be analyzed to identify course strengths and weaknesses as well as technical problems encountered by participants. These data can be used to improve the quality of distance courses and programs from their inception.

Methods Used to Evaluate the Course

Formative evaluations were developed (Willis 1992; Thorpe 1993; Preece et al. 1994) for the graphic mechanics course. These evaluations employed both quantitative and qualitative data-collection methods, including participant observations and questionnaires (Willis 1992; Thorpe 1993; Preece et al. 1994; Moore and Kearsley 1996).

In researching the methods used by distance education institutions (Head and Lockee 1994; Porter, Fallick, and Dagert 1994; Schick 1996), we noticed that the method often employed to obtain data and to determine strengths and weaknesses was questionnaires using a Likert scale. Therefore, questionnaires were developed and then administered during and after the course. The evaluations administered during the course identified aspects of the program that the participants considered successful and unsuccessful. The evaluations administered after the course helped to verify whether or not the difficulties were resolved, and if not, how they could be resolved in the future.

The questionnaire included open-ended and close-ended questions that were developed to assess the reactions of the students, the instructor (on-site teacher), and the mentor (distance teacher). A 5-point Likert scale (Peck and Wallace 1993; Preece et al. 1994) with the following point values was used: 1 = very poor, 2 = poor, 3 = average, 4 = good, and 5 = very good. The close-ended questions were designed to elicit responses on the use of technology, technical support, training, interaction between students/instructor/mentor, home page layout, and home page content. The open-ended questions focused on such topics as student preferences, improving instruction, comparison of the distance course to a traditional course, instructor and mentor responsibilities, strengths and weaknesses of the interaction, course strengths and weaknesses, and suggestions for the improvement of Programa Educ@r.

Results

In November 1996, the graphic mechanics course was offered for the first time in two public high school classes in Americana, State of São Paulo, Brazil. There was only one computer connected to the Internet, and due to time constraints, it was only possible to create and analyze the experiments on uniform rectilinear motion.

Questionnaires from the students, the instructor, and the mentor were used in the evaluation of the distance course (Magalhães 1996). In this pilot test, data were collected from twenty-one questionnaires administered during the course and thirteen questionnaires at the conclusion of the course. The data were compiled in an electronic spreadsheet and formulated graphically. The data from the open-ended questions were analyzed, and the common responses were selected, compiled, and then displayed graphically. Finally, the analyses were sent to the program staff to provide information on course strengths and weaknesses and on how to improve the course.

The first instructor evaluations of the graphic mechanics course in the Programa Educ@r revealed the following favorable instructional aspects of the project: it provided a stimulus to student understanding of the content, it allowed the actual use of the technology, it broadened student horizons, it facilitated communication with distance instructors, and it allowed for instructor improvement. The mentor indicated that the most successful aspects of the distance course were the interaction between students/instructor/mentor, the students' freedom to construct knowledge, and the support provided to both teacher and students as a supplement to the formal class. The mentor also emphasized that the information exchange between students/instructor/mentor and the outside world via the Internet makes this technology an important tool.

The students rated the following course aspects as "good" or "very good": the technology; the home page layout and content; and the instructor and mentor support. Most students thought that the distance course was better than the traditional course. Other positive aspects identified by the students were: responses given in the interactive tables; the indication of calculus errors; and the interaction with other people. We noticed that the students expressed a great deal of curiosity during the course about the identity of the mentor. Points for improvement that were mentioned included the Internet dial-up connection and the small size of the computation room. Students suggested that contact with the distance mentor should be immediate during the execution of the experiments. Therefore, we contacted the Internet provider support to try to resolve the connection problems. Improvements were implemented in time for the next course to be offered during the first semester of 1997. Figure 1 shows the results of the formative evaluations administered to a typical class during and after the course. The following point values correspond to a Likert scale where 1 = very poor, 2 = poor, 3 = average, 4 = good, and 5 = very good. As seen, there is little significant difference between the two results.

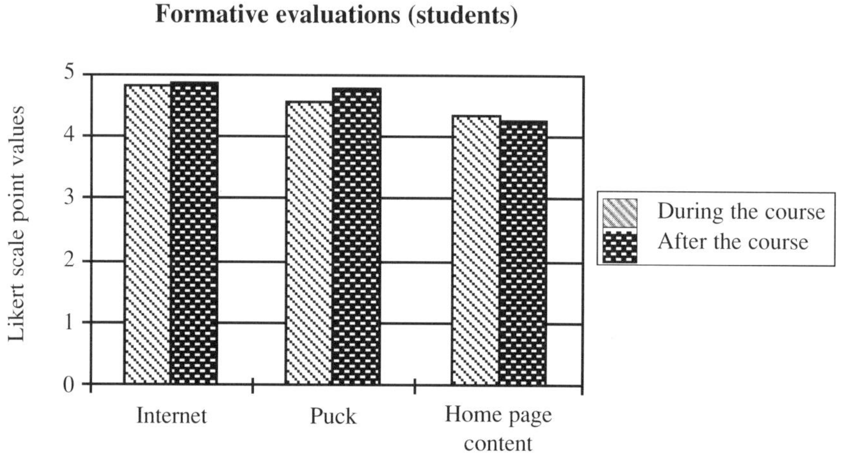

Figure 1. Formative Evaluations of a Typical Class

In January 1997, a training course was conducted for twenty teachers who will use this system in 1997. During the week of training, the first interactive table was completed. The greatest difficulty of the training was familiarizing teachers with Logo during such a limited time frame. Another point that caused some controversy concerned experimental errors; the teachers worried that the inexact results, a peculiar feature of any experimental work, would confuse the students. They are accustomed to problem resolution in which the results are not only exact, but also constitute integers, perfect squares, or trigonometric calculus with simple numbers. It becomes evident that developing a project such as the present one, which highlights errors and encourages discussion—necessary elements of experimental physics—is very important.

Conclusion

We have demonstrated in this paper the need for ongoing evaluation of distance education programs to control the quality of distance courses. It is our hope that this paper contributes to the present understanding in the field. The results of the applied evaluations showed that the Programa

Educ@r offered students the opportunity to examine data obtained with the puck and inserted into interactive tables and also to observe their errors through feedback of these tables. The pilot test also showed that Internet communications are effective for distance education.

Note

1. Supported by Vitae, FAPESP (Fundação Amparo e Pesquisa do Estado de São Paulo/The Foundation for Research Support of the State of São Paulo), and CNPq (Conselho Nacional de Desenvolvimento Cientifico e Tecnológico/National Council for Scientific and Technological Development).

References

Alves, J. R. M. 1996. Educação à distância e as novas tecnologias de informação na aprendizagem. Paper presented at the Engenheiro 2001, 7ª Teleconferência, October.

Head, T., and B. Lockee. 1994. Forming the future from the past: Student-centered evaluation of distance learning at Virginia Tech. Paper presented at the Tenth Annual Conference on Distance Teaching and Learning, August, Madison, Wisconsin.

Hessel, R. 1982. Discos sustentados por colchão de ar, uma nova proposta. *Revista Ensino de Física* 4 (3): 3–22.

Huggins, E. 1979. *Graphical Mechanics.* Wentworth, NH: COMPress, Inc./Dartmouth College.

Magalhães, M. G. M. 1996. *Avaliação de teste-piloto do programa de Física.* São Carlos, Brasil: Relatório Técnico CDCC-USP.

Moore, M. G., and G. Kearsley. 1996. *Distance education: A systems view.* Belmont, CA: Wadsworth Publishing.

Papert, S. 1980. *Mindstorms—Children, computers and powerful ideas.* New York: Basic Books.

Peck, R. M., and C. M. Wallace. 1993. Evaluating distance education courses: Initiative, methodology, and application. In *Distance education futures,* ed. T. Nunan, 527–38. Adelaide, Australia: Eleventh Biennial Forum of Australian and South Pacific, External Studies Association.

Porter, D., A. Fallick, and T. Dagert. 1994. New directions in distance learning: The year in review. *Open Learning Agency* (British Columbia, Canada).

Preece, J., Y. Rogers, H. Sharp, D. Benyon, S. Holland, and T. Carey. 1994. *Human-computer interaction.* Wokingham: Addison-Wesley.

Schick, J. A. 1996. Bridging distances between languages and cultures via distance education. *Gatherings Newsletter* (West Georgia College School of Education) 9, no. 2.

Thorpe, M. 1993. *Evaluating open & distance learning.* 2d ed. London: Longman.

Willis, B. 1992. *Instructional development for distance education.* ERIC Document Reproduction Service, ED 351 007.

Installation and Use of a Remote Electronic Bulletin Board in Teaching a Graduate-Level Course

C. Hugh Gardner and Murray H. Tillman

Vol. 2 No. 3 1988

Since the spring of 1982, The University of Georgia's College of Education has operated a doctoral program for health professionals on the campus of Armstrong State College in Savannah, Georgia. The program, which allows students to pursue a doctorate in education in the areas of curriculum or instructional development, was designed for health professionals who are involved in education or training. The purpose of this project was to examine systematically the process of introducing, maintaining, and using an innovation—the electronic bulletin board—within the off-campus doctoral program at Armstrong State College.

Who Were the Participants?

Fourteen doctoral students enrolled in an advanced course called "Research in Instruction" participated in this project. Students were employed, primarily as educators, in such health fields as nursing, dental hygiene, and radiological technology. They had been enrolled in this program for approximately four years and had taken, for the most part, the same sequence of course work. The group consisted of thirteen females and one male and ranged in age from thirty to fifty-two.

What Did We Do?

We conducted two major activities: installing and monitoring the electronic bulletin board and providing a training session on the use of the system.

Installation and Monitoring. A Tandy 1200 with 640Kb of RAM and a 10Mb hard disk was installed in the Armstrong Department of Nursing and was connected via modem to one of the departmental phone lines. We had previously tested the operation of this computer by running a campus bulletin board on it for a two-week period.

The software package used was the Remote Bulletin Board System for the IBM personal computer, or as it is more commonly known, the RBBS-PC. This program was developed and is still maintained by the Capitol PC User Group in Gaithersburg, Maryland. The RBBS-PC package is copyrighted but is available at no cost. For a modest contribution of $25 to the Capitol PC User Group, a user is registered and notified of further improvements in the package.

The major features of the RBBS-PC are message, bulletin, and filing systems. The message system allows up to 1,250 active messages, which may be private or available to anyone. The bulletin system is operated only by the system operator (SYSOP) and contains announcements or other information that is permanently posted. The filing system allows the uploading and downloading of text documents or programs. RBBS-PC also has an option for assigning different levels of security for users, which increases or decreases the user's access to the entire system.

A special program was written to initialize the program immediately when the computer was turned on, so that, with the flip of a switch, the system was ready for use. The board operated from 5:00 P.M. to 9:00 A.M. weekdays and twenty-four hours a day on weekends.

The logic of placing the host computer in Savannah was that it required only local calls for students. We would call long distance on GIST from Athens, thereby assuming the major phone expense. The system, then, had to be monitored remotely from Athens, which was a disadvantage to the SYSOP.

Training Session. A two-hour training session was held during the second class meeting of the fall quarter, 1985, on the same day that the computer was installed. Students met one of two SYSOPs, both graduate students enrolled in the on-campus program in instructional development, who then demonstrated the major features of the RBBS-PC package. An eleven-page description of the program was distributed. Major topics included signing on, the help file, reading messages, leaving a message, the utilities menu, and the filing system.

At the time the training session was conducted, an informal survey of students indicated that seven out of the eleven present owned a personal computer. Five students owned modems and communications software, and four had placed calls to an electronic bulletin board or electronic mail service. We made arrangements for a TRS-80 Model 100 computer, an inexpensive yet adequate computer with a built-in modem, to be made available to each student who did not own or have access to a computer.

What Data Did We Collect?

Students knew generally that we would collect data at the end of the quarter on the operation of the system and on their reactions to this experience. Upon further reflection, however, we concluded that this informal approach was unfair to the students. They should have known specifically what data we would collect, how it would be collected, who would do it, and what use would be made of it. We, therefore, developed a consent form that clearly explained our intentions. In all, three types of information were obtained: (1) self-report about their level of use of and reactions to the bulletin board; (2) response to the stages of concern questionnaire, or SoCQ, (Hall, George, and Rutherford 1979), which was used to measure students' concerns about the bulletin board as an instructional innovation; and (3) statistics on the use of the bulletin board, which came directly from the RBBS-PC program.

What Were the Major Outcomes?

In reviewing the findings, several important features of this project should be kept in mind. First, the introduction of the bulletin board came at a very stressful time for students, who were taking preliminary written and oral examinations. While students generally welcomed the board as a useful tool, it was clearly adjunctive or, for a few students, unnecessary at that moment. Second, the use of the bulletin board was purely voluntary. No minimum number of sign-ons were required. Third, at the time the host computer was installed, only five students had the necessary hardware to link up with the system. Although we would have preferred that all students have the necessary equipment at the start of the quarter, this could not be achieved without delaying the installation of the host computer. By the end of the quarter, most students had access to the bulletin board. In several cases, the availability of the board prompted students to purchase their own personal computers.

Findings are presented in four sections: summary of RBBS-PC usage, self-report results, responses to the SoCQ, and initial costs.

Summary of RBBS-PC Usage. The number of times each user signed on the RBBS-PC over a ten-week period from October to December can be summarized as follows:

Person	**Number of times signed on**
SYSOP 1	15
SYSOP 2	11
Instructor	13
Student 1	41
Student 2	11
Student 3	10
Student 4	5
Student 5	2
Student 6	1
Student 7	1
Others	5

These data show clearly that only half of the students signed on the bulletin board during the fall quarter. "Others" were callers who were checking out the new board. No files were uploaded or downloaded.

Self-Report Results. A survey of RBBS-PC usage was given during the last class meeting. Eleven of the fourteen students were present. Of those eleven, six had used the board and five had not. When asked, "Why did you not use the board?," four replied, "lack of equipment," and one "didn't know how." Three of the four who lacked equipment also mentioned that they did not need the board that quarter.

Of those who used the board, a variety of problems were encountered: (1) one student was tagged with a security violation and access was then withheld (apparently the student repeated an incorrect command three times, so the RBBS-PC program determined a "criminal" was at work); (2) several attempts to upload and download files were unsuccessful; (3) use of nicknames in addressing messages would result in undelivered messages; (4) a user would be knocked off the board automatically after two minutes of inactivity; (5) occasionally, the computer would not be turned on at 5:00 P.M.

Several suggestions for improvement in the system were obtained from those who used the board: (1) increase access time by having a separate phone line; (2) train other University of Georgia faculty in the use of the board; and (3) post more information of general interest to all.

And finally, students were asked two specific questions: (1) "How frequently do you plan to use the board next quarter?" Eight replied, "more than this quarter," and two, "about the same." (2) "Should the board be continued next quarter?" Ten replied, "yes"; one record was incomplete.

Responses to the SoCQ. Eleven students completed the SoCQ. For each record, raw scores for the seven stages were converted to percentiles then plotted. Two groups of student records were formed. One consisted of the three most frequent users of the bulletin board. The other consisted of five students who did not use the board. Profiles of these groups were averaged, plotted, and then compared. The resulting profiles conform to the predictions of the concerns model. For example, the nonuser group of five showed very high intensity of concerns in obtaining more information and in determining how they might use the bulletin board; they were not concerned about collaborating with others on the bulletin board. The user group, however, showed a different pattern of concerns—lower informational and personal but higher on collaboration. In short, concerns theory appeared to describe quite well the two user groups that we formed.

Initial Costs. Our original projection for equipment called for a budget of $9,600, which included one Tandy Model 1200 with accessories, ten Model 100 portable computers, and one printer. Our actual equipment expenses, however, were

1 Tandy Model 1200 HD with monitor, graphics adapter, and cables	$2,295
1 Modem	$350
3 Tandy Model 100 (24K) with cables, carrying cases, and AC adapter	$1,555
Total	**$4,200**

The SYSOP's salary for the quarter would add an additional $1,000 to this total (ten hours per week at $10 per hour for ten weeks) as well as the GIST phone calls to Savannah, estimated at $150 (GIST did not provide actual cost billing). The total expenses were $5,350. This figure does not reflect any equipment costs from Athens, because we already had the needed equipment.

Reflections on the Initial Installation

Our initial view of establishing a bulletin board focused on equipment, budget, and logistical problems. And indeed, it took virtually the entire quarter to develop an operational system, including installation and monitoring the system, training students in its use, and procuring equipment so students could have access to the system. After several weeks of operation, however, we became more aware of the students' view of the system. Some students, for example, needed additional practice in using the basic system. Yet, others wanted to share information about the bulletin board with colleagues and locate and use additional bulletin boards in their specialty areas.

How might this particular project have been more sensitive to a student's awareness, acceptance, and needs? We offer the following thoughts and suggest that others who might be anticipating a similar installation balance their concerns about hardware with their concerns for people who will use the system.

- Communicate the purposes of the project, data to be collected, and other important issues several weeks in advance of the actual installation.
- Obtain feedback from students about the proposed system. They should be able to express their views on accepting, rejecting, or establishing how the board should be used.
- Use the SoCQ or a similar questionnaire prior to the initial training session.

- Incorporate the results of the SoCQ into the initial training session. Thus, the training sessions would deal not only with the operation of the system, but also with the individual student's concerns about the system.
- Anticipate that each student's initial needs and concerns will change. The system should be responsive to those changes.

Reference

Hall, G. E., A. A. George, and W. L. Rutherford. 1979. *Measuring stages of concern about the innovation: A manual for use of the SoC questionnaire.* 2nd ed. Austin, TX: The University of Texas.

INTERVIEW

Vol. 11 No. 3 1997

Speaking Personally—with A. Frank Mayadas

Dr. A. Frank Mayadas is a program officer for the Alfred P. Sloan Foundation. Prior to joining the foundation in 1993, Dr. Mayadas spent twenty-seven years at the IBM Corporation, where he served as vice president of the Research Division, Technical Plans and Controls during his last years there. He is a fellow of The Institute of Electrical and Electronics Engineers, a member of The American Physical Society, and a past director of the Society of Engineering Science. He also serves as a member of the advisory board of the College of Engineering at the University of Illinois and at Vanderbilt University. Dr. Mayadas was interviewed by Gary E. Miller, associate vice president for distance education at The Pennsylvania State University.

Gary Miller: For the past several years, the Alfred P. Sloan Foundation has funded a large number of experiments and projects related to asynchronous learning networks (ALNs). How do you define "asynchronous learning networks," and why is the Sloan Foundation interested in ALNs?

A. Frank Mayadas: For many, many years, people have had the opportunity to learn at places away from campuses and other centers of learning. They have done this through the use of learning media, such as books and other print materials, and more recently, they have also been able to use videotapes, audiotapes, and various kinds of software, such as learning software built on rules-based or other systems. Learning software is often described as multimedia and is distributed on CD-ROM. All of these self-learning approaches are asynchronous in that they do not require the learner to synchronize his or her schedule with anyone else or with any other event. By this definition, attending a class, either face-to-face or through interactive TV, would not qualify as asynchronous learning. I usually do classify broadcast TV as asynchronous because this can be videotaped and played back at the learner's convenience with no loss in value.

We at Sloan have felt for many years that the relatively recent development of electronic asynchronous communication can have a huge impact on learning in combination with the above-mentioned asynchronous self-learning media. Probably the most common examples of asynchronous electronic communications are e-mail and voice-response systems. Somewhat less well-known are computer-conferencing systems that allow groups to communicate, discuss, and share information. So, our vision is that a remote learner should be able to learn through the use of self-learning media in much the same way that a campus learner does. Being connected to a peer group or cohort, an instructor, and perhaps, a tutor, the remote learner can also have the benefits of the important people-to-people communications that campus learners have always enjoyed and that self-learning alone does not provide. We can think of a group of geographically separated learners who use self-learning media and are connected through an electronic communication network as an asynchronous learning network. The term "network" is used here to refer both to a computer network and to the "people network" it enables.

Learning alone is difficult. We think that an ALN makes learning more accessible by bringing the many benefits of cohort-style learning to remote learners without regard to distance or time-synchronization constraints. It may bring to reality the vision that anyone should be able to access education at anytime or anyplace.

GM: What is the relationship of ALNs to distance education?

FM: I think of an ALN as a subset of the many delivery modes that make up the term "distance education," but in some ways, it is also a superset. It is a subset because approaches such as correspondence, interactive TV, and the various self-learning approaches that we discussed earlier, including broadcast TV, are all a part of what is called "distance education." So an ALN is a subset in that it is another entry, though one that I think may eventually prove to be the most important.

However, elements of ALNs can also be directly incorporated to benefit on-campus learners. We have supported a few projects that explore ways in which on-campus learning can be made more efficient through the introduction of ALN elements without sacrificing learning quality. With ALNs, a large part of the on-campus learners' communications with fellow students, tutors, and faculty would still be face-to-face, but significant portions would be asynchronous. The "distance education" term is usually not applied to on-campus learning.

My own view is that, eventually, ALNs will stretch seamlessly from the campus to remote environments but with differences in the way they are implemented as the distance from a campus increases.

GM: You mention that ALNs can be applied in many different environments—on campus and off—and that there are differences between single courses and programs. Taking all that into account, what criteria does the Sloan Foundation ask institutions to use to measure the success of ALN initiatives?

FM: As you note, we generally think of ALNs as falling into two basic varieties—on-campus ALNs and off-campus ALNs—although the latter can also be subdivided into near-campus and far-from-campus varieties.

For on-campus ALNs (i.e., those that are integrated into other, more conventional activities, such as face-to-face classroom sessions), it is important to attempt to measure outcomes since the overall cost of instruction can increase if an ALN is introduced. So, if improved learning quality is sought, it seems that this should be demonstrated through measurement. Another goal might be to improve student retention without sacrificing learning quality, but it should also be measured. I also believe that on-campus ALNs can be very active "laboratories" of experimentation in ALN pedagogy, something that is hard to do when teaching to off-campus students because of the increased complexity of the situation. With on-campus students, most of the interaction will still be face-to-face, and I can envision more experimental approaches being attempted in the ALN area, the best of which can then be carried over to the off-campus environment (perhaps with some modification).

With respect to the off-campus environment, we initially tried to encourage colleges and universities to just get into the game. Now, of course, a large number of institutions are involved, and some experience is being gained, so it becomes relevant to inquire about assessment. I think in terms of five assessment factors, all of which must show favorable outcomes and favorable progress in order for ALNs to succeed.

The first is access. I think the whole point of off-campus ALNs is to increase access to education to a pool of learners who currently do not have this access, and so we need to be able to assess whether increased access is, in fact, being provided. We should keep in mind that access has never been completely absent. Over the years, people have had the opportunity to learn on their own by reading books and other printed learning materials. All of us are familiar with stories of historical figures who mastered entire disciplines through their own efforts. That brings to mind the story of the impoverished postal clerk Ramanujam, who, in India at the turn of the century, taught himself mathematics and, subsequently, lectured at Oxford, developed a number of new theorems in number theory, and coauthored scholarly publications with the famous English mathematician G. H. Hardy.

So, access to education has, in some sense, always been there. But the flip side is that people like Ramanujam are very few in number, and for most people, access to self-learning materials is not really access at all. Correspondence is a step forward. But the question remains on the table: Do ALNs improve access beyond self-learning and independent study through correspondence? By how much? What can we do to further improve access?

Surely a part of the answer to the last question is to lower the cost of entry for learners (the below $1000 computer and $20 per month for Internet connections prices are a step in the right direction) and to increase the number of courses and disciplines available to remote learners. I think you get the idea that the degree of access provided in a particular ALN, as compared to some theoretically desirable figure, is a good thing to measure.

The second factor is learning effectiveness. This one is rather obvious. We need to do enough in the way of assessment to make sure that learning goals are being met. This does not necessarily mean that comparisons with classroom learning through control groups are necessary, only that learning mastery meets or exceeds goals set by faculty and the institution.

Third, it seems to me that, in order to have widespread adoption of ALNs and the increased access that I expect will follow, we need to strive toward making ALN teaching a satisfying experience for faculty—as satisfying as conventional classroom teaching or even more so. This should be true for most faculty, not just those that are sometimes called "early adopters." There is some symmetry here with what I said earlier about learners and access; just as we want to extend access to the learner, so, too, should we seek to make ALN teaching attractive to the average faculty member. And of course, this becomes an assessment factor; for example, what do we know about faculty satisfaction in a particular ALN implementation, and how do we go about improving it?

Fourth is cost-effectiveness. There is a cost associated with any kind of education, and although most faculty strive first and foremost for the highest quality, there is always the implied and real limitation imposed by cost. So I think the cost-effectiveness of various ALNs proposed for off-campus education is something that should be consciously thought through and measured. There are costs to the institution, such as ALN course creation, ongoing costs to maintain and provide courses and services for off-campus delivery, cost of infrastructure, and so forth. There are complementary costs to the student, such as tuition and fees, cost of Internet connection, cost of long-distance calls, and cost of computer and other equipment. And of course, the cost to the student and the cost to the institution have a relationship. We should think about these costs and begin to think about how to improve them without sacrificing quality.

Finally—and this is certainly not the least important—is student satisfaction. This is a broad category useful in thinking through all the ways in which a remote learner interacts with the university, ranging across academic matters from the full range of services to online social interaction with faculty and other students. Universities and students in traditional settings value the total "campus experience," which is a part of the learning experience. I see this category as focused on the "online experience" and its improvement. In the end, colleges and universities will want a loyal group of online graduates.

I've gone into some detail here because assessments patterned on these five factors made no sense as the ALN efforts were just starting. Now that many of these efforts are becoming established, it makes sense to begin considering these kinds of measurements. Some have begun, and we expect many more to get under way this year.

GM: What has the foundation learned about making ALNs successful within an institution?

FM: Success in ALNs can come at many levels, but the important ingredient is always "commitment" not factors of a technological nature, such as bandwidth.

Let me explain. A successful ALN course can be mounted by a single faculty member. An ALN degree program, however, requires more than the commitment of a single faculty member. A program that features multiple ALN programs and courses, for instance, one that aspires to resemble a university, requires very substantial institutional commitment. Multiple faculty must be involved, with the full support, financial and otherwise, of the president, provost, deans, as well as marketing, computing, and other support groups.

We have many examples of successful courses and degrees, and we are now seeing, in select cases, the necessary institutional commitment that can result in real ALN universities. Of course, an important part of this institutional commitment is to actively seek resources beyond the universities' own with which to carry out the task, and also to consciously mount an effort to learn from the work already under way at other places.

GM: We've talked a lot about success factors. However, we also learn from failures. What kinds of problems have you seen?

FM: The issue of successes and failures is an interesting one. I see it this way: Where we see successes, we know we have found one successful approach, but there may be many others. The field is in its infancy, so there is no reason to believe that even successful approaches are optimal. In some sense, that is why the measurements idea we discussed earlier is so important. Whatever seems to be working should be seen as something that might be improved. Similarly, where results are below expectations, we need to make an effort to find more favorable outcomes, rather than simply label the effort as a failure.

GM: In that case, where do you feel we need to focus more effort?

FM: Two areas come to mind where I think more efforts are needed. One is that I find enrollments are never as high as initially expected. We need to understand why this is and try to improve the numbers. It may be a matter of rethinking how to enhance awareness among the learner community and of marketing. It may be a matter of cost to the student. It may be that acceptance of these kinds of approaches among learners will be slow, just as acceptance has its own pace among faculty. We don't know the answers, but we need to keep looking.

A second area that needs attention is that of faculty satisfaction. The way in which most, if not all, ALN courses are designed and taught is generally more work for a faculty member than equivalent classroom courses. We need to stay focused on the area of work level and, more important, satisfaction level of faculty so that the faculty effort is equivalent to or less than that of classroom teaching.

At this early stage in the ALN field, the faculty involved are the more innovative and better ones, and I hear them saying that they have a high satisfaction level, even though it seems to be more work for them. I worry about this, however, when I look ahead and see that, for ALNs to be established and become large-scale, many more faculty, including those not presently participating, will have to get involved. Institutional incentives for faculty participation will help, but in the end, there will have to be high levels of satisfaction. So, we haven't yet found all the right answers on the pedagogy, design, or delivery of ALN courses.

GM: What do you see as the next step for ALNs?

FM: An excellent question, and a difficult one because there are so many next steps that come to mind. One is to expand, as fast as possible, the number of faculty involved and the number of disciplines covered. This way, much more research will be done in areas like pedagogy, and better teaching strategies will become more evident.

However, I think the one step that captures this and some other "next steps" is a move toward large-scale implementation of ALNs for off-campus learners. Higher education is a large-scale enterprise, and if the ALN approach is to be viable, I believe that it, too, must achieve large-scale implementation. As an ALN evolves toward large-scale operations, much will be learned in the process about pedagogy, student support, faculty attitudes, and the other issues we have been discussing.

An ALN that enrolls 10,000 students or more attending a single university, which isn't all that big in comparison to the campus enrollments at large universities, might be considered large-scale. Evolution toward large-scale will also force attention on issues of accreditation and licensure across state and national boundaries, and it will focus attention on issues of inter-institutional cooperation, possibly resulting in new kinds of organizations. It seems to me that a next step toward large-scale includes progress in many of the issues vital to the future of ALNs in higher education.

Gary E. Miller